Perspectives

Academic Reading Skills and Practice

Marina Rozenberg

OXFORD
UNIVERSITY PRESS

OXFORD
UNIVERSITY PRESS

Oxford University Press is a department of the University of Oxford.
It furthers the University's objective of excellence in research, scholarship,
and education by publishing worldwide. Oxford is a registered trade mark of
Oxford University Press in the UK and in certain other countries.

Published in Canada by
Oxford University Press
8 Sampson Mews, Suite 204,
Don Mills, Ontario M3C 0H5 Canada

www.oupcanada.com

Copyright © Oxford University Press Canada 2015

The moral rights of the author have been asserted

Database right Oxford University Press (maker)

Library and Archives Canada Cataloguing in Publication
Rozenberg, Marina, author
Perspectives : academic reading skills and practice / Marina
Rozenberg.

ISBN 978-0-19-900954-1 (pbk.)

1. Reading (Higher education).   2. English language—Textbooks
for second language learners.   3. English language—Study and teaching—
Foreign speakers.   I. Title.

PE1128.R688 2015   428.64   C2013-902760-2

Cover image: iStock/Thinkstock

Printed and bound in Canada

4 — 17

CONTENTS

PART II CROSS-DISCIPLINARY READINGS

ACKNOWLEDGEMENTS

I would like to thank the OUP Canada editorial staff especially Nadine Coderre, as well as copy editor Cindy Angelini, for sensitive guidance, wise advice, and amazing expertise, which made writing this book a stimulating and fun experience. I also want to thank my family who patiently waited for me and on me while I was spending hours on the computer.

–Marina Rozenberg

Oxford University Press Canada would like to express appreciation to the EAP instructors who graciously offered feedback on *Perspectives* at various stages of the developmental process. The following reviewers shared their valuable insights with the author and editorial department:

Pamela Barkwell, Brock University

Joan Birrell-Bertrand, University of Manitoba

Tatiana Galetcaia, University of Manitoba

Scott Jamieson, University of Guelph

Kristibeth Kelly Delgado, Fanshawe College

Claire Marin, Fanshawe College

Julian Z. Martin, Seneca College

Yuliya Miakisheva, York University ELI

Janice Romyn, Mohawk College

David Schwinghamer, Collège Ahuntsic

Michele Secret, Simon Fraser University

Marlene Toews Janzen, University of Ottawa

INTRODUCTION

Perspectives: Academic Reading Skills and Practice will put you on the path to the challenging but satisfying world of post-secondary studies. Reading is fundamental to your academic career: you read to prepare for classes and exams and to write papers. In addition, academic reading expands your horizons as a well-educated individual, and *Perspectives* will help you to achieve just that. Quite often during their studies, students are comfortable with the texts they encounter in their major discipline but find they lack a basic understanding of fields that are outside their major. In modern academia, where experts from different disciplines collaborate, a good reader should be able to look at an issue across a range of disciplines—that is the idea behind this book. For instance, if you are studying biology, you will certainly come across the topic of the origin of cancer and its treatments from the point of view of a biologist, but most likely not be exposed to an engineer's view of cancer as a mechanical problem in the human body or to a cancer survivor's perspective that emphasizes the psychological burdens of fighting and surviving the disease. To bridge the gap between disciplines, *Perspectives* offers three reading selections per reading unit, centred around one theme.

Part I of the book presents essential academic reading skills and strategies. These are the tools that enable you to read effectively and efficiently. Part I contains five units covering the following topics:

- Smart reading strategies
- Smart vocabulary strategies
- Main ideas and supporting details
- Inferences, facts, and opinions
- Assessing an argument

Academic reading strategies, such as making connections between your instructor's assignment and the text, annotating the text, making predictions, and summarizing the text, will set you on the course of active engagement with your reading material. The ability to differentiate between main ideas and supporting details is useful when outlining the text in preparation for a paper or oral presentation. Understanding how main points are supported by and connected to details, and learning to infer main points that are sometimes implicit, aids in seeing the bigger picture of what you are reading. The units on inferences, facts, and opinions, and assessing an argument will contribute to your becoming a critical and careful reader: you will learn to judge whether an issue is presented objectively, and whether or not an argument is adequately supported. In other words, you will learn not to accept ideas in print at face value, but rather to assess them critically.

A word on vocabulary learning: research shows that no matter what reading strategies you use, the critical element for success is the number of words in your active vocabulary. Therefore, *Perspectives* places a specific emphasis on vocabulary development. Unit 2 offers instruction and practice in vocabulary strategies, such as keeping a personal vocabulary notebook, recognizing terms and their definitions, guessing words in context using word part knowledge, and ignoring less-important unfamiliar words while reading. You will have the opportunity to put these strategies into practice in Part II of the book, where each selection concludes with an academic vocabulary exercise.

Part II of *Perspectives* provides a wealth of reading selections that allow you to apply the skills and strategies taught in Part I. There are eight themed units with three reading selections; each reading is followed by comprehension and vocabulary questions. At the end of the unit, there is a Unit Reflection and Synthesis section. Here, you are asked to assess the common ground between the three selections as well as that which makes each unique. This activity sharpens your critical and analytical thinking. This section involves sharing of ideas—many of the questions may have more than one answer, and group work on these questions will lend some fascinating and unexpected perspectives to you and your classmates. My hope is that you will be able to see how the topics in the book connect to your life: your studies, your future career, and maybe even your personal and social identity. Therefore, I have selected interesting and relevant texts, many of them about modern Canadian or North American realities. You will encounter readings from a variety of sources—many of them are excerpted from textbooks, but you will also find additional materials from sources including academic journal articles and newspapers.

It is my hope that you will find *Perspectives* thought-provoking and practical as a resource for your academic progress. I also wish that the book will inspire you to read and think critically beyond a prescribed, conventional formula and develop an informed, multi-faceted approach to academic issues. Enjoy!

–Marina Rozenberg

PART ONE

Academic Reading Skills and Strategies

Smart Reading Strategies

Reading is probably the most common activity that you, as a college or university student, engage in: you read to prepare for classes, tests, presentations, and papers. Reading provides the basis for your academic success, and therefore it makes sense to think about the following questions: *How does a successful student read? What reading strategies does he or she use?*

1. Look at the pictures above and discuss the differences between the ways in which the two students read.

2. Imagine reading a novel, a biography, a magazine, or a blog—anything that you would enjoy reading in your leisure time. How is the process of reading this type of text similar to and different from reading a textbook for class?

3. In the chart below, fill in the similarities and differences between the process of reading purely for enjoyment and the process of reading an assigned textbook chapter for class.

	READING FOR ENJOYMENT	READING A TEXTBOOK CHAPTER
Similarities		
Differences		

You have probably found more differences than similarities. Although it is possible that you enjoy reading your textbook as much—or almost as much—as what you choose to read in your leisure time, when you read academic material for class, you do many things that you do not do when reading purely for enjoyment. That is because your goals in these two activities are different: with the book, magazine, or website, you may be reading for personal interest, but with the academic assignment, your goal is to understand and remember the ideas in the textbook for future use.

Study the five smart academic reading strategies discussed on the following pages. You will have a chance to work on each of these strategies in more detail in the reading activities that follow.

READING WITH PURPOSE

Often your academic reading will be connected to a specific assignment or a set of questions. The way you read will depend on what you are expected to do with the information after you've read it. Therefore, you should always keep the purpose in mind while reading.

If you've been given an assignment that requires you to write a paragraph or participate in a discussion related to the reading material, analyze the assignment to which your reading is connected *before* starting to read. Ask yourself what you already know about the topic and what information you'll need to take from the reading in order to help you complete the assignment.

If the assigned text is followed by vocabulary, comprehension, or discussion questions, you have different reading options depending on the context.

- If you are reading at home, take the time to read slowly and carefully, using all the smart reading strategies discussed in this unit. Then answer the questions following the text.
- For an in-class reading assignment or an exam, you will often be given limited time to read and answer the questions. In that case, choose one of two answer-completion strategies:
  A. Preview the text, read the whole text, and then approach the questions. This strategy gives some readers more confidence in answering the questions because they start with the "big picture" of what the text is about.
  B. Preview the text, then go straight to the questions. Work your way through the relevant parts of the text to locate information to answer each specific question. This strategy might save you time— when reading, you can narrow your focus to the information needed to answer each question.

Both methods for answering questions can be effective, so it's important to experiment with both and see which one works best for you. In either case, you'll need to employ the smart reading strategy discussed below: interact with the text by previewing, making predictions, and marking up the text.

Sometimes you will be assigned reading material that isn't connected to a specific assignment or set of questions. Although it may be more difficult, it is still important to read with purpose in order to ensure that you understand and retain the material. Before and while you read, imagine the types of questions that an instructor may ask based on the reading material and try to answer these questions.

INTERACTING WITH THE TEXT

Actively interacting with a text will help you process and retain the information you read more effectively. Specific tips for interacting with the text include the following:

- Preview before reading. Previewing makes reading more efficient as you are better prepared to deal with the information the text presents. To preview a text, look at the title, section headings, and visuals, and read the first paragraph. You may also find it helpful to read the last paragraph. You should also study any other prominent features that a text contains (subtitle, author's credentials, textboxes, charts, *italicized* key words, or words in **bold**).

- Make predictions before and while reading. You may find it helpful to write questions or predictions in the margins.
- Make notes in the margins. These could be about the text's key points or topics, some unclear ideas, or any ideas from your own experience or knowledge associated with the reading.
- Underline, highlight, or circle key terms, main ideas, and important supporting details.
- Try to guess unfamiliar words in context. Verify your guesses and look up unclear key words in an English-English dictionary.

All these activities will help you to review the text more efficiently at a later point, if necessary, and to connect the ideas to your previous knowledge.

SUMMARIZING TO LEARN AND REMEMBER

Some reading activities will be connected to a specific assignment or set of follow-up questions, which provide an opportunity to test your comprehension. However, instructors do not test students on every reading task they assign. Rather, they expect students to take responsibility for learning the material on their own and to integrate this material into a major assignment, such as a paper, an exam, or a class discussion. Therefore, you should make efforts to monitor your own learning, and one way to do that is to summarize the text by creating an outline of key points.

Get into the habit of creating simple text summaries. Mentally or in writing, summarize the main points after you finish reading. You do not have to write a full-length text summary each time you read. Simply compose a bullet-point outline that describes the key points: key terms, main ideas, and important supporting details. Your text mark-up, done as a part of your interaction with the text, will make summarizing easier.

When creating a simple point-form summary, try not to look back at the text—work from memory. If you have unfilled blanks after you have worked through the whole summary, go back to the text to check for any points you do not feel sure about.

Your outline of key points will help you see which ideas from the text you remember perfectly well and which you need to review. Ultimately, summarizing helps you to learn and remember the material.

These three smart reading strategies—reading with purpose, interacting with the text, and summarizing—will help you get the most out of every reading assignment. Along with these strategies, you should practise the following essential study habits to help ensure academic success.

MONITORING YOUR READINESS TO START THE ASSIGNMENT

Approach your reading assignment, like all of your assignments, with a positive attitude and confidence that you can complete it successfully. An optimistic mindset and self-confidence regarding a task help to handle the task with success.

Concentrate on your assignment fully. Eliminate all possible distractions from your working space and make sure you allocate a sufficient amount of time to your task.

EXPANDING YOUR VOCABULARY

You'll learn more about smart vocabulary strategies in Unit 2. Before we get to those specific strategies, there are two techniques for expanding your vocabulary that every EAP student should practise.

- Start a personal vocabulary notebook where you will write down new words and their meanings. The words may come from your English class, from your other classes, or from any source of English you encounter: newspapers, TV, books, conversations. Review your word lists several times a week.
- Read extensively. In addition to your academic reading assignments, read English magazines, websites, and books for fun.

Let's practise these smart reading strategies and effective study habits, as you read the following passages and complete the pre- and post-reading activities that accompany each one.

Activity 1

The passage on p. 9 is from a sociology textbook. Imagine that, based on this passage, your sociology instructor has given you the following assignment: *Write a paragraph defining the term "social role." Include your own example of a social role and explain what expectations we may have of a person in this social role. How do these expectations influence social interactions?*

PRE-READING

1. Monitor your readiness to start the assignment:

   a) Are you sitting in a quiet, comfortable place?

   b) Are you physically comfortable (not hungry, for example)?

c) Have you allocated enough time (at least 45 minutes) for this assignment?

d) Have you turned off your TV, computer, and phone?

2. Try to get into a positive mindset regarding your successful completion of the assignment. Hard work leads to effective results, so prepare to do some serious work and you will complete your assignment with success.

3. In order to ensure that you are reading with purpose, start by analyzing the assignment task on page 7.

a) What term (specific to the subject you are studying in this assignment) do you need to understand in order to write the paragraph?

_____

b) Is it enough to use only the textbook passage to write a good paragraph in response to the assignment? If not, what additional information will you need to include?

_____

_____

c) What do you think social roles are?

_____

_____

_____

READING

The first two paragraphs in the following reading selection have been marked up for you as an example of how you should interact with a text. Read the rest of the text and continue to mark it up.

- Highlight the terms you need to know and their definitions.
- Underline the main point of each paragraph and circle important examples.
- Mark anything you are unclear about with question marks.
- Make notes in the margins if an idea in the text reminds you of something in your own experience.
- Guess and/or look up unfamiliar vocabulary.

While reading and interacting with the text, and *before* you start the post-reading activities, write down any questions you imagine an instructor might ask you about the reading. There is space on page 10 to write these questions.

Status and Role

[handwritten: script: movie scenario? plan?]

[handwritten: What does the writer mean by age roles?]

01 Throughout a lifetime of establishing identities, we act parts in the game of life by playing out scripts organized in the form of normative social expectations called *roles*, which are attached to social positions, or *statuses*. These roles include gender roles, age roles, occupation roles, and a multiplicity of others.

[handwritten: my examples of occupation roles: clerk/customer in a bank]

02 On the one hand, roles provide scripts that permit and oblige us to behave in certain ways. For example, at a party everyone can say, "It's getting late; I've got to go to sleep"— except the host. On the other hand, roles can be thought of in a more dynamic fashion, as expectations that emerge in the give and take of social interaction. For example, a student reports that during an exam he was passed a note by his friend sitting in the next seat requesting "help" for a particular question. Terrified that the instructor might notice the interaction, the student attempted to resolve the dilemma by eating the note, mercifully "very short and written on a small piece of paper" (Albas and Albas, 2005).

[handwritten: How would I behave in this situation?]

03 Thus, *role enactment*, or *role-playing*, can be viewed either structurally, in terms of fixed expectations, or interactionally, as dynamic and developmental. In other words, we can view social behaviour as the learned performance of scripts that follow agreed-on rules or as negotiated arrangements that people work out with one another to solve unique problems of spontaneous interactions.

04 What is the use of studying the concepts of roles? As agreed-to expectations for behaviour, roles generally facilitate interaction in society. We don't realize just how dependent we are on *role expectations* to coordinate our acts with others until those expectations are violated. Similarly, in order to play roles, we need to know the identities of others as well as our own. Roles may also polarize and distance people from one another. The expectations that persons may hold of others can work as barriers to both communication and socialization. We need to understand roles in order to avoid being unwitting[1] slaves to them.

05 Consider an example of how roles work. The American sociologist Harold Garfinkel (1997) believed that we could best understand the constraints of social structure by breaking the hidden rules. To do this, he instructed his university students to return to their homes and behave in ways that breached the normal expectations of their family lives: by acting as if they were boarders and their parents were the landlords. Students were to be extremely polite, addressing their parents formally as "Mr" and "Mrs" and speaking only when spoken to. Approximately 80 percent of students who actually went through with the experiment reported that their parents were stupefied, shocked, and embarrassed. Many worried that their children had "lost their minds"—that the pressures of school, work, and everyday life had "gotten to them." Others thought their children were being mean, inconsiderate, and impolite. In short, parents couldn't make sense of this rule-breaking behaviour.

Source: L. Tepperman & J. Curtis, *Principles of Sociology: Canadian Perspectives*, 2nd edition (Don Mills, ON: Oxford University Press Canada, 2009), p. 82.

---

[1] not aware of what you are doing or of the situation you are involved in

POST-READING

Vocabulary

1. While reading, you may have been puzzled by some or all of the following words:

   a) script (par. 1)

   b) spontaneous (par. 3)

   c) facilitate (par. 4)

   d) polarize (par. 4)

   e) constraint (par. 5)

   f) breach (par. 5)

   g) stupefied (par. 5)

Some of the words you could guess in context—more about guessing in context in Unit 2—and others you had to look up in the dictionary. Now, match each word with its definition.

_____ to create distance or interfere with communication between people

_____ to help; to make something easier

_____ a set of words or actions prepared in advance

_____ to break; to violate

_____ extremely surprised

_____ happening on the spot, without a plan

_____ restriction, limitation

Make sure you have started a personal vocabulary notebook; enter any new words from the above reading and their definitions. Continue filling your notebook with new vocabulary and review your word lists several times a week. Bring your notebook to class: your instructor may want to check your progress.

QUESTIONS AN INSTRUCTOR MIGHT ASK BASED ON "STATUS AND ROLE"

_____

_____

_____

_____

_____

Are any of these questions similar to those in the Comprehension section below?

Comprehension

1. In the example of the student who received a note in the middle of an exam (par. 2),

   a) he behaves according to the social expectations of his friend.

b) he relies on a set script to help him to resolve a conflict in a predictable manner.

c) he helps his friend with the difficult questions.

d) he reacts spontaneously, based on his understanding of his instructor's expectations of a good student.

2. What are the two perspectives on role enactment?

_____ and _____

3. The purpose of studying roles is

a) to create barriers in social interactions.

b) to avoid following them blindly.

c) to violate social expectations.

d) to develop dynamic and spontaneous arrangements.

4. Garfinkel's experiment was designed to prove that

a) social roles are disrupted in the families of students and their parents.

b) most students comply with the expectations of their professors.

c) social structures are based on certain rules of behaviour.

d) polite behaviour can sometimes cause problems in communication with parents.

5. The author includes several examples of social roles in the passage. Fill in the chart below with expectations related to the social roles listed. Use ideas from the text or from your own experience. Use the notes you made in the margins. The first role has been explained for you.

ROLE	EXPECTATIONS
Student in an exam	Does not cheat
A friend	
A young adult living at home with parents	
A nurse (an example of an occupation role)	

Discussion and paragraph writing

As part of the process of reading with purpose, think about how the information in the text helps to complete your assignment. Look at the task again: *Write a paragraph defining the term "social role." Include your own example of a social role and explain what expectations we may have of a person in this social role. How do these expectations influence social interactions?*

1. You have found examples of social roles in the text. Now think of your own example of a social role and list the expectations you may have of a person in this role.

    Role: _____

    Expectations: _____

    _____

2. How can the role you chose be viewed in terms of fixed expectations and how can it be viewed as dynamic and developmental? How do expectations about this role facilitate social interaction and how do these expectations create barriers between individuals? Explain.

3. Now you are ready to write a paragraph to complete the task. After you have finished writing, share your paragraph with a classmate.

Activity 2

The next reading explores the dangers of social interactions in which people rely too heavily on predetermined scripts or expectations rather than expressing their own individuality. (You have just learned about scripts in the first reading.)

After reading this text, you will have to participate in a discussion on the following topic: *What are the problems associated with decision making when the group of decision makers all tend to think in a similar way? What should be done to help committees at work or school make good decisions? Use the excerpt on groupthink from Baumeister and Bushman's* Social Psychology and Human Nature *(3rd ed.) and your own ideas in your discussion.*

PRE-READING

A) Read with purpose. Before you start reading, analyze the topic of the discussion.

    1. Have you ever been a part of a decision-making committee (at your school or workplace, or in your community)? Was the work of your committee effective?

    2. In order to complete the task above, which key term do you need to know?

3. What is your initial response to the discussion topic? Can you predict why problems might arise if decision makers do not express different views?

4. While reading the text, notice the definition of the key term mentioned in the discussion topic. Pay attention to the disadvantages of decision making by similarly minded decision makers. Notice also whether the text suggests ways to overcome these disadvantages. Your ideas will be helpful for having an active discussion following the reading.

B) Interact with the text

1. Preview the text. Remember that your preview should include any of the following elements the text contains: title, subtitle, author's credentials, section headings, textboxes, images, charts, *italicized* key words or words in **bold**, and the first and last paragraphs.

2. Based on your preview of the text below, make predictions about its contents before reading it in its entirety. Answer the following questions:

    a) Locate the source for this text. Can the reader trust the source?

    b) What is *groupthink*?

    c) Why do you think the authors call committees foolish?

READING

While reading, continue to make predictions about ideas in the text. The questions and comments in the margins of the text will help you. In the future, try to write notes or mentally ask yourself similar types of questions.

Continue marking up the text as demonstrated in Activity 1.

Groupthink

01 The term *groupthink* was borrowed from novelist George Orwell, who used it in his novel about totalitarianism called *1984*. The term refers to the tendency of group members to think alike. Social psychologists use it specifically to mean a style of thought in which the group clings to a shared but flawed or mistaken view of the world rather than being open to learning the truth. In decision making, groupthink means that the group sticks to its preferred course of action, refusing to consider alternatives fairly and refusing to recognize the dangers or flaws in its plan.

How are groupthink and totalitarianism connected?

Does this sound like any of my experiences as a group member?

02   The roots of groupthink probably lie in the desire to get along. Members of a group do not want to spend all their time arguing, nor do they want the other members to dislike them. They most enjoy being together and working together when they all agree. In principle, a group will have the most information if people bring diverse viewpoints and air conflicting opinions, but such discussions can be difficult and unpleasant. Hence, people become reluctant to criticize the group, attack its basic beliefs, or question each other. This creates the illusion that everyone is in agreement.

Examples of groups with these characteristics? Examples of movies or books that show groupthink in practice?

03   Several aspects of a situation make groupthink more likely. First, the group tends to be fairly similar and cohesive to start with (and then becomes more so as a result of groupthink). That is, the members of the group share many views and ideas in common, and they tend to get along well with each other. Second, a strong, directive leader makes groupthink more likely. Third, the group may be isolated in some sense from others, so that it is not exposed to disturbing facts or contrary views. Fourth, the group may have high self-esteem, regarding itself as a superior, elite collection of people who do not need to worry about what outsiders think or want.

Foolish committees

04   Most organizations rely on committees to study issues and make decisions. This approach is based on an eminently sensible principle: it may be hard for a single person to know all sides of an issue and all aspects of a problem. By bringing together a group of people with different knowledge and different viewpoints, the outcome can be improved. Ideally, each person contributes something different, the group members respect each other's opinions, and the committee can achieve a broad level of wisdom and understanding that is above and beyond what anyone working alone could accomplish.

Does my experience confirm the authors' prediction?

05   But ask anyone with extensive experience whether committees generally achieve high levels of wisdom and understanding. Most likely, the answer will be a laugh or a roll of the eyes. What goes wrong?

06   Careful laboratory studies of group decisions have begun to reveal the problems that cause committees to fail to live up to their promise. One important factor is that members of a committee want to get along with each other, so they focus more on what they have in common than on their different perspectives. These pressures toward group harmony end up stifling the free exchange of information.

07   In one set of studies, the experimenter told a group of participants to decide which of two job candidates should be hired. Each member of the group was given some information about the two candidates. There were seven reasons to hire Anderson and only four reasons to hire Baker, and the group had all of the

reasons—so, logically, the committee should have chosen Anderson. Yet, most groups ended up choosing Baker, who was objectively the poorer candidate.

Why did they choose Baker?

08   The roots of the wrong decision lay in how the information was distributed. The researchers gave each member of the group the same four reasons for choosing Baker, but they gave each person only one of the reasons for choosing Anderson. Each person got a different reason for choosing Anderson, so if the committee members managed to pool their knowledge, they would realize that there were more reasons to hire Anderson. After all, that is how committees are supposed to work, by bringing together all the different information that the various members have.

09   But they didn't manage to pool their information. Instead of talking about all seven different reasons for hiring Anderson, they mainly talked about the four reasons for hiring Baker. That is, their group discussion focused on what they all knew in common, rather than on the unique information each person had.

How does this demonstrate the negative effects of groupthink?

10   Thus, a committee can end up being less than the sum of its parts, even in purely informational terms. Instead of bringing together different views and information, committees often narrow their focus to what they have in common. Information is lost rather than gained.

Source: R.F. Baumeister & B. Bushman, *Social Psychology and Human Nature*, 3rd edition (Belmont, CA: Wadsworth Cengage, 2014), pp. 524–526.

POST-READING

Vocabulary

1. While reading, you may have been puzzled by some of the following words:

    a) totalitarianism (par. 1)

    b) flawed (par. 1)

    c) air (par. 2)

    d) reluctant (par. 2)

    e) cohesive (par. 3)

    f) eminently (par. 4)

    g) stifling (par. 6)

    Enter any new words into your personal vocabulary notebook. This should become a habit every time you encounter new vocabulary; you will not continue to be reminded after every reading.

Some of the words you could guess in context and others you had to look up in the dictionary. Now, match each word with its definition.

_____ express opinions publicly

_____ preventing something from happening

___ a political regime with only one party that has complete power and control over the people

___ defective; problematic

___ unwilling

___ very; extremely

___ forming a united whole

Comprehension

1. a) Do the authors describe groupthink in paragraph 1 in a positive or a negative light? _____

   b) Highlight the words in the paragraph that support your answer to question a.

2. What may cause groupthink? Circle all that apply.

   a) People's wish to be polite and pleasant with each other

   b) People's unwillingness to get into conflicts

   c) People's desire to have an enjoyable time with each other

   d) People's need to be liked by group members

3. Mark the statement as T (true) or F (false). If false, correct the statement.

   ___ Members of a group experiencing groupthink truly agree with each other.

4. Paragraph 3 describes four characteristics of groups that are more likely to engage in groupthink. Each is marked by a connector (*First*, *Second*, etc.). Match each of the following examples with one of the characteristics from paragraph 3.

   First: _____   Third: _____

   Second: _____   Fourth: _____

   a) The student council in a Toronto all-boys private school consists solely of students who come from white upper–middle class Anglo-Saxon families who have been in Canada for many generations.

   b) The board of a large financial consulting company includes wealthy brokers who see themselves as more successful and privileged than the average Canadian. They are well-connected to people in power and are confident that even if they break a few rules, they will not be caught or punished.

   c) A group of college students is working on a project for their business course. Michael is the first to share his views with the group and to offer suggestions on how they should proceed with the project, even recommending who should complete specific tasks. Soon, all group members fall in line with Michael's instructions.

d) Jessy and his friends grew up in the inner city in a neighbourhood ridden with poverty, drugs, and crime. Most of their family members joined gangs at a young age and, although they have witnessed gang violence, these boys are convinced that being gang members is the only way to live their lives.

5. The authors present two different views on the effectiveness of committees. Fill in the following diagrams contrasting ideal and real committees.

Ideal committee

People in the committee express different knowledge and different viewpoints.

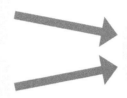

The committee can achieve a broad level of wisdom and understanding.

Real committee

People want to agree with each other.

The committee has a narrow focus of the situation; information is lost.

6. In the study described in paragraphs 7–9, what happened as a result of the group members' wish to get along with each other?

a) They chose to hire the best candidate.

b) They focused on the knowledge they all shared.

c) Each participant was given the same four reasons for choosing Baker, but the researchers gave each person only one of the reasons for choosing Anderson.

d) The group as a whole benefited from the unique information that each member contributed.

7. The authors of the text use an example of a hiring committee to illustrate the risks of groupthink. There are many other situations in which groupthink occurs, some much more serious than others. Could each of

the following be considered an example of groupthink? Why or why not? What other examples did you come up with while reading?

a) The Nazi movement

b) A high school clique of the most popular students

c) A recreational softball team

d) Other: _____

Discussion

Study the discussion topic presented before Reading 2 again: *What are the problems associated with decision making when the group of decision makers all tend to think in a similar way? What should be done to help committees at work or school make good decisions? Use the excerpt on groupthink from Baumeister and Bushman's* Social Psychology and Human Nature *(3rd ed.) and your own ideas in your discussion.*

As a part of the process of reading with purpose, you should have been thinking about how the text would help you to participate in the discussion. What does the text say about similar thinking of group members? What can you conclude about ways to prevent groupthink? In small groups, or as part of a class debate, share your opinions on the discussion question.

Activity 3

You have learned that people involved in groupthink fail to express personal opinions openly; in fact, they may even lose their sense of personal control as they are swayed by the will of the group as a whole. The next reading, taken from a psychology textbook, explores the issue of the loss of personal control. There are a number of questions following the text; you will be given a limited amount of time (determined by your instructor) to answer them. Use this opportunity to try out one of the answer-completion strategies (A or B) on page 5. You will also practise making a brief summary outline of the text.

PRE-READING

1. Preview the text: study the title, figure, picture, and italicized terms, then read the first paragraph.

2. Based on your preview, make predictions about the text's contents before reading.

   a) Explain the idea of *learned helplessness* in your own words.

   b) Do you think that having a great variety of products to choose from in a supermarket makes shopping more or less stressful (see the picture on p. 20)?

c) How might the idea of abundant choice be related to the topic of personal control?

READING

1. With a partner, experiment with the two different answer-completion strategies recommended when you have limited time to read and respond. You can review these strategies on page 5.

   Student A: Having previewed the text, read it in its entirety. Interact with it while reading. Then complete the questions following the text.

   Student B: Having previewed the text, go to the questions. Study each question and then look for the answer in the text. While reading, interact with the text.

   Students A and B: After completing the questions, compare your answers and check them with your instructor for accuracy. You may put your score below in the blank on page 23 after the post-reading questions. Share your thoughts about the positive and/or negative points of the strategy you used.

2. Use the same text mark-up strategies that you used in Activities 1 and 2 to interact with the text.

Learned Helplessness versus Personal Control

01 In studying how we interact with our environment, social-cognitive psychologists emphasize our sense of *personal control*— whether we learn to see ourselves as controlling or controlled by our environment. People who feel helpless and oppressed often perceive control as external. This perception then deepens their feelings of resignation, as experimenter Martin Seligman (1975, 1991) found. Dogs strapped in a harness[1] and given repeated [electric] shocks, with no opportunity to avoid them, learned a sense of helplessness. Later placed in another situation where they *could* escape the punishment by simply leaping a hurdle, the dogs cowered as if without hope. In contrast, animals able to escape the first shocks learned personal control and easily escaped the shocks in the new situation.

02 It's not just animals. When repeatedly faced with traumatic events over which they have no control, people come to feel helpless, hopeless,

---

[1] a set of leather strips for controlling an animal's ability to move

Negative experiences that one has no control over

⬇

Feeling out of control

⬇

Sense of overall helplessness

Figure 1.1 Learned helplessness

People can become accustomed to feeling helpless, and therefore acting helpless, when they continually experience negative situations in which they cannot exert control.

and depressed. Psychologists call this passive resignation *learned helplessness* (Figure 1.1).

03   Part of the shock we feel in an unfamiliar culture comes from a diminished sense of control when unsure how others will respond (Triandis, 1994). Similarly, people given little control over their world in prisons, factories, colleges, and nursing homes experience lower morale and increased stress. Measures that increase control—allowing prisoners to move chairs and control room lights and the TV, having workers participate in decision making, offering nursing home patients choices about their environment—noticeably improve health and morale (Humphrey et al., 2007; Wang et al., 2010). When Gallup pollsters asked workers whether they were allowed to personalize their workspace, those who said they could were 55 percent more likely to report high work engagement (Krueger & Killham, 2006).

04   In one famous study of nursing home patients, 93 percent of those encouraged to exert more control became more alert, active, and happy (Rodin, 1986). As researcher Ellen Langer

(1983, p. 291) concluded, "Perceived control is basic to human functioning." No wonder so many people like their iPads and DVRs, which give them control of the content and timing of their entertainment.

05   The verdict of these studies is reassuring: under conditions of personal freedom and empowerment, people thrive. Small wonder that the citizens of stable democracies report higher levels of happiness, and others have become happier with democratization (Inglehart, 1990, 2009; Ott, 2010). Shortly before the democratic revolution in the former East Germany, psychologists Gabriele Oettingen and Martin Seligman (1990) studied the telltale body language of working-class men in East and West Berlin bars. Compared with their counterparts on the other side of the Wall, the empowered West Berliners much more often laughed, sat upright rather than slumped, and had upward- rather than downward-turned mouths.

06   Some freedom and control is better than none, notes Barry Schwartz (2000, 2004). But does ever-increasing choice breed ever-happier lives? Actually not. Schwartz notes that the "excess of freedom" in today's Western cultures contributes to decreasing life satisfaction, increased depression, and sometimes decisional

Abundant consumer choice

paralysis. Increased consumer choices, as when buying a car or phone, are not an unmixed blessing. After choosing among 30 brands of jam or chocolate, people express less satisfaction than those choosing among a half-dozen options (Iyengar & Lepper, 2000). In the middle of the last century, an average supermarket carried 3750 items, notes Sheena Iyengar (2010), while today's Walmart and other big-box stores offer more than 100,000, and Amazon offers 24 million books and millions of other products. This *tyranny of choice* brings information overload and a greater likelihood that we will feel regret over some of the unchosen options.

Source: D. Myers, *Psychology*, 10th edition (New York: Worth Publishers, 2012), pp. 538–539.

POST-READING

Comprehension

1. The dogs in Seligman's experiment did not try to escape further shocks because **(1 point)**

   a) the harness was fit too tightly around their bodies.

   b) they felt they could not control the situation.

   c) it was pointless to try to escape from something that was inevitable.

   d) the hurdle was placed too high.

2. Seligman's experiment with dogs demonstrates that **(1 point)**

   a) it is always useful to learn how to escape from a difficult situation.

   b) repeated electric shocks cause helplessness in animals.

   c) lack of control over traumatic happenings makes dogs feel helpless.

   d) people and dogs behave differently in similar situations.

3. Which is NOT an example of an environment where individuals may feel that they have little or no personal control? **(1 point)**

   a) Living in a nursing home with strict rules

   b) Working in an autocratically managed factory

   c) Studying in a liberal college

   d) Arriving in a country with a very different culture

4. Allowing prisoners to move chairs in their rooms may **(1 point)**

   a) make them feel less helpless.

   b) boost their physical strength significantly.

   c) increase success chances in their rehabilitation process.

   d) increase the control of guards over the prisoners.

5. Allowing workers to personalize their workspace in a car manufacturing factory may result in **(1 point)**

   a) control over production processes.

   b) great satisfaction in work.

   c) ineffective human resources management.

   d) increased work engagement.

6. The reader may conclude from paragraph 5 that **(1 point)**

   a) democracies offer a sense of freedom and empowerment.

   b) under democratic governments, most people feel very happy.

   c) West Germany was less democratic than East Germany.

   d) people had a better time in the bar in East Berlin than in West Berlin.

7. Mark each statement as T (true) or F (false). **(1 point each)**

   ＿＿ Increasing the number of product options always results in increasing consumer satisfaction.

   ＿＿ Freedom of choice in modern Western cultures does not have any negative consequences.

8. What are the negative effects of the "tyranny of choice" (par. 6)? **(1 point)**

   _____

   _____

9. Choose the best meaning of the word in the text. **(0.5 point each word)**

   i. resignation (par. 1):

   a) helplessness

   b) oppression

   c) personal control

   d) quitting a job

   ii. morale (par. 3):

   a) goodness

   b) participation

   c) fairness

   d) confidence

iii. counterparts (par. 5):

a) friends

b) city residents

c) people of the same position in a different place

d) opponents

iv. breed (par. 6):

a) grow

b) create

c) species

d) diminish

10. Based on your understanding of the text, give your own example of each of the following:

a) a situation in which a person learns to be helpless **(0.5 point)**

_____

_____

b) a situation or an item that gives more control to a person, thus helping to overcome a sense of helplessness **(0.5 point)**

_____

_____

Your score: _____/12

Discussion

Discuss your results with your partner. Did you feel comfortable using the answer-completion strategy you were assigned? Did you have enough time to complete the questions? Do you think your strategy helped you to complete the questions correctly? Would you follow this strategy in the future or would you prefer to try the strategy your partner used?

Summary Outline

Create a basic summary to help reinforce your learning. The activity included comprehension questions, but many reading tasks will not include a set of questions or a specific assignment. You will still be expected to understand and remember the material, and creating a text summary outline can help. Review the section on summarizing on page 6, and then complete a simple point-form summary of the text "Learned Helplessness and Personal Control."

- *Personal control* definition: _____

  _____

- Learned helplessness chart: _____

  _____

- Experiments on learned helplessness and personal control:

  Dogs: _____

  Prison: _____

  Nursing home: _____

- Study of people in democratic and non-democratic societies

  _____

  _____

- Effects of too much choice in the West: _____

  _____

Smart Vocabulary Strategies

Answer these questions in pairs or small groups.

1. Study the picture above. What are the essential building blocks required to construct a house? How is building a house similar to learning a new language?

2. What are your favourite strategies for expanding your English vocabulary?

3. Do you always use a dictionary when encountering an unfamiliar word in a text? Why or why not? What strategies, in addition to using a dictionary, do you use to decipher unfamiliar words?

It is impossible to build a solid house without enough building materials. Similarly, you cannot express yourself or understand others fully without a sufficient vocabulary. Like the bricks that make up a house, words are the building blocks that make up language. A strong vocabulary is essential to decoding ideas in reading. In fact, no smart reading strategy, like those suggested in Unit 1, will help you read fluently and accurately if your vocabulary is limited. An extensive vocabulary is a cornerstone of reading, especially academic reading, which employs high-level vocabulary you cannot learn simply by watching movies or participating in everyday conversations.

Unit 1 provides two simple but effective ways to expand your vocabulary: keep a vocabulary notebook and read extensively. In your vocabulary notebook, write down all the new words you encounter in your academic surroundings and review your lists regularly. By reading in English as much as possible, you will engage with new or unfamiliar vocabulary in various contexts, thereby improving your chances of remembering them.

Although you might be armed with a strong vocabulary, you will still continue to meet some unfamiliar words in your academic readings. This unit focuses on four strategies to help you approach those unfamiliar words:

1. Identifying terms and their definitions
2. Analyzing word parts
3. Guessing meaning in context
4. Ignoring less-important unfamiliar words

IDENTIFYING TERMS AND THEIR DEFINITIONS

Study the following passage.

> Some bacteria are "good," aiding digestion and cleaning up waste, whereas others are "bad," causing infection. There are helpful forest fires, which clean out dangerous accumulations of underbrush, and harmful ones, which threaten lives and property. In the same way, some *conflicts* can be beneficial, or *functional*. They provide a way for relationships to grow by solving the problem at hand. Other *conflicts* can be harmful, or *dysfunctional*, causing pain and weakening a relationship.

Would you need a dictionary to determine the meaning of the phrases *functional conflict* and *dysfunctional conflict*? Why or why not?

In many academic texts, writers use specialized words that have specific meanings within their fields of study. These words are called *terms*. In introductory-level texts, terms are usually explained to the reader, and so using a dictionary is unnecessary. Often, terms are *italicized* or set in **bold** type. Their definitions are introduced with the help of special expressions and/or punctuation (see the passage on page 26).

In many cases, a regular college dictionary may not include precise definitions of technical terms used in particular fields of study, so using a dictionary would be less helpful than working through the definition given in the text.

Activity 1

A. The passages below describe ways in which people deal with personal conflict. In each passage, circle the key term and underline its definition. Highlight the words and punctuation that signal each term and definition. The first is done for you.

1. The inability or unwillingness to express thoughts or feelings in a conflict is referred to as non-assertion. Non-assertion can often come from a lack of confidence, but in many cases, people lack the awareness or skill to use a more direct means of expression.

2. Non-assertion can take the form of avoidance or accommodation. Avoidance, i.e. choosing not to face a conflict, may take a physical form (steering clear of a friend after having an argument) or a conversational form (changing the topic, joking, or denying that a problem exists). Accommodation is defined as dealing with conflict by giving in, putting the other's needs ahead of one's own.

3. Passive aggression, or the expression of dissatisfaction in a disguised manner, is designed to punish another person without direct confrontation. An example of passive aggression involves someone agreeing with you face-to-face but then showing a different agenda behind your back—such as the teenager who says he'll clean his room, then doesn't do so as a means of getting back at the parent who grounded him.

4. Whereas a non-asserter under-reacts, a directly aggressive communicator does just the opposite. Direct aggression—lashing out to attack the source of displeasure openly—can have a severe impact on the target.

5. Unlike a communicator with an aggressive message, an asserter does not attack the other person. That is, in assertion a speaker's statement expresses thoughts and feelings clearly but without the intent to hurt another person. For example, "I get the idea that you are mad at me" is an assertive statement as opposed to "You are always mad at me," which is an aggressive statement.

6. If both partners treat one another with matching hostility, one threat or insult leads to another (in a so-called escalatory spiral of conflict). If the partners both withdraw from one another instead of facing their problems, a complementary de-escalatory spiral results, in which the satisfaction and vitality seep out of the relationship, leaving it a shell of its former self.

7. When people have been in a relationship for some time, their communication often develops into conflict rituals—unacknowledged but very real repeating patterns of interlocking behaviour. An example of this is the following: A couple fights. One partner leaves. The other accepts the blame and begs forgiveness. The first partner returns, and a happy reunion takes place. Soon, they fight again.

B. Read the following scenarios. Based on your understanding of the terms used in the passages above, match each term with the situation that best illustrates it.

a) non-assertion   e) direct aggression

b) avoidance   f) assertion

c) accommodation   g) escalatory spiral of conflict

d) passive aggression   h) conflict ritual

_____ 1. As often happens, Jane is unhappy with her friend Trish: Trish does not return Jane's calls and behaves as if she does not care about Jane. Jane withdraws until Trish asks what's wrong. "Nothing," she replies. The questioning persists until the problem is finally out in the open. The friends then solve the issue and continue happily until the next problem arises, when the pattern repeats itself.

_____ 2. Twenty-five-year-old Jacob lives with his mother who is controlling, often preventing Jacob from spending time with his friends in the evenings. Jacob is unable to express his dissatisfaction because he lacks confidence and is afraid of his mother's anger.

____ 3. Eli resents the fact that his wife is a perfectionist and likes their house to be spotless. He has promised his wife he won't leave his dirty socks on the floor of the washroom but he keeps breaking his promise.

____ 4. Feifei criticizes her colleague's sloppy work on a project in front of their boss and co-workers. She calls her colleague lazy, careless, and incompetent in an attempt to ridicule and intimidate him.

____ 5. Whenever Mirabel raises the topic of spending too much money on eating out and clothes, her partner, Jack, jokes about it and tries to change the subject.

____ 6. Chen is habitually late for meetings with his friend Alistair. Alistair decides to discuss the problem directly without being confrontational. He politely tells Chen that he is upset and feels disrespected when Chen is late.

____ 7. Cindy and Fatima work together. Cindy dislikes Fatima, saying that she interferes in things that are not her business, that Fatima is bossy and arrogant. Fatima answers back, accusing Cindy of having poor cooperation skills and being unable to share work with others. They fight more and more, and their relationship worsens.

____ 8. Samantha and Terry have been friends and neighbours for years. Samantha has started travelling regularly for work and has been asking Terry to water her plants, take care of her pets, and mow the lawn. She also expects rides to and from the airport. Although Terry feels annoyed by Samantha's demands, she continues to do what is asked, wanting to be a good friend.

ANALYZING WORD PARTS

Would you describe yourself as a *bibliophile*? Or maybe, you happen to be a *bibliophobe*? If you chose to attend post-secondary school, where reading is required for most courses, and you signed up for a reading course, you are likely not a *bibliophobe*.

Confused? A close look at the parts making up these two words will help to understand their meanings. *Biblio-* is a word root that comes from the Greek and it means "book." *Phile* and *phobe* are also of Greek origin, and they have opposite meanings: "to love" and "to hate." Therefore, a *bibliophile* is a person who loves reading, looking at, and maybe collecting books, while a *bibliophobe* is someone who hates or distrusts books.

Analyzing word parts is a smart vocabulary strategy. Many prefixes, roots, and suffixes in English are found in numerous words and so if you recognize one or more word parts in an unfamiliar word, you can often make an educated guess about its meaning. For example, if you know that the word *bibliography* means "a list of books," then you should remember that *biblio-* means "books." Knowing the meaning of that root will help you decode many other unfamiliar words (*bibliophobe*, *bibliophile*) with the same root.

Activity 2

The exercise below will give you a taste of how helpful knowing word parts may be. Each group of words contains the same word part, the meaning of which is given. Make an educated guess about the definition of each word, based on the context in the example sentences. Then complete each chart by writing down another word that includes the same word part and adding your own definition along with an example sentence.

1. The prefix *sub-* means "under."

WORD	DEFINITION	EXAMPLE
subconscious		Some advertisements work on us at a subconscious level, so that we do not notice their effects.
subtitle		The subtitle explained the subject of the book in more detail.

2. The prefix *omni-* means "all."

WORD	DEFINITION	EXAMPLE
omniscient		Many religions believe in an omniscient being.
omnivorous		Black bears are omnivorous: they eat berries and hunt small animals.

3. The prefix *circum-/circul-* means "around."

WORD	DEFINITION	EXAMPLE
circumference		The circumference of this auditorium is 100 metres.
circulate		The bad news circulated quickly throughout the office, upsetting everyone.

4. The root *volve* means "turn" or "roll."

WORD	DEFINITION	EXAMPLE
evolve		Life on planet Earth has been evolving for millions of years.
revolve		Earth revolves around the sun.

5. The root *vert/vers* means "turn."

WORD	DEFINITION	EXAMPLE
reverse		The government succeeded in reversing the economic downturn.
divert		The course of the river was diverted to create a dry area in order to construct a dam.

6. The root *chron* means "time."

WORD	DEFINITION	EXAMPLE
chronic		This experienced nurse prefers working with patients who suffer from chronic diseases because she is able to build long-lasting relationships with them.
synchronize		In group swimming competitions, it is important that team members synchronize every movement.

7. The root *ver* means "true."

WORD	DEFINITION	EXAMPLE
veracity		The judge doubted the veracity of the witness's testimony.
verify		Before bringing the customer a particular model of camera, the salesperson had to verify that the camera was in stock.

8. The suffix *-ize* means "to make something have a certain quality."

WORD	DEFINITION	EXAMPLE
customize		If you buy this house now, while it is still under construction, we can customize the colours, bathroom fixtures, and kitchen cabinets for you.
familiarize		The public library has a course to familiarize seniors with Internet tools.

A list of common roots, prefixes, and suffixes and their meanings can be found on many English language learning websites. If you do an online search for *word parts and meanings* or *prefixes, suffixes, and root words*, you will find a number of helpful sites that contain comprehensive lists. The appendix on page 286 contains a concise list of word parts that you should familiarize yourself with.

GUESSING MEANING IN CONTEXT

How many of the words below do you know?

ostracism	stub	ruminate
despise	dull	hinder

Probably not many, because these words are not used very often in everyday speech or writing. Looking at each word on its own, you have no clues to help you work out its meaning. However, if you see the words in context, you should be able to guess their meanings because you are assisted by the following context clues: words with a similar meaning (synonyms), words with a contrasting meaning (antonyms), examples, and other general details in the text that suggest the meaning of a target word. To notice and make use of context clues, you must carefully read not only the sentence that contains the target word, but also the sentences before and after.

A. The following passage discusses the pain of social exclusion, and contains all of the words listed in the box on page 33. After reading, choose the correct word to complete each of the sentences that follow the text. You might need to change the form of the word to fit the grammar of the sentence.

Rejection, social exclusion must be the same or close in meaning to "ostracism".

There is a contrast between "people we like" and "people we despise", so "despise" must mean dislike.

Stubbing your toe is an example of physical pain.

A pain reliever such as acetaminophen dulls pain, i.e. reduces or makes something (e.g. pain) less intense.

"Ruminate" must be similar to "relive something over and over again in our minds"; perhaps a way of thinking intensely about something.

Shy people try to avoid social interactions. Their painful experience hinders, or makes it more difficult, for them to interact with others.

Why do we seek approval from others and why does it hurt so much when they reject us? Kipling Williams has conducted a great deal of research on social exclusion and *ostracism*, and he and his colleagues have found that not only is it painful when other adults choose not to play a cyber ball game with us, it is also painful just to watch others be rejected from the online game (Wesselmann et al., 2009). We feel pain when we are rejected by the people we like. Incredibly, it is painful even when we are rejected by groups of people we *despise* (Gonsalkorale and Williams, 2007). In an extensive review of the literature regarding social and physical pain, Geoff MacDonald and Mark Leary (2005) suggest that some of the same brain mechanisms that signal physical pain (e.g., *stubbing* your toe) are also activated by social pain (e.g., not being invited to a party). In fact, taking a pain reliever such as acetaminophen *dulls* the social pain of rejection and exclusion just as it does physical pain (DeWall et al., 2011). It is interesting that we seldom *ruminate* about episodes of physical pain that we have experienced, but we frequently relive social pain over and over again in our minds, often reconstructing the argument or incident and replacing what we said with what we wish we had said. . . . Some researchers suggest that the pain of social exclusion may be at the heart of what *hinders* shy and anxious people from engaging in social interactions. People with shy temperaments may learn to avoid social interaction because of the painful feelings they have experienced during social interactions in the past (Panksepp, 2011).

1. After a few glasses of wine, we sat on the porch, watching the sunset and _____ about the meaning of life.

2. I _____ my toe when I was moving the new furniture. It was very painful.

3. A few years ago, two brothers committed a horrible murder. Since then the whole family has suffered social _____.

4. His inability to speak English fluently _____ Juan from finding a well-paying job in sales.

5. After she was mugged, Joan thought she would never feel safe again; only time helped _____ the shock of the trauma.

6. Benny _____ himself after he cowardly watched the struggling kitten drown instead of diving into the river to save it.

Although context clues are helpful when decoding unfamiliar words, they work only if the reader approaches the text armed with an extensive vocabulary. In addition, even if you guess the meaning of the word correctly, it generally will not stay in your memory for long. To retain new words, you need to actively learn their forms and meanings, enter them into your vocabulary notebook, and review them regularly.

Context clues can help you work out the meaning of a word used in a particular context, but many words can mean different things in different contexts. For instance, above, the meaning of *stub* as in *to stub your toe* is "to hurt your toe by hitting it against something hard." But, *stub* can also mean "a short piece of a cigarette, pencil, etc., when the rest of it has been used," as in *a pencil stub*, or "the small part of a ticket," as in *a ticket stub*.

B. Select the best meaning of the italicized word or phrase in each sentence or passage. Use context clues.

1. We decide who we are on the basis of how others react to us. *Deprived of* communication with others, we would have no sense of identity.

    a) without

    b) enjoying

    c) reacting to

2. We spend a *staggering* amount of time communicating with others. For example, college students spend approximately 13 hours a day engaged in some type of interpersonal communication.

    a) small

    b) astonishing

    c) reasonable

3. He could not speak but *uttered* only weird cries.

    a) kept silent

    b) suppressed

    c) made a sound

4. Imagine that a friend says "I'm sorry" after showing up two hours late for a pre-arranged meeting. There are several possible "meanings" that this expression might have: a genuine apology, an insincere attempt to defuse your anger, or even a sarcastic *jibe*.

    a) request for forgiveness

    b) insult

    c) smile

5. Disputes over apparently *trivial* subjects, such as who will take out the garbage or whether we will play tennis or swim, are important. We are arguing about the nature of our relationship: who is in control? How important are we to each other?

    a) essential

    b) fascinating

    c) of little importance

6. Sometimes, after a fight between friends, further explanation can clear up the confusion and an apology can *mollify* another person's hurt feelings.

    a) reduce

    b) intensify

    c) trigger

7. When you decline an unwanted invitation by saying "I can't make it," you probably want to create the impression that the decision is really beyond your control. (If your goal were to be perfectly clear, you might say, "I don't want to get together. In fact, I'd rather do almost anything than accept your invitation.") In fact, we often *equivocate* precisely because we want to hide our true thoughts and feelings.

    a) speak clearly

    b) insult others

    c) use ambiguous language

8. There are other times when talking too much actually *aggravates* a problem. In one study, college roommates revealed that thinking and talking about conflicts actually increase relational problems.

    a) solves

    b) makes worse

    c) reduces

9. Even the most *tyrannical*, demanding, by-the-book boss might show an occasional flash of humanity.

   a) gentle

   b) clever

   c) controlling

10. We sometimes wish that we could go back in time, erasing words or acts and replacing them with better alternatives. Unfortunately, such reversal is impossible. Words said and deeds done are *irretrievable*.

    a) regrettable

    b) preventable

    c) impossible to take back

IGNORING LESS-IMPORTANT UNFAMILIAR WORDS

In the previous activities you have learned to use different clues—definition markers, word parts, context signals—to figure out the meaning of unfamiliar words in a text. The last piece of advice in this chapter is, strangely, to learn when to overlook certain unfamiliar words when reading. In some cases, the reader might understand the text well enough even if it contains some unknown words.

Study the following example:

It is important to remember that other people will have perspectives different from yours; it is critical that you understand and respect those perspectives. Many of the problems among people exist or are exacerbated because one group of people is ignorant or intolerant of the perspectives of others.

- What does the writer encourage the reader to do in this passage?
- What happens if people are ignorant of the perspectives of others?

If you can answer these questions, you understand the gist of the passage. You might not have known what *exacerbated* means but this did not prevent you from understanding the main idea. Here, we see that some words are less important

Even if you understand the passage without using a dictionary, look up the word in question if you have the opportunity. Then write the word down in your vocabulary notebook—after all, your goal is to expand your English vocabulary, and the not-so-important word in one passage becomes very important in another. (By the way, *exacerbate* means "to make something worse.")

than others in making up the meaning: you have to know what *perspective*, *respect*, and *ignorant* mean but the definition of *exacerbated* is not as important. Therefore, to ignore the word and continue reading may be the best strategy, especially when readers are under time pressure or unable to look up new words in the dictionary, specifically in a test situation. Before you decide to ignore an unfamiliar word, read the entire passage and ensure that you feel confident in your understanding without knowing the meaning of that specific word.

Activity 4

The following passages contain words that may be unfamiliar to you. Cross them out. Then try to answer the questions, ignoring the unfamiliar vocabulary.

1. Alternative media sources are small organizations, not connected to large corporations, and they offer alternative views to those found in mainstream sources. They may provide points of view that advocate a specific social perspective or political leaning.

   a) Why are some media sources considered "alternative"?

   _____

   b) Is it possible for alternative media sources to influence social or political events?

   _____

2. Because of modern communications technology, the amount of information available to us about world issues has increased exponentially, often making it difficult to determine what is true.

   What difficulty has modern communications technology created? Why?

   _____

   _____

3. Facts are indisputable truths: knowledge that is certain, concrete, and incontestable. They can be verified by accurate observation and measurement; for example, the types and amounts of chemicals found in a lake.

   a) Which statements do we call "facts"? Explain in your own words.

   _____

b) Why is the following statement a fact? "The level of asbestos in the lake was measured at 18 to 37 million fibres per litre (MFL)"?

_____

4. Polling companies ask people questions to determine their beliefs or opinions about a particular issue. When the opinions of a small number of people have been obtained, the information is extrapolated to represent the opinions of a much larger group of people.

How do polling companies determine the opinions of large groups of people?

_____

5. In the 1950s, when DDT (a chemical insecticide) was in wide use, birds were negatively affected. As they accumulated greater levels of DDT in their tissues, some birds began laying eggs with very thin shells. DDT was interfering with their production of calcium carbonate, a mineral necessary for sturdy eggshells. As a result, fewer eggs than normal were surviving the incubation period, and many birds faced extinction.

a) What happened to some birds' eggs in the 1950s?

_____

b) Why did some birds face extinction in the 1950s?

_____

6. Rachel Carson, a biologist and writer who studied the effects of exposure to DDT, died of cancer in 1964, before she could see the banning of DDT. In 1980, she was posthumously awarded the Presidential Medal of Freedom, the highest civilian honour in the US.

a) Why did Rachel Carson get a medal?

_____

b) Was Rachel Carson alive when the government awarded her a medal?

_____

INTEGRATING THE STRATEGIES

Activity 5

Read the following excerpt from an anthropology textbook. Then answer the questions.

Use all the smart vocabulary strategies you learned in this unit:

- Identifying terms and their definitions
- Analyzing word parts
- Guessing meaning in context
- Ignoring less-important unfamiliar words

Variety in Curing Practices

01 When we are faced with a mild disease, illness, or injury, we often take care of the treatment for ourselves. For example, for a cold we might take over-the-counter medication; for a cut, we might use commercial bandages and antiseptics. We might also resort to home remedies or folk cures recommended by a member of our family or our community. On your grandmother's assurance that "it has always been done that way," you may swallow some vile cough syrup she has concocted or some soothing chicken soup she has prepared with care. Frequently, we find that these home remedies are effective—if only through the *placebo effect* (i.e. feeling a physical change after taking a treatment, because of a belief in the treatment, even though it has no actual medical benefits)—and we do not need to venture far beyond our home for a cure. Families are often our frontline, our fortitude, our foundation in health care regardless of the cultures in which we live.

02 When we feel that treatment requires more than home remedies, we will seek outside help from someone with advanced knowledge of our condition. If we are part of a culture that relies on traditional knowledge, we might appeal to a medicine woman or man or a shaman (male or female) for assistance. To a Western observer, traditional curative measures may seem no more effective than a home remedy; yet traditional cures can be highly effective for reasons not often considered in Western medicine. Marilyn Walker (2003), for example, notes that shamanistic music used in Siberia induces altered states of consciousness, allowing the shaman to access the patient's unconscious as well as various forces (spirits) in the transcendental world(s). Other cultures use similar ceremonial activities to mediate inner and outer worlds and thus rebalance the patient in these worlds.

03 In other cases, even trained medical practitioners may not be able to help. For example, if you are bitten by a black mamba (*Dendroaspis polylepis*) in a remote area, you may not be able to find medical assistance before it is too late. The venom of the black mamba is full of neurotoxins that quickly shut down voluntary and autonomic nerve functions such as those that control breathing. If left without treatment, an adult who is bitten will generally die within an hour; even with treatment, small children never survive a black mamba bite. What can anyone do for the patient if there is no hope of finding antivenom and medical evacuation to a hospital in time? They can comfort the victim as he or she dies and hope that coma or death will come before the worst of the symptoms can manifest. This is a horrific and, in some sense, extreme example, but similarly hopeless situations may arise after a traffic accident or when a patient is in the final stages of an incurable disease.

A black mamba

04 Sometimes—all too often in some places—the treatment a patient seeks may depend on his or her financial resources rather than the severity of the condition. Medical treatment can be very expensive, and the harsh reality is that class and geopolitical disparities affect an individual's access to and quality of treatment.

05 The reality of such disparities is clear when we examine the various statistics on HIV/AIDS generated by national and pan-national organizations. Consider that in excess of 95 percent of all new infections of HIV/AIDS occur in countries commonly classified as "developing" and that at least 50 percent of these infections are in women. Consider also that the number of childhood cases being reported is increasing, not only among children born to infected mothers but also among children forced to work in the sex trade. Indeed, we can wonder what "development" can mean to communities where so many people are dead or dying of this disease. Socioeconomic disparity is also a significant factor in HIV transmission in more affluent Western nation-states. In Canada, rates of transmission are highest in Aboriginal communities, where many live in what could be considered "developing" conditions. Health Canada (2010) estimates that between 6 and 12 percent of HIV/AIDS infections occur in Aboriginal people, while Aboriginal people make up only 3.3 percent of the Canadian population.

Source: E. Schultz, R. Lavenda, & R. Dods, *Cultural Anthropology: A Perspective on the Human Condition*, 2nd Canadian edition (Don Mills, ON: Oxford University Press, 2012), pp. 230–232.

1. Explain the meaning of the following words from the text. Do not use a dictionary. In small groups, discuss your answers and the strategies you used to reach them.

   a) antiseptics (par. 1): _____

   b) soothing (par. 1): _____

   c) placebo effect (par. 1): _____

   d) shaman (par. 2): _____

   e) induces (par. 2): _____

   f) venom (par. 3): _____

   g) disparities (par. 4): _____

   h) pan-national (par. 5): _____

2. a) What example of a home remedy does the text give?

    _____

   b) Give an example of a home remedy used by your family.

    _____

3. What is an example of geopolitical disparity in people's access to medical care?

   _____

4. Mark the statement as T (true) or F (false). If false, correct the statement.

   ____ It is only in developing countries that people are at great risk of being infected with HIV/AIDS.

5. List any words that were unfamiliar to you but did not prevent you from understanding the meaning of the text.

   _____   _____   _____

Main Ideas and Supporting Details

1. Study the picture. The mighty trunk of this beautiful old tree bears the weight of many twisting branches—some thick, others thinner—filled out with leaves. Compare the organization of ideas in a paragraph to the arrangement of branches and leaves on this tree.

a) What are the essential parts of a tree? What are the essential parts of a paragraph?

b) Which parts are less important for the tree's survival? Which parts are less important in a paragraph?

2. How do you locate the main idea in a paragraph? Is the main idea always explicit in a paragraph?

3. What do you know about organizational patterns of paragraphs?

Some ideas in a paragraph are more important than others; without them the paragraph simply falls apart, just as the tree is not really a tree if we cut off all its heavy branches. If, however, we omit the less-important ideas in a paragraph, such as examples and specific details, the paragraph will still hold, although it will not be as clear and informative. Something similar happens to a tree in the fall when it sheds its leaves: its branches are visible but the tree looks naked without the rich green foliage. It loses some of its richness and substance without the leaves. Likewise, a well-written paragraph needs main ideas and a variety of supporting details to be complete.

This unit explores the organization of main ideas and supporting details in a paragraph, focusing on these specific reading skills:

1. Distinguishing between main ideas and supporting details

2. Identifying an implied main idea

3. Distinguishing between major and minor supporting details

4. Identifying organizational patterns

5. Studying graphical information

DISTINGUISHING BETWEEN MAIN IDEAS AND SUPPORTING DETAILS

When reading complex academic material, breaking down a paragraph or a section of a reading into main ideas and supporting details is a useful way of processing information. It is impossible to remember everything you read, but you can improve retention of key concepts by focusing on main ideas, whether you are drawing up an outline of a text or simply reviewing the points mentally.

The paragraph below demonstrates how main ideas differ from supporting details. Read it and answer the questions that follow.

[1]Providing a meaningful one-sentence definition of any academic discipline is a real challenge. [2]In the case of human geography, however, the American geographer Charles Gritzner has suggested a useful definition in the form of three closely related questions: "What is where, why there, and why care?" (Gritzner, 2002). [3]Every exercise in human geography, regardless of which theme it highlights, begins with the spatial question: "where?" [4]Then, once the basic environmental, regional, and spatial facts are known, the geographer focuses on understanding, or explaining, "why there?" [5]Finally, the third part of the question—"why care?"—draws attention to the pragmatic nature of human geography: geographic facts matter because they reflect and affect human life. [6]This is true of any geographic fact, whether it is something as seemingly mundane as the distance between your home and the nearest convenience store or something as far-reaching or serious as a drought or a civil war that causes peasant farmers in Ethiopia to lose all their crops.

1. Are all ideas in this paragraph equally important? Explain.

2. Underline the sentence that expresses the main idea of the paragraph.

3. Which sentences provide information to support—explain and give details about—the main idea?

4. What is the role of the last sentence?

5. Provide your own example of a geographic fact, explaining "what is where," "why there," and "why care."

In the paragraph you've just read, you should have recognized the most essential information was in the second sentence: the term *human geography* is defined by its three elements. Sentences 3, 4, and 5 provide specific details related to each of the three elements, and sentence 6 offers examples of geographic facts that impact people's lives. Both the main idea and the supporting details are necessary in this paragraph. Omit the definition in the second sentence and the paragraph loses its purpose; omit the explanation and the examples and the paragraph loses its substance and becomes hollow.

Without a main idea, the details the author provides will not make sense. To locate the main idea, disregard a popular misconception that the main idea is always the first sentence in a paragraph. In fact, it may be located at the beginning, at the end, or in the middle of the paragraph. To identify a main idea, ask yourself "What is the essential message that I should take from this text?"

A. In this activity, you will practise locating main ideas in a paragraph. In each paragraph below, underline the main idea sentence(s) and answer the question following the paragraph.

1. Gerardus Mercator (1512–1594) was undoubtedly the most influential of the map-makers due to his ingenious idea of how to represent large geographical spaces on paper. He tackled the crucial problem of projection: how to represent a sphere on a flat surface. His answer was the famous 1569 Mercator projection, still used extensively today. This projection, which showed the earth as a flat rectangle with a grid of latitude and longitude lines, was enormously useful to sea travellers because a straight line on the map was a course of constant compass bearing. By the early seventeenth century, Mercator's map had replaced all earlier charts used at sea.

Why is Mercator famous?

   a) He invented the concept of maps.

   b) He was a skillful navigator at sea.

   c) He developed a new approach to map-making.

   d) He put down geographical spaces on paper.

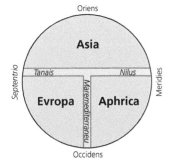

Figure 3.1 Example of a T-O map

2. Certain early European maps known as "T-O" maps,[1] created between the twelfth and fifteenth centuries, clearly reflect medieval Christian values, with Jerusalem placed at the centre of the world. Other maps from that place and time show terra incognita (unknown lands) to the south. Nineteenth-century European maps reflect the political and economic concerns of their creators: colonial possessions, for example, are prominently displayed. These maps established the conventions that most of us take for granted today: north at the top, 0° longitude running through Greenwich, England, and the map centred on either North America or Western Europe. These conventions are totally arbitrary—and yet their influence is enormous, because in effect they tell us that certain countries are world centres and others

are outliers. In sum, maps reflect the assumptions of their creators, and the viewer must understand their subjective limitations.

---

[1] consisting of a T drawn within an O, these maps show the world as a circle divided by a T-shaped body of water

Why does the author mention the fact that some early European maps represent the space to the south of Europe as *terra incognita*?

a) To show that geographical knowledge of the mapmakers at the time was limited

b) To show that maps rarely have subjective limitations

c) To show that the map-makers expressed their religious beliefs through the map

d) To show that maps are created based on their creators' subjective views

3. A geographic information system (GIS)—a computer-based tool that combines the storage, display, analysis, and mapping of spatially referenced data—has numerous and varied applications. Biologists analyze the effect on wildlife of changing land-use patterns. Geologists search for mineral deposits. Market analysts determine trade areas. Defence analysts select sites for military installations. The common factor is that the data involved are spatial. In brief, compared to traditional maps, a GIS achieves a whole new range of mapping and analytical capabilities—additional ways of handling spatial data.

How are the capabilities of GISs different from those of traditional maps?

a) GISs enable a computer-based analysis of data.

b) GISs display spatial data.

c) GISs are made for biologists, whereas traditional maps have a general usage.

d) GISs do not map spatially referenced data.

4. Both GISs and traditional maps have spatial data at their core. They both display geographical spaces, in small and large scales. However, a GIS challenges one of the most basic geographic conventions,

namely, the idea that regions are separated by lines. Of course, we know that this is not the case, but the very act of drawing maps with boundaries effectively creates both boundaries and the regions they circumscribe—it misleads us into thinking of them as fixed realities. A GIS is much more capable than a conventional map of depicting continuous spatial change, and thus requires users to think about geographic worlds without precise boundaries.

What is one distinct feature of a GIS?

    a) It can depict spaces in small and large scales.

    b) It can draw changing spaces but keep track of the boundaries they had.

    c) It is able to represent spatial data without assigning boundaries.

    d) It challenges our idea of regions as having no boundaries.

B. As seen in the paragraphs above, the location of the main idea in a paragraph varies. Although many paragraphs start with the main idea—this is a convention that most writing instructors expect—some paragraphs will have the main idea at the end, in the middle, or both at the beginning and at the end. The diagrams below represent the location of main ideas in a paragraph. Match each one to a paragraph above.

Paragraph ____

| Main idea opens a paragraph |
| Supporting details explain the main idea |

Paragraph ____

| Supporting details |
| Main idea as a summary or conclusion |

Paragraph ____

| Main idea |
| Supporting details |
| Main idea paraphrased |

Paragraph ____

| Introduction |
| Main idea, especially after a connector of contrast |
| Supporting details |

IDENTIFYING AN IMPLIED MAIN IDEA

Study the following paragraph. What is its main idea?

Easter Island, in the Pacific Ocean, was settled by the seventh century and possibly as early as the fifth century; the first settlers were likely Polynesians. They arrived at an island with few species of plants and animals and limited opportunities for fishing, but with considerable areas of woodland. Their diet consisted of sweet potatoes (an easy crop to cultivate) and chicken. The considerable amount of free time available allowed the Easter Islanders to engage in elaborate rituals and construct huge stone statues, called the *moai*. Agricultural activities, cooking food, cremating the dead, and building canoes required the removal of some trees on the island, but most of the deforestation was carried out for the purpose of moving the statues. By about 1550, the population peaked at roughly 7000. Deforestation, which would, over time, have led to soil erosion, reduced crop yields, and caused a shortage of building materials for both homes and boats, probably was complete by 1600. Without wood, Easter islanders were unable even to build canoes to catch porpoises (their principal source of protein) or to escape the remote island.

1. Are you able to locate one sentence that expresses the main idea of the paragraph? _____
2. What do you think is the purpose of telling the reader details of the Easter Islanders' way of life?

   _____

   _____

The example above demonstrates that some paragraphs do not contain a single sentence that expresses the main idea. Yet, the reader can **infer** the main idea based on the supporting details provided. To do that, the reader should ask the following questions: *What is the overall purpose of the paragraph? What is the one common idea underlying the details?*

Looking specifically at the details in the paragraph above, the reader must ask, *Why does the writer tell us that there were considerable areas of woodland when the Polynesians first arrived to Easter Island? Why does the writer tell us that many activities of Easter Islanders, especially* moai-*building, required a lot of wood?* Answers to these questions will lead to a conclusion about the main idea, which is **implied** in the text.

infer: to reach an opinion or decide that something is true on the basis of information that is available

imply: to suggest that something is true, without saying so directly

3. What is the implied main idea in the paragraph you have just read? Look at your answer in question 2 above, compare the options below, and select the best answer.

   a) Easter Island has a long and rich history.

   b) Creating the *moai* statues demanded a lot of work and resources, especially wood.

   c) Easter Islanders were creative people but had problems obtaining food.

   d) Easter Islanders destroyed their natural environment and way of life through deforestation.

Activity 2

In the paragraphs below, the main idea is implied. Study the supporting details and ask yourself which details are most significant and how they are connected. Then conclude what main point is implied in the paragraph.

1. Two facts about human impacts on climate are clear: humans are adding greenhouse gases to the atmosphere, and an increase in global temperature is therefore inevitable. But public understanding of these two incontrovertible facts is not helped by what is best described as the politicization of climate science. Most notably, individuals and organizations with a vested interest in the continued burning of fossil fuels (and they are legion in today's profit-oriented economy) have routinely questioned, even rejected, these two facts. Consider the comments made by Chrysler's chief economist in 2007 to the effect that any climate change is a far-off risk of uncertain magnitude. The publication of such comments suggests to many people that a legitimate scientific debate continues about whether humans are adding greenhouse gases and whether global warming is resulting.

Implied main idea: _____

_____

2. In the aftermath of the Chernobyl nuclear accident in 1986, about 350,000 people have been resettled away from the worst affected areas,

but another 5.5 million remain. For several years it was estimated that as many as 7,000 people died and up to 3.5 million suffered from diseases related to the release of radioactive material. More recently, a United Nations report estimated the number of deaths that had resulted as of 2005 at less than 4,000. However, a 2006 report from Greenpeace claimed that in the coming years about 100,000 will die of cancer, especially thyroid cancer, caused by the accident.

Implied main idea: _____

_____

3. Animal domestication serves many purposes, providing foods such as meat and milk (cows, pigs, sheep, goats), as well as draft animals (horses, donkeys, camels, oxen), and pets (dogs, cats). Once domesticated, animals have often been moved from place to place, both deliberately and accidentally. Whalers and sealers were probably the first to introduce European rabbits into the Australian region, but the key arrival was in 1859, when a few pairs were introduced into southeast Australia to provide so-called sport for sheep-station owners. Following this introduction, rabbits spread rapidly across the non-tropical parts of the continent, prompting a series of "unrelenting, devastating" (Powell, 1976) rabbit plagues. Rabbits consume vegetation needed by sheep and remain a problem today.

Implied main idea: _____

_____

DISTINGUISHING BETWEEN MAJOR AND MINOR SUPPORTING DETAILS

In many paragraphs, ideas can be categorized by their importance and level of generality. You already know that main ideas are the most general and most important within the paragraph. Among the supporting details, however, it is also possible to distinguish between general and specific points. The more

Outlining a text, as you learned in Unit 1, is a smart reading strategy. It forces the reader to process the information, thereby facilitating learning and retention.

general supporting details are called *major details*, and the more specific ones *minor details*.

Although not all paragraphs lend themselves to it, outlining main ideas, major supporting details, and minor supporting details is a useful habit.

Activity 3

A. Read the paragraph and fill in the blanks in the outline on page 53 with the main idea, and major and minor supporting details. Some are already completed for you.

Fertility is high throughout tropical Africa—in several countries the total fertility rate[1] (TFR) is between 6 and 7—but the national statistics mask some remarkable variations within countries. For some areas, TFRs are as low as 2 to 5. Various explanations have been offered for the fact that fertility rates in some areas are impaired (abnormally low for the region). Four will be noted here. First, there are cultural variations in the length of time a baby is breast-fed; breastfeeding limits ovulation and often extends the period of infertility following birth from about 2 months to 18 months. The second cause of localized areas of low fertility is the impact of diseases such as gonorrhea and syphilis, which can cause sterility and also tend to reduce the likelihood of sexual intercourse. Poor nutrition is the third cause: fertility declines following famine and is consistently low in areas experiencing chronic undernutrition. The fourth cause relates to marriage. Although almost all women marry, and the age at first marriage is usually in the mid-teens, there are exceptions. For example, among the Rendille of northern Kenya, cultural practices result in one-third of the women not marrying until their mid-thirties; and among nomadic pastoralists, periods of prolonged spousal separation are not uncommon.

_____

[1] the average number of children a woman will have, assuming she has children at the prevailing age-specific rates

Major supporting detail: TFRs within African countries vary greatly.

MAIN IDEA: Several factors influence impaired fertility rates.

Major supporting detail I: _____

Major supporting detail II: _____

    Minor supporting detail: Examples of diseases: gonorrhea and syphilis

Major supporting detail III: _____

Major supporting detail IV: _____

    Minor supporting detail: Some Rendille women marry in mid-thirties.

    Minor supporting detail: _____

B. Read the paragraph and fill in the blanks in the outline below with the main idea, and major and minor supporting details.

The total fertility rate for Germany (1.4) reflects an unprecedented trend in the former East Germany, which appears to have come as close to a temporary suspension of child-bearing as any large population in the human experience. Eastern Germans have virtually stopped having children. The explanation is not an increase in abortions, which have also fallen abruptly. One possible explanation is the trauma associated with the transition from communism to capitalism, and specifically, concern about employment opportunities for future generations in a region with high levels of unemployment. It may be appropriate, then, to interpret the low fertility rate in Germany—actually a form of demographic disorder—as one temporary outcome of the transition from the "old" to the "new" political order. This suggestion appears to have some merit, as fertility also declined between 1989 and 1993 by 20 percent in Poland, 25 percent in Bulgaria, 30 percent in Romania and Estonia, and 35 percent in Russia (*The Economist*, 1993: 54)

MAIN IDEA: _____

Major supporting detail: _____

    A. *Minor supporting detail*: _____

    B. *Minor supporting detail*: _____

    C. *Minor supporting detail*: _____

    D. *Minor supporting detail*: _____

IDENTIFYING ORGANIZATIONAL PATTERNS

Main ideas and supporting details are often organized in specific patterns, depending on the writer's purpose. For example, if the purpose is to show several effects of climate change, the writer will probably state the goal in the main idea sentence and outline the specific effects as supporting details. Certain words and phrases, including *as a result of*, *causes*, *because*, and *due to*, will point to the fact that the organizational pattern of this paragraph is cause-effect.

The following are the most common organizational patterns used in academic writing. Often, a paragraph will have one central pattern, with elements of other patterns supporting it.

Cause-effect: explores the causes and/or the effects of an event or state

Process: describes steps in a process, so that each step leads to the next one

Classification: divides items into groups

Definition: defines a term or concept

Comparison: describes similarities between items

Contrast: describes differences between items

Problem-solution: illustrates a problem and its solution

Description: describes an event, state, person, or item

Activity 4

Read the following paragraphs and identify which organizational patterns they follow. Think about the writer's purpose in each paragraph. Underline the words or phrases that help you see the central pattern. Highlight the main idea. The first paragraph is marked for you.

1. Organizational pattern: _____Definition_____

"Gaia" is the Greek name for the goddess of the earth. Today the term is used to denote a self-regulating system, with all components of the ecosphere—chemical, physical, and biological systems—in a stable balance that keeps the planet habitable. This remarkable concept was first introduced in a book by James Lovelock (1979). In brief, Gaia is seen as a self-regulating entity that keeps the environment relatively constant and comfortable for life; earth and all life on it have evolved together as one.

2. Organizational pattern: _____

The principal response to the fact of global warming and its probable consequences has been an effort to implement policies that will reduce the emission of greenhouse gases. Most notably, the UN-sponsored Kyoto Protocol established goals that, if met, were expected to slow the rate of global warming. This Protocol, a legally binding agreement to cut greenhouse gas emissions, was reached in 1997 by about 150 countries but only came into force in early 2005 with most participating countries agreeing to reduce emissions by a specific percentage.

3. Organizational pattern: _____

There are many different opinions about the impact of human activities on the environment. At one extreme are catastrophists, who view the current situation and future prospects in totally negative terms. At the other extreme are cornucopians,[1] who believe that the gravity of current problems has been greatly exaggerated and that human ingenuity and technology will overcome the moderate problems that do exist.

_____

[1] this term is derived from *cornucopia*, the magical "horn of plenty" in Greek mythology that provides its users with food and drink that never end

4. Organizational pattern: _____

According to Fagan (2004), it is possible that the early civilization in Mesopotamia was prompted by a period of reduced rainfall that began about 3800 BCE, causing many farmers to abandon their fields and seek work in a few favoured locations where irrigation was a practical possibility. Reduction in rainfall also obliged farmers in irrigated areas to innovate and intensify, for example, by using draft animals for the first time. This concentration of increasingly intensive grain production in a few advantaged areas may then have encouraged urban growth and other characteristics of civilization.

5. Organizational pattern: _____

In the course of history, our societies have been organized into several types. Feudalism was a non-centralized system of governance and social and economic organization that developed in Northern Europe over the centuries following the collapse of the Roman Empire (c. 375). Under the feudal system, all land was owned by the king, who effectively delegated control of it to his warrior lords (vassals) in return for their military and political support. Peasants worked the land and were permitted to live on the land in exchange for their labour. Capitalism was a new type of social and economic organization that began to emerge as early as the late sixteenth century and that was fully in place in many parts of Europe by the eighteenth century. Capitalism is characterized by the transformation of labour into a commodity that can be bought and sold, and the separation of the producer (the worker) from the means of production, which are owned by the capitalist class. Today, capitalism is the dominant form of economic and social organization. In the twentieth century, a number of societies rejected capitalism in favour of socialism, a form of social and economic organization based on common ownership of the means of production and distribution of products. Socialism focuses on community, equality, the well-being of society as a whole, and the vision of a classless society.

STUDYING GRAPHICAL INFORMATION

Many academic texts contain tables, graphs, or charts. These graphic elements of a text are a useful way of presenting information because they illustrate trends or specific details related to a topic in a visually clear way. Moreover, providing a chart with statistical details is often the most concise way to support main ideas in the text.

The first step in working with a chart, graph, or table is studying its title, which explains *what* information is being illustrated. After looking at the title, read the headings in the table or on the x- and y-axis of the graph. These will indicate *how* the data is being illustrated and will often show the units of measurement in which the statistics are expressed (people, millions of dollars, percentages, etc.)

After reading the data contained in the chart, graph, or table, reflect on it by drawing connections between the ideas in the text and the supporting information presented in the chart. Doing so will help you form a full picture of the text.

Visual aids may reflect data at a fixed point in time or data changing with time. Pie charts, tables, and bar graphs most often reflect data at a fixed point in time, while linear graphs illustrate data changing over time.

Read the following text, study the chart accompanying it, and answer the questions.

01 Like many cultural variables—indeed, like culture itself—language began as a single entity (or at most a few different ones) and diversified into many. Over the long period of human life on earth, many languages have arisen and many others have died out. During the past several hundred years, however, a new language is a rarity while the disappearance of a language is commonplace. Of the roughly 7,000 distinct languages (not counting minor dialects) that existed 400 years ago, approximately 1,000 have disappeared, leaving about 6,000 languages today. Many more may vanish over the next few hundred years. Current estimates by UNESCO suggest that about 3,000 languages are endangered and that one language dies about every two weeks. None of these numbers are certain. For example, some sources put the current number of languages at closer to 7,000.

02 Most languages are spoken by relatively few people. Indeed, about 96 percent of the world's population speaks only 4 percent of the world's languages. Table 3.1 identifies the nine languages spoken that have more than 100 million native speakers. Mandarin has more native speakers than any other language, with Spanish ranking second. Different sources often suggest different data on numbers of speakers because some sources focus on all speakers rather than on native speakers; if this method of estimating is employed, then the number of English speakers increases markedly from that noted in Table 3.1.

03 Languages die for two related reasons. First, a language with few speakers tends to be associated with low social status and economic disadvantage, so those who do speak it may not teach it to their children. In some cases this results in people choosing to speak a different language associated with economic success and social progress. Also, when a language has few speakers the specific reason for disappearance might be a natural disaster, such as drought or the spread of disease. Second, because globalization depends on communication between previously separate groups, it is becoming essential for more and more people to speak a major language such as English or Chinese. Already, a very few dominant languages effectively control global economics, politics, and culture.

LANGUAGE	NUMBER OF SPEAKERS (MILLIONS)
Mandarin	1,213
Spanish	329
English	328
Arabic	221
Hindi	182
Bengali	181
Portuguese	178
Russian	144
Japanese	122

Table 3.1 Languages with more than 100 million native speakers, 2010

Source: "Statistical summaries." Ethnologue: Languages of the World, Statistical Summaries, www.ethnologue.com/ethno_docs/distribution.asp?by=size

1. What is the main idea of paragraph 1?
    a) A language disappears almost every two weeks.
    b) It is not exactly clear how many languages exist on Earth today.
    c) Multiple languages in use today have evolved from one or two ancient languages.
    d) In modern times, there is a tendency for languages to disappear.

2. Are the statistical details mentioned in paragraph 1 reflected in Table 3.1?

    _____

3. Complete the following sentence.

    The main idea of paragraph 3 is _____,

    _____

    and the two major supporting details are _____

    _____ and

    _____

4. Mark the statement as T (true) or F (false).

    ___ Table 3.1 supports the idea that a large portion of people on Earth speak only a small fraction of world languages.

5. According to Table 3.1, how many people speak Portuguese as a native language? _____

6. Does the table describe data at a fixed point in time or data changing with time?

    _____

7. Does Table 3.1 show how many people speak English as their second language?

    _____

8. Give your own example or explanation of how a dominant language controls global culture.

    _____

    _____

Activity 6

Read the following text, study the visual aids accompanying it, and answer the questions.

01 As in most of the world, urbanization is continuing in Canada. Changes in total, urban, and rural population between 1950 and 2000 and projected through to 2030 are shown in Table 3.2 and graphed in Figure 3.2. From 60.8 percent in 1950, Canada's urban population for 2030 is projected to reach 87.2 percent.

02   The urban centres increasing most in population are those located relatively close to the US border, those attracting immigrants both from elsewhere in Canada and from overseas, and those with economies based on manufacturing or services. Newfoundland and Labrador is the only region in Canada that is experiencing a declining urban population.

03   The projected decrease in rural population is not simply a reflection of rural-to-urban migration but also indicates anticipated urban sprawl and rural growth, so that locations and households presently classified as rural will have been enveloped by urban growth and expansion, and thus be reclassified.

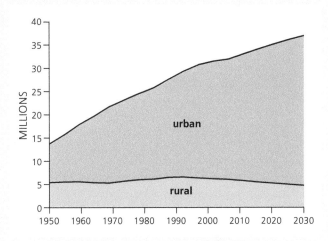

Figure 3.2 Rural and urban populations, Canada, 1950–2030

Source: Produced using data from United Nations Department of Economic and Social Affairs, Population Division, *World Population Prospects: The 2002 Revision and World Urbanization Prospects: The 2003 Revision*. At: esa.un.org/unup

YEAR	TOTAL POPULATION	URBAN POPULATION	PERCENTAGE URBAN	RURAL POPULATION	PERCENTAGE RURAL
1950	13,737	8,356	60.8	5,381	39.2
2000	30,769	24,429	79.4	6,340	20.6
2015	34,133	28,667	84.0	5,467	16.0
2030	36,980	32,251	87.2	4,729	12.8

Table 3.2 Canada: Total, urban, and rural population (000), 1950–2030

Source: Adapted from United Nations Department of Economic and Social Affairs, Population Division, *World Population Prospects: The 2002 Revision and World Urbanization Prospects: The 2003 Revision*. At: <esa.un.org/unup>

1. Compare Table 3.2 and Figure 3.2.

   a) Do these charts reflect some identical data? _____

   b) Why does the author choose to include both a table and a graph here?

   _____

   _____

2. According to paragraph 1, from 60.8 percent in 1950, the proportion of Canada's population living in urban areas in 2030 is projected to reach 87.2 percent. Highlight the data described in this sentence on the relevant chart.

3. a) Is the information described in paragraph 2 reflected in either the table or the graph?

   _____

   b) Why do you think the population is increasing in cities close to the US border?

   _____

   _____

4. a) Which paragraph of the text offers explanations for the trends illustrated in the charts? _____

   b) What are the causes of the projected decline in rural population?

   _____

INTEGRATING THE SKILLS

Use all the reading skills you learned in this unit:
- Distinguishing between main ideas and supporting details
- Identifying an implied main idea
- Distinguishing between major and minor supporting details
- Studying graphical information
- Identifying organizational patterns

Activity 7

Read the following excerpt from a geography textbook. Then answer the questions.

The Geography of Happiness

01 An interesting recent focus is on the idea of happiness. Notoriously difficult to measure, happiness is clearly related to, but different from, the idea of well-being. Essentially, it is how we perceive ourselves, and thus cannot be measured objectively. It is not unusual in some countries for surveys to be conducted that ask us, to put it simply, whether we are very happy, just happy, or not so happy. There is even a regularly updated World Database of Happiness housed in Erasmus University, Rotterdam. Those who conduct these surveys and those who then interpret and publish their thoughts on happiness are at the forefront of what *The Economist* (2006: 13) humorously described as the "upstart science of happiness," blending economics, psychology, and geography.

02 Two general points that emerge from this work are, not surprisingly, that the rich report greater happiness than do the poor, and, perhaps surprisingly, that people in affluent countries have not become happier as they have become richer. The latter finding might be because: (1) for many people, happiness is having things that others do not have, so as others become wealthier then the already wealthy become less happy; (2) when people achieve a better standard of living they are unable to appreciate its pleasures.

03 Of particular interest to human geographers is research that focuses on the spatial distribution of happiness. The first world map of happiness at the country scale, published in 2006, showed Denmark first, followed by Switzerland, Austria, Iceland, Bahamas, Finland, Sweden, Bhutan, Brunei, and Canada. Least happy of the 178 countries included were DR of Congo, Zimbabwe, and Burundi (Figure 3.3). There is a close relationship between happiness and measures of health, prosperity, and education. These results are much as expected, and much of the interest in this work is on the detailed differences between countries, on how happiness might be more scientifically measured, and on whether or not individual responses reflect reality. With this latter point in mind, a geography of happiness project has been set up in Britain involving geography teachers travelling through Europe to determine how happy people are and whether these informal surveys accord with the published data.

Source: W. Norton, *Human Geography*, 8th edition (Don Mills, ON: Oxford University Press, 2013), pp. 319–320.

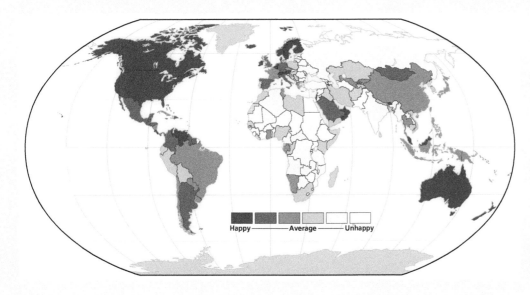

Figure 3.3 World distribution of happiness

1. A. What is the main idea of paragraph 1?

   a) A recent interest in measuring happiness points to the establishment of a new science of happiness.

   b) Happiness and well-being are not the same thing.

   c) Some countries conduct surveys on happiness.

   d) There is a regularly updated database of information on the state of happiness in different countries.

   B. Is this main idea implied or explicit? _____

2. Reread paragraph 2 and mark the following statements with MI (main idea) or SD (supporting details).

   a) ____ People wish to have things that others do not have, and this makes them happy.

   b) ____ The fact that rich people report greater happiness than poor people is not surprising.

   c) ____ People do not always appreciate a high standard of living.

   d) ____ On one hand, rich people seem to be happier than poor people; on the other hand, the level of happiness in rich countries does not rise with increasing wealth.

3. What is the organizational pattern of paragraph 2?

   a) Classification

   b) Effect-cause

   c) Description

   d) Contrast

4. Study paragraph 3 and identify the main idea, and major and minor supporting details. Use the prompt questions below the lines to help you.

   Main idea: _____

   Is there research on the connection between happiness and location?

   A. Minor supporting detail: _____

   Which countries are high on the scale of happiness?

   B. Minor supporting detail: _____

   Which countries are low on the scale of happiness?

   Major supporting detail I: _____

   Is there a correlation between happiness and indicators of social development of a country?

Major supporting detail II: _____

What are some specific questions researchers have?

C. Minor supporting detail: _____

What has been done to verify the current data on happiness?

5. Study Figure 3.3.

a) Does the map, in general, support the idea expressed in the text that there is a relationship between happiness and the measures of health, prosperity, and education? Explain.

_____

_____

_____

b) There are a number of countries shaded in grey on the map; however, there is no grey on the happiness scale at the bottom. What do you think the grey areas might represent?

_____

_____

c) Find your home country on the map. Where on the scale of happiness is it located? _____

Do you feel the map describes your home country correctly? Explain.

_____

_____

_____

Inferences, Facts, and Opinions

"There aren't any icons to click. It's a chalk board."

Study the cartoon and check the statements that you agree with.

____ The teacher has asked the student to write his response or solution to a problem on the board.

____ The student spends a lot of time on the computer.

____ The teacher would like her students to read a lot.

____ The teacher never uses computers in her classroom.

____ Today, many children love using computers.

____ Children should not spend too much time on the Internet because this activity discourages them from reading books.

When assessing situations, in real life or in texts, we differentiate between several kinds of information. Some information is **explicitly** expressed. For example, we see that the two characters in the cartoon are the teacher and the student, and the teacher is explaining that the chalkboard has no icons. The humour in the cartoon relies on **implicit** information—the reader has to use clues to draw a conclusion, or **inference**, to understand the joke. You should be able to infer, based on the teacher's response, what the boy's question or statement was. Although the cartoon does not explicitly tell you that the boy spends a lot of time on the computer, you can draw this inference based on the clues provided: the boy is shocked that he has to write with chalk rather than click an icon, which is what he is used to doing. You can also infer, based on the poster next to the chalkboard, that the teacher would like her students to read a lot.

> **explicit**: clear and easy to understand
> **implicit**: suggested without being directly expressed
> to **infer**, or to **make an inference**: to reach an opinion or decide that something is true on the basis of information that is available.

In order to make correct, or *valid,* inferences, you have to assess all the clues carefully. If you do not find sufficient clues to support your inference, the inference is probably incorrect, or *invalid*. For example, the idea that the teacher never uses computer technology in her class is an invalid inference; although the classroom has a chalkboard, which the teacher is using at the moment, it is possible that the teacher does have computers that she also uses.

Write down an example of an inference you have made in the last several days. It could relate to your everyday life or studies.

Example: When my father walked into our apartment, I did not hear him unlocking the door. I must have left the door unlocked after I came in from school.

_____

_____

fact: a piece of information that can be proved true by objective evidence
opinion: a subjective belief in a person's mind

In addition to thinking about information as implicit and explicit, we can categorize information into facts and opinions. For instance, the idea that many children, like the student in the cartoon, love computers is a **fact** that can be verified using objective evidence, such as a survey of a large group of children. In contrast, that children should not spend too much time on the computer is an **opinion**, a personal belief. People have different opinions on the same subject: some may think using computers is a great skill for children to master and should be pursued without any time limitation, while others will disagree. Both opinions are valid as long as they are backed up by solid evidence.

Write two sentences: one expressing a fact and the other an opinion. Make an effort to come up with significant information in your sentences. Then read them to your partner and let him or her guess which sentence is a fact and which is an opinion.

Fact: _____

Opinion: _____

Why do you think it is important to be able to make inferences from the information you read? Why is it important to differentiate between facts and opinions?

This unit explores the following strategies in learning about inferences, facts, and opinions:

1. Assessing valid and invalid inferences
2. Distinguishing between facts and opinions
3. Learning about informed opinions
4. Identifying biased opinions

ASSESSING VALID AND INVALID INFERENCES

Inferring information is a fundamental reading skill: a specific text is usually part of a larger discourse—a part of a textbook or a discussion started earlier, for example—and so the reader has to make inferences based on his or her knowledge outside that particular text. In addition, the author usually does not explain every single connection between ideas in a given text and so expects the reader to make connections between ideas independently.

Making valid inferences requires you to use logical reasoning, that is, the ability to trace causes and effects. Also necessary are some general knowledge—the knowledge of scientific, cultural, or historical facts or events, for example—and an awareness of social context.

Activity 1

Study the following passages, note the remarks on the margins, and mark each inference as V (valid) or I (invalid). The first passage is done for you.

1. Astronomers have found a new planet, the closest yet outside our solar system, and just an astronomical stone's throw away at four light years, raising the chances of finding a habitable planet in Earth's neighbourhood.

   Making inferences from this passage requires the knowledge of the scientific term "light year."

   a) __I__ The newly found planet is geographically close to Earth. (*Four light years refers to an astronomical distance so the planet is definitely not geographically close to Earth.*)

   b) __I__ The planet is habitable. (*According to the text, this discovery improves the "chances of finding a habitable planet," which indicates that this planet is not habitable.*)

   c) __V__ Astronomers have found planets outside our solar system before. (*This new planet is "the closest yet outside our solar system" which means that others have been found before.*)

2. Researchers say the new planet is too close to its sun to support known forms of life, with a surface temperature estimated at 1,200°C. But previous studies suggest that when one planet is discovered orbiting a sun, there are usually others in the same system.

   a) ____ Forms of life that are familiar to us cannot exist in temperatures of 1,200 °C.

   b) ____ It is a rare case when only one planet orbits its sun.

   c) ____ The extreme heat on the new planet is created by its closeness to the sun.

   d) ____ Scientists hope life is possible on one of the planets in the discussed solar system.

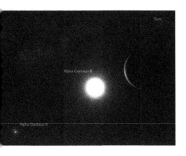

3. Alpha Centauri is a three-star system consisting of two stars similar to our sun and a faint red star called Proxima Centauri. The planet orbits Alpha Centauri B. Astronomers have speculated about planets orbiting these suns since the 19th century but small planets like this [recent discovery] are hard to find, and instruments have only recently become sensitive enough to detect them.

   a) ___ Astronomers in the nineteenth century could see planets in other systems.

   b) ___ Astronomical instruments in the past were very primitive.

   c) ___ Astronomers today can detect a distant planet of a small size.

   d) ___ Recently, there has been an advance in the development of sensitive astronomical instruments.

4. A drug made from a plant known as "thunder god vine," or *lei gong tei*, that has been used in traditional Chinese medicine wiped out pancreatic tumours in mice, researchers said, and may soon be tested on humans.

   a) ___ Traditional Chinese medicine is rich in plants that cure cancer.

   b) ___ All drugs are made from plants.

   c) ___ There is hope that "thunder god vine" will help to fight cancer in humans.

Making inferences from this passage requires some previous knowledge of how fingerprinting is used by law enforcement, ie. police.

5. Biometrics is the science of humans' physiological or behavioural characteristics, and it is being used to develop technology that recognizes and matches unique patterns in fingerprints, faces and eyes and even sweat glands[1] and buttock pressure. As technologies advance, the use of biometrics in everyday life is shifting from traditional law enforcement and government security to a host of more consumer-friendly applications. For example, BIOPTid Inc. created a device that users can hook up to their computers and mobile electronics to replace passwords for Internet logins and banking. The

cube reads a personal sweat gland barcode to verify identity from the moisture on a user's fingertip. "With one touch, you can log right into your social networking site, right onto your page. You can instantly purchase something without having a credit card or form of ID," says the representative of the company.

---

[1] organs in a person's body that produce sweat

a) ____ Biometrics may help to identify a person who committed a crime and left fingerprints on the scene.

b) ____ Online bank accounts might be at risk for fraudulent activity.

c) ____ Human sweat contains characteristics that are unique to each person.

d) ____ The invention of the BIOPTid device will completely replace passwords in the future.

e) ____ More people will use Internet banking services or social networking sites with the spread of biometric identification.

6. The simplest way to stick to your calorie intake goals is to track what you eat, but how many calories are hiding in that spinach salad anyway? MealSnap is a fun new application released this year that lets you track your calories simply by snapping a picture of your plate. The app analyzes the food it detects in the photo and produces a calorie estimate. . . . The app runs rather slowly, the calories are just estimates, it costs $3 to download and it's only available on iPhone. But the fun factor may make you more inclined to use it and help you keep a rough idea of your calorie intake.

Making inferences from this passage, as from most other texts, requires sharing a common social context and values, such as the idea that one should watch one's caloric intake and be slim.

a) ____ MealSnap ensures that a person does not overeat.

b) ____ MealSnap helps to control one's caloric intake.

c) ____ The application has a few disadvantages.

d) ____ The creators of MealSnap developed their product knowing that many people watch their weight.

Read the passages below. Each is followed by an invalid inference or inferences. Explain why the inference is invalid and write a valid inference related to the same idea. Remember that in order to make a valid inference, one has to find sufficient support in the text to back up that inference.

1. *Openness*, probably the most important [design] feature [of human language], is the ability to talk about the same experiences from different perspectives, using different words and various grammatical constructions. This feature allows people to conceptualize, label, and discuss the same experience in different ways. Thus no single human interpretation of an experience is necessarily more correct in every respect than all others. To understand how truly significant the feature of  openness is to communication, compare our spoken language to the vocal communication systems (or *call systems*) of monkeys and apes. Whereas our language allows us to endlessly combine and recombine elements of our experiences in new and various ways, the possibilities of meaning are much more limited when it comes to call systems. Primates have several calls, all of which are appropriate to specific situations: when the animal is in the presence of food; when it is in danger or pain; when it wants to show friendly interest or the desire for company; when it wants to mark its location; and so on. Each call is appropriate in only one situation, and primates cannot combine one call with another to express more complex messages.

Invalid inference: Because their communication system is limited, primates do not develop social relations with other members of the group.

Why invalid? _____

_____

Valid inference: _____

_____

2. Sociolinguist Deborah Tannen (1990) has gained much popular attention in the media with her study of speech patterns of men and women in the United States. Tannen focusses on typical male and female styles of discourse, arguing that men and women use language for different reasons: men tend to use language as a competitive weapon in public settings, whereas women tend to use language as a way of building closeness in private settings. Tannen shows what happens when men and women each assume that their rules are the only rules without realizing that the other gender may be defining appropriate language use from a different perspective. For example, when a husband and wife get home from work at the end of the day, she may be eager to talk while he is just as eager to remain silent. She may interpret his silence as a sign of distance or coldness and be hurt. He, in contrast, may be weary of the day's verbal combat and resent his wife's attempts at conversation, not because he is rejecting her personally but because he believes he has a right to remain silent.

Invalid inference: Deborah Tannen discovered the primary reason why couples have marital problems.

Why invalid? _____

_____

Valid inference: _____

_____

3. Anthropologist Colin Turnbull worked among the Mbuti of the northeastern Democratic Republic of the Congo (formerly Zaire) for many years. He discovered that these people, who live all their lives in a dense forest, have no experience of distance greater than a few feet and are therefore not accustomed to taking distance into consideration when estimating the size of an object in the visual field. Turnbull took one of his informants,[1] Kenge, on a trip that brought them out of the forest and into a game park. For the first time in his life, Kenge faced vast, rolling grasslands. Kenge's response to this experience was dramatic: "When Kenge topped the rise, he stopped dead. Every smallest sign of mirth[2] suddenly left his face. He opened

---

[1] a person from whom an anthropologist obtains information about local culture
[2] happiness

his mouth but could say nothing. He moved his head and eyes slowly and unbelievingly." (Turnbull 1961: 251) When Kenge finally saw the far-off animals grazing on the plain, he asked Turnbull what insects they were. When told that they were buffalo, Kenge laughed and accused Turnbull of lying. Then he strained to see better and inquired what kind of buffalo could be so small. Later, when Turnbull pointed out a fishing boat on the lake, Kenge scoffed at him and insisted it was a piece of floating wood.

Invalid inference: Kenge had never seen a buffalo before.

Why invalid? _____

_____

Valid inference: _____

_____

DISTINGUISHING BETWEEN FACTS AND OPINIONS

We state facts and express opinions on a daily basis. Newspaper items describing current events might include both facts and opinions. Academic textbooks and articles also include both facts (hard data objectively proven by research) and opinions (the authors' predictions or subjective comments).

The main distinction between facts and opinions is that a fact can be supported by solid, objective evidence, while an opinion cannot be proved true or false conclusively by objective evidence. Rather, an opinion is subjective, a belief that might be true for one person, but false in the eyes of another.

It is important to distinguish between facts and opinions because doing so will help the reader to critically evaluate the text. A competent reader assesses the support that writers present for their ideas to decide whether the writers are stating facts or opinions.

Activity 3

Read each passage, along with the remarks in the margins. Mark the statements following each passage F (fact) or O (opinion).

1. Suicide is contagious among youth for at least two years, a new study shows: when children commit suicide, their school peers are more likely to consider or attempt suicide, the study, published in the *Canadian Medical Association Journal*, concluded. Dr. Ian Colman, Canada Research Chair in Mental Health Epidemiology and senior author of the study, said the results were "shocking" and should influence the way school boards handle grief counselling. Colman studied the results of a decade-long Statistics Canada survey of more than 20,000 children 12 to 17 years old; he found 12- and 13-year-olds exposed to suicide are five times more likely to "seriously consider attempting suicide." Colman said counselling should be schoolwide, rather than for the "closest friends or immediate classmates or team members," and available long-term, not just for a few months.

This passage came from a newspaper. A newspaper report may include both facts and opinions, although traditionally a reporter should not express a personal opinion, reporting the events from a neutral perspective.

a) ____ If a child commits suicide, his or her peers are more likely to consider doing the same.

b) ____ The results of Colman's research are shocking.

c) ____ The Statistics Canada survey lasted 10 years.

d) ____ Post-suicide school counselling should last longer than a few months.

2. To some people, the mention of globalization inspires visions of the global village—a world where every person is linked by the latest high-technology communications systems and where free trade and the efficient operation of the world's economy contribute to growing wealth for all. To others, globalization is the reason a local factory shuts down, only to reopen thousands of kilometres away in a country with cheaper labour, poor labour practices (for example, child labour and no tolerance of labour unions), and weaker environmental laws. To critics, globalization means the destruction of local cultures and the weakening of traditional religious beliefs, only to be replaced by a homogenized (blended into a uniform state), largely American-dominated culture.

This passage from a social studies textbook lists several interpretations of globalization. Each interpretation is unique to a certain group of people. In other words, they have different opinions about globalization.

a) ____ Globalization ensures people have more opportunity to accumulate wealth.

b) ____ Some companies exploit child labour.

c) ____ Some factories are relocated to countries where production costs are low.

d) ____ Local cultures are eroded by the global dominance of American culture.

Scientific theories can also be opinions if they have not been proven by objective evidence. Notice how opinions about chemical elements have changed in the course of history.

3. The Greek philosopher Aristotle thought everything on Earth was made from four elements—earth, air, fire, and water. This four-element theory existed for more than 2000 years. Although it is true that basic substances, called elements, comprise all objects and living things on Earth, Aristotle was wrong about the specific elements he chose and the idea of what an element is. He could not know that an element is matter made up entirely of atoms with the same atomic number—the same number of protons[1] in the nucleus of an atom. We have identified more than 100 elements, and earth, air, fire, and water are not among them. The three most abundant elements in the Earth's crust are oxygen, silicon, and aluminum.

_____

[1] positively charged particles

a) ____ Everything around us is made up of elements.

b) ____ Aristotle considered earth, air, fire, and water elements.

c) ____ There are at least 100 elements.

d) ____ Aristotle's thinking was simplistic.

LEARNING ABOUT INFORMED OPINIONS

As discussed earlier, opinions are different from facts in that they reflect subjective beliefs, not objective truths. However, this does not detract from the validity of opinions. Opinions backed up by solid evidence can be considered valid: we call them *informed opinions*. In your textbooks and lectures, you will often encounter informed opinions. Usually, an academic's goal is to verify an opinion by studying a problem and finding evidence to support the opinion. As a student, you are expected to have a perspective on the subject matter you study and to demonstrate that your opinion is well-considered and valid. In other words, you will be encouraged to produce informed opinions.

Sometimes it is impossible to find objective, empirical support for an opinion. In that case, other kinds of support for an informed opinion may be acceptable.

KINDS OF SUPPORT FOR AN INFORMED OPINION

- **Research results**: may include statistics or may be simply a statement of fact
- **Statistical data**: information shown in numbers; may or may not be connected to a research project
- **Expert opinions**: the opinion of an expert in a *relevant* field can be used to support an informed opinion
- **Logical reasoning**: used to trace rational connections between causes and effects
- **Relevant examples and anecdotes**: used to illustrate or personalize a situation
- **Personal experience**: not all personal experiences will support an informed opinion; they are generally not considered appropriate in academic texts

Activity 4

Read each passage and underline the opinion expressed. Then decide which types of support are used to make the opinion informed, highlighting the relevant words and phrases.

1. Francesca Gino and her colleagues (2010) randomly assigned female students to one of two groups to perform a series of very difficult puzzles while wearing sunglasses. The first group believed they were wearing authentic designer sunglasses, while the second group believed the sunglasses they wore were designer knockoffs[1]. Actually, all participants wore authentic designer sunglasses while completing the puzzles. The participants were told they would be rewarded for the number of puzzles they solved and that the investigators were using the honour system—participants would tally up their own scores and submit them. In fact, the experimenters tracked the number of puzzles each participant solved and the number each claimed to have solved. As predicted, participants lied about their performance, reporting more solved puzzles than they actually completed. The surprising finding was that significantly more participants in the "fake sunglasses" group cheated (71 percent) compared to the participants in the "authentic sunglasses" group (30 percent). . . Francesca Gino and her colleagues conclude that there are negative consequences of wearing designer knock-offs, including a greater likelihood of behaving dishonestly. . .

---

[1] a cheap version of an expensive, brand-name item

Support: _____

2. One of the foundational insights provided by sociology is that our lived realities are constructed socially. We become human through a social process, and our understanding of the world is forever framed by these social experiences. For example, a new friend offers to give us a ride home. When we approach her car in the parking lot, we do not simply register the fact that here is a vehicle with four wheels and an engine. Rather, we immediately and unconsciously run through a whole gamut of socially constructed meanings—meanings embedded in patterns of social inequality. The age, make, and upkeep of the car are all instantly noted. That our new friend drives a brand-new, sparkling BMW evokes a whole range of social reactions and connections that are quite different from those we would experience if a rusty, dented Toyota Corolla were sitting there.

Support: _____

3. Social stratification—the hierarchical arrangement of individuals based upon wealth, power, and prestige—is an issue in Canadian society.

I grew up in one of the many postwar suburban developments that sprang up as the federal government provided low-cost housing to ex-soldiers. The subdivision was filled with streets of families living in similar economic circumstances. Social class was apparently a non-issue. However, when asked in a first-year sociology course to find out my social class, reality revealed its complexities. From my mother's viewpoint, we were "working-class," while my father embraced the North American ideal of classlessness—we were "middle-class." For my mother, a war bride who grew up in hard-scrabble working-class London, England, being a member of the working class was a statement of pride—we worked for a living and didn't rely on others. For my father, being a member of the middle class reflected Canada's openness—here everyone was equal and had the same opportunity to advance.

Class was an issue—even within my own family.

–Ann Duffy

Support: _____

4. Despite public beliefs about the random nature of violence, sociologists have known for decades that the risks of becoming a victim of crime are anything but random. Like disease, accidents, and other kinds of negative life events, violence seems more likely to afflict some of us than others.

Sociological researchers have been able to document the "social structure of violence" through large-scale studies that ask a representative sample of the population about crimes they may have experienced during some defined period of time (e.g., the previous six months or the previous year). These studies allow the researchers to compare the profiles of victims and non-victims and therefore to identify the factors that seem to be associated with the risk of becoming a victim of violence.

The most recent such Canadian study was conducted by Statistics Canada in 2009. . . . Among the findings relating to the differential risk of violent victimization are the following:

- Younger Canadians were more likely than older Canadians to become victims of violence. . . .
- With respect to marital status, single people were most likely to be victims and married people were least likely.
- Rates of violent victimization were lower for people who identified as a visible minority than for non-visible minorities. Rates of victimization were also lower for immigrants than for non-immigrants.
- Violent victimization was associated with higher levels of alcohol consumption.

Support: _____

IDENTIFYING BIASED OPINIONS

The *Oxford Advanced Learner's Dictionary* defines **bias** as "a strong feeling in favour of or against one group of people, or one side in an argument, often not based on fair judgement."

This definition clearly illustrates the difference between an informed opinion and a biased opinion: while a writer presents credible support for an informed opinion (and

All writers bring a certain point of view or perspective to their texts, often stemming from their political, cultural, or ideological backgrounds. All writing is influenced by the writer's point of view. Here, however, we are assessing writers' bias, which goes beyond point of view or perspective. When identifying bias, the reader's concern is whether the writer's approach is unfair, misleading, unsupported, or illogical.

may be willing to consider the opposite point of view), he or she presents a one-sided argument in the case of a biased argument. Often, the holder of a biased opinion is not willing to consider the disadvantages of or alternatives to his or her point of view. A critical reader should be able to identify biased opinions.

Consider the following texts and answer the questions that follow.

A. "Offensive." "Grotesque." "Revolting." "Repugnant." "Repulsive." These are the words most commonly heard these days regarding the prospect of human cloning. Such reactions one hears both from the man or woman in the street and from the intellectuals, from believers and atheists, from humanists and scientists. Even Dolly's[1] creator, Dr. Wilmot, has said he "would find it offensive" to clone a human being. People are repelled by many aspects of human cloning: The prospect of mass production of human beings, with large clones of look-alikes, compromised in their individuality; the idea of father-son or mother-daughter twins; the bizarre prospects of a woman giving birth to a genetic copy of herself, her spouse, or even her deceased father or mother; the creation of embryonic genetic duplicates of oneself, to be frozen away in case of later need for homologous organ transplantation; the narcissism of those who would clone themselves, the arrogance of others who think they know who deserves to be cloned or which genotype any child-to-be should be thrilled to receive; the Frankensteinian[2] hubris to create human life and increasingly to control its destiny; man playing at being God. Almost no one sees any compelling reason for human cloning; almost everyone anticipates its possible misuses and abuses. Many feel oppressed by the sense that there is nothing we can do to prevent it from happening. This makes the prospect all the more revolting.

---

[1] the first mammal, a sheep, to be cloned from an adult cell in 1996
[2] Frankenstein is a fictional scientist who created a monster.

1. What is the author's opinion about human cloning?

   _____

2. Which adjectives does the author use to describe human cloning? Underline them in the text.

3. Whose opinion, in addition to Dr. Wilmot's, does the author mention to support his argument?

   _____

4. Does the author discuss the advantages of human cloning?

_____

The author of the text holds a very strong opinion against human cloning. He uses emotionally loaded language to express his extreme opposition. He draws sickly pictures of the future, such as a woman giving birth to a genetic copy of her deceased father. The author refers to the "prospect of mass production of human beings," suggesting that this is an inevitable future.

However, defenders of human cloning would probably support the growing of tissues or organs for transplantations in case of organ failure, rather than "mass production." This and other potential advantages of human cloning are ignored by the author. Also, the author confidently cites the opinions of "almost everyone" to suggest it is obvious to all that human cloning is a bad idea. Yet, to say that "almost everyone" is against the idea is a sweeping generalization. Indeed, there are those who defend human cloning.

To identify bias, ask the following questions:

- What type of support, if any, is provided for the opinion?
- Does the author consider the disadvantages of the favoured point of view?
- Does the author consider an alternative to the favoured point of view?
- Does the choice of vocabulary indicate extreme emotional engagement masking the lack of factual support?
- Does the choice of vocabulary indicate generalizations?

Compare the previous text with the one below. It comes from on online fact sheet written by the National Human Genome Research Institute, an American government agency. Do you think the author is biased?

B. **What are the potential applications of therapeutic cloning?**

Researchers hope to use embryonic stem cells, which have the unique ability to generate virtually all types of cells in an organism, to grow healthy tissues in the laboratory that can be used to replace injured or diseased tissues. In addition, it may be possible to learn more about the molecular causes of disease by studying embryonic stem cell lines from cloned embryos derived from the cells of animals or humans with different diseases. Finally, differentiated tissues derived from embryonic stem cells are excellent tools to test new therapeutic drugs.

What are some of the ethical issues related to cloning?

Gene cloning is a carefully regulated technique that is largely accepted today and used routinely in many labs worldwide. However, both reproductive and therapeutic cloning raise important ethical issues, especially as related to the potential use of these techniques in humans.

Reproductive cloning would present the potential of creating a human that is genetically identical to another person who has previously existed or who still exists. This may conflict with long-standing religious and societal values about human dignity, possibly infringing upon principles of individual freedom, identity and autonomy. However, some argue that reproductive cloning could help sterile couples fulfill their dream of parenthood. Others see human cloning as a way to avoid passing on a deleterious gene that runs in the family without having to undergo embryo screening or embryo selection.

Therapeutic cloning, while offering the potential for treating humans suffering from disease or injury, would require the destruction of human embryos in the test tube. Consequently, opponents argue that using this technique to collect embryonic stem cells is wrong, regardless of whether such cells are used to benefit sick or injured people.

1. a) What contrasting opinions are presented about the ethics of reproductive cloning?

   _____

   b) What contrasting opinions are presented about the ethics of therapeutic cloning?

   _____

2. Do you think that person who wrote this text approves or disapproves of cloning? Would you consider the writer biased?

   _____

Both texts present facts and opinions about human cloning. However, while text A condemns all human cloning, text B takes a more careful approach: it offers the benefits of gene cloning, but notes the ethical issues that some people have with it. The tone of text B is reserved, as opposed to the inflammatory rhetoric of text A.

Activity 5

Read the following texts on controversial topics and answer the questions that follow.

A. I would like to begin with the compelling story of Sarah McKinley. Home alone with her baby, she called 911 when two violent intruders began to break down her front door. The men wanted to force their way into her home so they could steal the prescription medication of her deceased husband, who had recently died of cancer. Before the police could arrive, while Ms. McKinley was on the line with the 911 operator, these violent intruders broke down her door. One of the men brandished a foot-long hunting knife. As the intruders forced their way into her home, Ms. McKinley fired her weapon, fatally wounding one of the violent attackers and causing the other to flee the scene. Later, Ms. McKinley reflected on the incident: "It was either going to be him or my son," she said. "And it wasn't going to be my son."

Guns make women safer. Most violent offenders actually do not use firearms, which makes guns the great equalizer. In fact, over 90 percent of violent crimes occur without a firearm. Over the most recent decade, from 2001 to 2010, "about 6 percent to 9 percent of all violent victimizations were committed with firearms," according to a federal study. Violent criminals rarely use a gun to threaten or attack women. Attackers use their size and physical strength, preying on women who are at a severe disadvantage.

Guns reverse that balance of power in a violent confrontation. Armed with a gun, a woman can even have the advantage over a violent attacker. How do guns give women the advantage? An armed woman does not need superior strength or the proximity of a hand-to-hand struggle. She can protect her children, elderly relatives, herself, or others who are vulnerable to an assailant. Using a firearm with a magazine holding more than 10 rounds of ammunition, a woman would have a fighting chance even against multiple attackers.

–Gayle S. Trotter

1. What is the main opinion expressed (implicitly or explicitly) by the author? It is against

    a) strict gun control.

    b) violent attackers.

    c) the police who respond slowly to emergencies.

    d) women's access to firearms.

2. What kinds of support does the author use to back up her opinion? Circle all that apply.

    a) Study results

b) An account of a real event

c) A citizens' survey

d) An appeal to the reader's emotions

3. What counter-argument may be made against the author's viewpoint?

a) Only about 6 percent to 9 percent of all violent victimizations were committed with firearms between 2001 and 2010.

b) Women are physically weaker than men, so they may be easily harmed by male attackers if unarmed.

c) A woman's gun may be used by her attacker against the woman herself.

d) An armed woman may protect not only herself but her children if attacked.

4. Would you consider the author's opinion biased? Why or why not?

_____

_____

_____

_____

B. While bottled water itself has been around for centuries, the last 100 years or so saw the creation of what we see today as a vital source of healthy, convenient hydration. The vast majority of bottled water companies in the United States are very small, about ten employees or less, and generate less than $10 million in sales annually. These are local family entrepreneurs with deep roots and strong ties to their communities.

People choose bottled water because it is a safe, reliable, and convenient source of healthy hydration. Whether bottling spring water from protected underground aquifers or producing high-quality purified bottled water from a municipal source, America's bottled water companies consistently meet consumer demand for safe, quality drinking water at home, at work, on the go, and when emergencies and natural disasters strike.

1. What opinion does the author of this text express?

   _____

   _____

   _____

2. How does the author try to appeal to the reader? The author suggests
   that. . . (Circle all that apply.)

   a) bottled water producers are local families with strong ties to their
      communities.

   b) bottled water has been around for centuries.

   c) bottled spring water comes from underground aquifers.

   d) bottled water will help keep us safe during emergencies or natural
      disasters.

3. Are there any disadvantages of bottled water that the author overlooks? You
   many need to do some online research to answer this question.

   _____

   _____

   _____

   _____

4. Would you consider the author's opinion biased? Why or why not?

   _____

   _____

   _____

   _____

INTEGRATING
THE SKILLS

Activity 6

Read the following article from a newspaper and answer
the questions that follow.

Use all the skills you have learned in this unit:
- Assessing valid and invalid inferences
- Distinguishing between facts and opinions
- Identifying informed opinions
- Identifying biased opinions

Drug Addicts Should Be Sent to Isolated Work Camps

01 I prosecuted a lot of drug dealers in Vancouver during my career. Those at the wholesale level were not usually addicts. At the retail level of drug dealing, many were addicts, peddling drugs to anyone, including kids, to obtain money to fuel their addiction. Of course, the addicts engaged in many other crimes to get money for more drugs. They mugged old ladies, broke into homes and cars, stole from stores and family, broke their parole and probation terms, abused the welfare system, prostituted themselves, and generally led a degenerate, lawless life.

02 In one case I argued before the B.C. Court of Appeal, I presented several authoritative studies that showed an indisputable correlation between criminal activity and drug addiction. I have, as a result of my prosecution career, never seen addicts as victims. I see them as victimizers, who make victims of their families and children, and their friends, as well as the general public, all for the sake of the next fix.

03 When it comes to sentencing drug addicts for their crimes, the addiction is often presented by defence counsel as a mitigating factor. I don't see it that way. An addict chooses to be an addict. Sure, some of them have had a rough or even tragic life, some not, but escaping into drug addiction is the action of an amoral fool.

04 When it comes to sentencing those who are convicted of a crime, I have always been pragmatic. The sentence should be one which first of all does the best job of protecting the public. Consideration for the criminal is secondary.

05 During the 1970s, the late unlamented Trudeau government reversed these priorities. Pierre Trudeau's solicitor-general, Jean-Paul Goyer, said to Parliament in 1971: "We have decided from now on to stress the rehabilitation of individuals rather than the protection of society." Since then, the increase of crime has conclusively demonstrated the failure of this policy, and the endangerment of the public that resulted. Despite that, many cling to the concept of rehabilitation because it seems more humane and uplifting—even if it fails most of the time and the public suffers.

06 That brings me to the safe house shooting gallery called Insite, and the handing out of free crack pipes in Vancouver. Those with good intentions think they are helping drug addicts to be healthy. In fact they are paving a freeway to hell for the addicts, and endangering the public as a result of the crimes those addicts will commit to get more drugs.

07 Should we just allow addicts to use dirty needles or crack pipes and die in the gutter? No, we aren't that indifferent in this country. We need to do something effective to rid them of

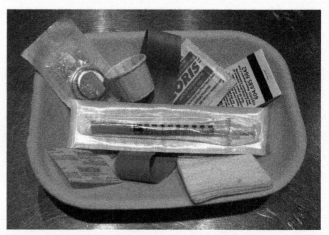

An injection kit handed out to addicts at Insite

the addiction, and protect the public from drug-related crime so long as they are addicted. That means addicts should be segregated from society until they are no longer addicted. Put them in jail for long terms? No, that is expensive, and it is too easy to get drugs in our jails.

08   I suggest isolated work camps, where drug addicts will go cold turkey or are weaned off drugs in a medically supervised way. They will be taught a work ethic, by doing work of a meaningful type, such as farming or manufacturing. They will be required to pass a basic education course, and a technical course to make them employable, before they are released. They will remain in the camp until they have become drugfree, physically and psychologically, and have passed the work and education tests. Some, of course, would never qualify for release. They would, however, have room and board, and free medical care at taxpayer expense for their lifetime, even though most will never have contributed a dime in taxes. That's better than continuing to be a criminal and an addict even if you do have a clean needle or crack pipe.

09   I can already hear words like "gulag" and "concentration camp" being hurled about by those who want to help stray animals and broken people. Just remember, though, that stray animals are put into animal shelters. They are locked into those shelters until they can be released into a new environment. Think of the addict camp as a shelter, but one with the ability to make a drug addict into a drug-free person with some reasonable prospect of a productive life. The alternative is a life of crime, and the destruction of the addict and all those close to him. Which is better?

Brian Purdy, Q.C., spent more than 30 years working in criminal law. He is a retired general counsel with the federal Department of Justice and lives in Calgary.

Source: B. Purdy, "Drug addicts should be sent to isolated work camps." *Vancouver Sun*, 14 September 2011.

1. Mark each inference as V (valid) or I (invalid), based on the text.

    a) ＿＿ Crime rates among drug addicts are higher than among the non-using population.

    b) ＿＿ Difficult life experiences leave no other choice for a person but to escape into the world of addiction.

    c) ＿＿ In matters of criminal punishment, Canadian governments have always favoured society at the expense of an individual.

    d) ＿＿ The author believes that all addicts can be rehabilitated with medical supervision, education, and work experience.

2. Mark each statement as F (fact) or O (opinion).

    a) ＿＿ Crime rates have increased since 1971.

    b) ＿＿ The rehabilitation policy directed towards drug addicts has failed.

    c) ＿＿ Handing out free crack pipes to drug addicts in Vancouver helps them to be healthier.

    d) ＿＿ It is possible to get drugs in Canadian jails.

3. What is the author's opinion about Insite?

_____

4. What is the way to best deal with drug addicts, according to the author?

_____

5. Look at the various techniques that the author uses to support his opinion and decide whether it is an informed opinion or a biased opinion. Explain why.

_____

_____

6. How do you think Brian Purdy's professional experience shapes his opinion?

_____

Consider the opposite point of view to Purdy's. The first paragraph below is taken from the website of Vancouver Coastal Health, a large governmental health authority. It is followed by an expert opinion—a few paragraphs excerpted from an opinion piece written by a doctor familiar with Insite.

Since opening its doors in 2003, Insite has been a safe, health-focused place where people inject drugs and connect to health care services—from primary care to treating disease and infection, to addiction counselling and treatment, to housing and community supports. Insite is North America's first legal supervised injection site. The BC Ministry of Health Services provides operational funding for Insite through Vancouver Coastal Health, which operates the facility in conjunction with PHS Community Services Society. Insite operates on a harm-reduction model, which means it strives to decrease the adverse health, social and economic consequences of drug use without requiring abstinence from drug use.

The strict rules at Insite preclude the possibility of a used syringe being passed between users since nurses police the program to ensure clean needles are used in every injection. Not only do injections take place out of public view and away from vulnerable youth who may be curious about injecting, but onsite disposal also ensures used needles cannot find their way into public spaces. Insite further forces its clients to temporarily remain onsite after injecting and where an addiction treatment program is co-located. As a result, a study published in the

New England Journal of Medicine demonstrated how the opening of Insite coincided with a 40 percent increase in addiction treatment admissions among its clients.

The desire for greater control over the behaviour of intravenous drug users explains why centres of commerce and tourism in Europe have embraced supervised injecting facilities. More than 90 supervised injecting facilities exist in over 60 cities.

Public health and financial constraints are a further consideration, given that each HIV infection costs on average approximately $500,000 in medical costs. Insite has contributed to a 90 percent reduction in new HIV cases caused by intravenous drug use in British Columbia, which is why the B.C. government has been such a strong supporter of the program.

Of course, regardless of how one's view of Insite is framed, caught in the middle are desperately addicted Canadians just trying to find help and avoid acquiring a life-threatening infectious disease.

Evan Wood MD, PhD, is a professor of medicine at UBC where he holds the university's Canada Research Chair in Inner City Medicine.

1. Mark each inference as V (valid) or I (invalid) based on the two texts above.

   a) ＿＿ The purpose of Insite is to help drug users quit their addiction.

   b) ＿＿ The funding for Insite comes from taxpayers' money.

   c) ＿＿ All Canadian health professionals are in favour of safe injection sites.

2. Mark each statement as F (fact) or O (opinion).

   a) ＿＿ There had been no medically supervised drug injection sites in North America before Insite.

   b) ＿＿ Insite is trying to reduce the negative consequences of drug abuse.

   c) ＿＿ Insite has been highly successful at reducing the negative consequences of drug abuse.

3. How do you think Evan Wood's professional position shapes his opinion?

   _____

4. After you have compared the two opinions on Insite, explain your personal view on this supervised drug injection site. Should it continue to operate?

   _____

   _____

5

Assessing an Argument

IF CANADA IS A LAND OF OPPORTUNITY,
WHY IS AN MBA SERVING FAST FOOD?   hireimmigrants.ca

IF CANADA IS A LAND OF OPPORTUNITY,
WHY IS A PROFESSOR DRIVING A CAB?   hireimmigrants.ca

Study the photos, part of an advertising campaign, and discuss the following questions in small groups.

- What is the purpose of these ads?
- What audience is being addressed?
- What techniques are used to get the message across?
- Do you think these ads make a strong impact on the viewer?

These ads address discrimination against immigrants in the Canadian job market. Thus, Canadian employers are the target audience of the ad campaign. The message of discrimination is made clear by highlighting the mismatch between the education level of the newcomers and their present employment (i.e. a fast food restaurant cashier with an MBA degree and a taxi driver with a PhD). This absurdity is accentuated by the question referring to Canada as "a land of opportunity." The question calls for a correction of the injustice: these individuals would contribute much more to the country's economy if their status as highly qualified specialists were recognized.

Like advertising professionals, writers often make an argument for or against an idea. Depending on the argument being made, a text may target a specific audience or may address the general public. To make a successful argument, authors must firmly support their point of view and make sure that the concerns of their audience are fully addressed. For this reason, authors must be familiar with both the subject and the audience involved in the issue.

Skillful readers are able to conclude whether an author's argument makes sense. This unit deals with several important strategies that help readers make this assessment:

1. Identifying the purpose of a text
2. Identifying the audience
3. Identifying techniques of persuasion
4. Assessing an argument's support and logic

IDENTIFYING PURPOSE OF A TEXT

As the introduction of this unit shows, one possible purpose of a text is to *persuade* the reader. There are two other main purposes of writing: to inform and to entertain the reader. The writer *informs* the audience by providing information to educate readers about a specific topic. The writer *entertains* the audience when the text is fun to read—when it is interesting or humorous, for example. Sometimes a text has more than one purpose: for example, humour may be used both to entertain and to educate the audience.

Activity 1

The three readings that follow all have different purposes. Read the texts, answer the questions, and identify the purpose of each text.

Census: One in Five Speaks a Foreign Language at Home in Canada

01 As the Canadian government moves to toughen language requirements for newcomers, the latest census figures suggest that more than two million people speak neither English nor French at home. According to Statistics Canada, the figure more than doubles when individuals are asked about the non-official language they speak "most often" at home. Overall, one-fifth of Canada's population reported speaking a foreign tongue at least some of the time at home.

02 More than 200 languages were reported in the 2011 census, with Chinese languages continuing to dominate, with more than a million people saying they speak either Mandarin, Cantonese or Chinese (a non-specified category that includes Mandarin or Cantonese). Punjabi was listed as the next most common foreign language spoken in Canadian households, with 460,000 reporting it as their mother tongue. Tagalog, a Philippines-based language, saw a huge jump in popularity in Canada in 2011 with 279,000 people reporting speaking it at home—a 64 percent increase over 2006. The use of Mandarin (51 percent),

Arabic (47 percent), Hindi (44 percent), Creole (42 percent), Bengali (40 percent), Persian (33 percent) and Spanish (32 percent) also saw significant growth since 2006. The vast majority of those who said they speak an immigrant language at home live in a major Canadian city.

03 While the use of foreign languages in Canadian households has gone largely unchanged since 2006, the government has started to crack down on immigrants who aren't proficient in at least one official language. This year, Immigration Minister Jason Kenney unveiled tough new language requirements for those seeking citizenship or permanent residence. Strong language skills are thought to improve newcomers' chances of getting a good job and integrating into society. Kenney has also noted a correlation between immigration fraud and regions that don't make proficiency in one of Canada's official languages a priority.

Source: Adapted from T. Cohen, "Census: One in five speaks a foreign language in Canadian homes." Postmedia News, www.canada.com, 24 October 2012.

1. Mark each statement as T (true) or F (false).

   a) ____ More than four million people in Canada speak a language other than English or French most frequently at home.

   b) ____ The Chinese languages, including Mandarin and Cantonese, are the predominant non-official languages in Canada.

   c) ____ Tagalog is the second-most common non-official language in Canada.

   d) ____ Thirty-three percent of immigrants to Canada speak Persian.

   e) ____ Immigrants who continue speaking the language of their home countries tend to concentrate in big cities.

   f) ____ The Canadian government's attitude toward the language requirement for prospective immigrants is quite relaxed.

2. What two reasons are given for requiring higher language proficiency scores for immigrants?

   _____

   _____

3. What is the purpose of the article?

   a) To persuade

   b) To inform

   c) To entertain

Speak English, s'il vous plait! Or One of 200 Other Languages

Multilingualism has stepped in to fill the bilingual void

01 Pardon my English, but has anything ever bedevilled[1] this country more than language? It's the membrane that separates us. It's the crux on which our history has turned. Or, if you prefer, the cross we've always borne.[2] If language can be said to have had any unifying force in Canada, it would have been its power to inspire episodes of grudging accommodation—usually

---

[1] caused a lot of problems over a long period of time
[2] having a cross to bear means having a difficult situation that you have to accept or endure

at the end of a gun or government fiat.[3] The one constant that backdrops these accommodations has been our mutual resentment. In 145 years of nationhood, language hasn't brought us any closer to understanding one another. And that was just with two languages. Now, according to the latest Statistics Canada census, we speak more than 200.

02   This is hardly news. Walk the streets, go to any public school, and you'll hear as much. What is news is Statistics Canada's recent profile this week of the concentration of that multilingualism. The 2001 Census found one-sixth of the population spoke a language other than French or English at home. The 2011 census found that percentage had increased to one-fifth of the population. That is astounding growth. That growth is continuing.

03   Most of those 200 languages were spoken in small enough numbers to be statistically negligible, but a significant few—most of them Asian—were being spoken in such great numbers and have been so concentrated in the country's major cities that their use has, effectively, nullified Canada's policy of two official languages.

04   Bilingualism is dead. Or at least it's been relegated to the status of charming relic. While bilingualism statistically is holding its own, allophones[4] will soon outnumber francophones in Canada. The federal government might continue to observe the niceties of bilingualism in the face of this fact, but the real world will ignore it. True bilingualism has always been an Ottawa pipe dream,[5] anyway, and I'm pretty sure not even Ottawa buys into it any more.

05   Multilingualism has stepped in to fill that void. Or more precisely, stomped in. The official version of this complete and radical transformation of the country's fabric—accomplished in the space of a generation—goes thus: Multilingualism is a wonderful thing, the diversity of which is evidence of Canada's enlightened tolerance.

06   "When I look at the globalized world that we live in," *The Sun* quoted Doug Norris, chief demographer at Environics Analytics, as saying, "the fact that we ourselves are becoming more diverse and reflecting all of those languages is a real asset to us as a country today. I think it strengthens us as a nation as opposed to a country which was very singular in terms of its language or ethnicity."

07   This is a lovely view of the world, and not necessarily untrue, though I can think of a few countries, some of them economic powerhouses, that despite a distaste for diversity have had no trouble operating in a global market. But given the strife that language has caused in Canada, and given our historical track record, you would think there might be a more skeptical and frank discussion about multilingualism. Which is to say, Canadians do not live in a "globe." They live in neighbourhoods. And Canada isn't a corporation. It's a nation. There is a big difference.

08   So, the question should be, does multilingualism work at the street level, and has it made us stronger as a society? Or has it made our society less cohesive? Are we becoming a truly multicultural nation unified by a global vision, or are we fracturing into a collection of tribes? Does multilingualism and multiculturalism work, not at the corporate board level and in feel-good government press releases, but practically in our cities and our neighbourhoods?

09   We step carefully around those questions, ever so sensitive to charges of racism. We are such a nice people, at least in public. But there have been more and more news stories

---

[3] an official order given by somebody in authority

[4] a resident of Canada, especially Quebec, whose first language is neither French nor English

[5] a hope or plan that is impossible to achieve or not practical

examining the phenomenon of self-ghettoizing,[6] and the concentration of linguistic groups and cultures in such great numbers that the need or compulsion to speak one of the two official languages in public has lessened. This used to be a concern unique to Quebec. It no longer is.

10   The corollary to these doubts harbours an even greater question, which is, will our growing linguistic diversity change our belief system? Language, after all, is only the vehicle for culture. And my culture, the one I believe in, is a society that embraces women's rights, sexual tolerance, a healthy skepticism of authority (rather than a deference to it) and a belief in the Canadian brand of socialism. I don't want to see these beliefs eroded.

11   The question is—and it's one we shouldn't be afraid to ask—in the future we've embarked upon, are we going to be on the same page on those issues, or will we be speaking a different language?

Source: P. McMartin, "Speak English, s'il vous plait! Or one of 200 other languages." *The Vancouver Sun*, www.vancouversun.com, 24 October 2012.

---

[6] choosing to live in an area of a city where many people of the same ethnic background live, separately from the rest of the population

1. Mark each statement as T (true) or F (false).

   a) ____ The history of Canada shows that its citizens who speak English and French have been coexisting peacefully.

   b) ____ The writer is surprised by the fact that, according to Statistics Canada, people speak a great variety of languages in the country.

   c) ____ According to the writer, bilingualism continues to have a healthy presence in Canadian society.

2. Which two different views of multilingualism does the author present in this text?

   a) _____

   _____

   b) _____

   _____

3. Which view on multilingualism and multiculturalism (2a or 2b above) does the writer of this text appear to favour? _____

4. A. How does the writer support his opinion that multilingualism may not be strengthening our society?

   _____

   B. Would you consider the author's opinion to be informed (see Unit 4, page 74)?

   C. What kind of support does the author use for his view?

   _____

D. Note some stylistic choices the author uses to make his argument more powerful.

    i. Why does he use French in the title of the article?

    ii. What is the difference between the two verbs the writer uses in paragraph 5: *to step in* and *to stomp in*?

5. What is the author's concern about the future of Canadian culture?

6. What is the purpose of this text?

    a) To persuade

    b) To inform

    c) To entertain

What's in a Name?

To my Scottish father—plenty

01 The silence was deafening. "Patrick? *Patrick*?? You want to name him Patrick?" My father was upset. Very upset. "Well," I replied weakly, my voice rapidly losing steam. "It was just an idea."

02 "Patrick," said Fayther, simply and forcefully, "is an *Irish* name." He made it sound like an affliction. For my father, Scottish to the core, the very worst thing you could say about someone or something was that they had an "Irish" quality. Fayther, as my sister Margaret dubbed him, was a great mountain of a man, with a booming voice and a stare that could melt tar off a roof.

03 Now, my wife and I were expecting our first child any day, a baby boy, and we still hadn't chosen a name. My wife is from Japan and we had already selected our son's Japanese name: Genki, meaning "lively or full of life." But after that we hit an impasse. The list grew more and more fanciful: Mortimer, Gilgamesh, Hewlett. But none of them had the right ring, and we finally settled on Patrick, which is a good strong name, even if it is a wee bit "green." "Give him a proper Scottish name," said Fayther. "Alexander or Duncan or Murdoch. Anything but Patrick."

04 Here's the odd part. For all his bite and bluster, my father was only half Scottish. His mother was from Norway, which makes *me* a quarter Viking. It gets even worse. Our dark family secret is this: I'm Irish. And so are all my siblings. My grandfather on my mother's side was from Belfast, which means I have exactly as much Irish in me as I do Scottish. But Fayther

refused to accept this. He had four sons and he tried to name each one of them Angus.

05 "Angus MacFergus," I said. "It sounds like a bull with a bagpipe." "It's a fine name," said Fayther. "It has the scent of the Highlands[1] about it."

06 Mom, meanwhile, was whispering encouragements in my ear. "Name your baby Patrick," she'd say, her voice smooth as honey. "Or maybe Paul." Later that evening, exhausted and head still spinning, I turned to my wife and said, "What do you think about Angus? You know, for the baby." She frowned. "Angus," she said. "It sounds like a cow."

07 As noted, my wife is from Japan. There are no hyphens in her identity. She is Japanese, plain and simple. Her parents were Japanese. Her grandparents were Japanese. Her great-grandparents, her great-great-grandparents and so on, all the way back into the mists of time. For my wife, Canada's mongrel mélange[2] of cultures is endlessly fascinating.

08 At one point, she sat down with a calculator and figured out the exact percentages. "Our son will be 50 percent Japanese, 12.5 percent Scottish, 12.5 percent Irish, 12.5 percent Norwegian, 6.25 percent Czech and 6.25 percent miscellaneous."

09 We looked at each other. "A mix like that," I said, "you realize what it means?" She nodded. "He'll be 100 percent Canadian." Our son was born a few weeks later. We named him Alexander.

Source: W. Ferguson, "What's in a name?" *YorkU*, October 2003, p. 34.

---

[1] a region in Scotland
[2] a mixture or variety of different things

1. Mark each statement as T (true) or F (false).

   a) ____ *Fayther* is an accidental misspelling of *father*.

   b) ____ The author's father is a strong, imposing man who usually asserts his opinions quite clearly.

   c) ____ Angus is a typical Irish name, while Patrick is a Scottish one.

   d) ____ The author's father has Scottish and Irish roots.

   e) ____ The author's "dark family secret" is about some infamous, evil family ancestors.

   f) ____ It was easier for the author and his wife to choose a Japanese name for their son than an English name.

   g) ____ It can be inferred from the text that many Canadians have mixed ethnic origins.

   h) ____ The author and his wife finally choose a non-Scottish name to spite his father.

2. What is the purpose of this text?

   a) To inform

   b) To persuade

   c) To entertain

You have just read three different texts on the topic of multilingualism, cultural diversity, and Canadian identity. What is your opinion about the future of the Canadian society in view of its growing multiculturalism? Will it stay united by a common national identity or will it split into different ethnic groups? Discuss these questions in a small group.

IDENTIFYING THE AUDIENCE

Authors usually address a certain *audience* with their texts. They write to persuade, inform, or entertain these target readers. For example, if a text on upcoming American presidential elections is published in a Canadian newspaper, it will probably inform Canadians about the implications of each candidate's presidency on Canada. Such a text would interest the Canadian public because our close relationship with the US is affected by the American leadership. A similar text published in an American newspaper will have a different purpose and audience: it may highlight possible roles of presidential candidates for the future of the US, trying to persuade Americans to cast their vote one way or another. Thus, the purpose and the audience of the two texts are different.

If the reader understands that the text is addressing a specific audience to persuade it to accept a certain point of view—such as to vote for one candidate and not another—the reader should also examine whether the author's view is presented objectively, without bias. Thus, an awareness of a text's purpose and audience will help the reader assess the writer's arguments more critically.

Activity 2

The following readings are all about online commerce but each one addresses a different audience. Read the texts, answer the questions that follow, and identify the intended audience of each text.

Ways to Turn Your Website into a Sales Machine

Your online presence is a vital part of any sales strategy. But is your website the sales powerhouse it should be? Replicating the effectiveness of the face-to-face sales process online—and getting customers to go from clicking to buying—can be difficult. The good news is that there are a few simple tricks and tweaks that can improve your site's revenue-generating capabilities.

Here are some tips that can help turn a business website into a sales machine:

- **Build an effective shopping cart.**
  Some small businesses use services such as PayPal for making and receiving online payments. But building a full-featured shopping cart directly into your website might be a better option. Shopping carts allow for more customization and the potential to provide more product information. This will ultimately encourage your customers to buy more products.

- **Recommend related products.**
  Even if you can't interact face-to-face with web customers, you still can demonstrate old-fashioned salesmanship. An online store can include a "recommendation engine" that suggests complementary products, upgrades and additional services. For example, if a customer puts a grill in his online shopping cart, he can be prompted to also consider buying tongs and a spatula.

- **Start a contest or promotion.**
  An online contest or promotion can help attract attention in social media channels and lure potential customers to your site. Giving away a high value item can stir up the most attention but frequent, simple contests with smaller perks can also be effective.

Source: J. Blum, "Five ways to turn your website into a sales machine." *Entrepreneur*, www.entrepreneur.com/article/223348, 16 April 2012.

1. What is the purpose of the tips the writer offers?

   _____

2. Do you think having an online shopping cart is a valuable feature for a customer? Why or why not?

   _____

3. If you were buying online, would you like to have products recommended to you? Why or why not?

_____

4. Who is the intended audience of this text?

_____

Warnings about Online Shopping

There's growing interest in the Internet as a place to shop. But this type of shopping has its own dangers, and the rules of smart shopping are as important in the electronic marketplace as they are on your doorstep.

One problem is that consumers have little control over what happens to personal information used when shopping online. Each transaction leaves an information trail that can be used by hackers and other unauthorized individuals to assemble financial and personal profiles on you. This information can be sold or stolen and used for criminal purposes. You have every right to feel vulnerable when your credit card number and other financial information go sailing into cyberspace.

Please review our helpful advice and understand your rights before you make a purchase online.

- Don't fall for offers that sound too good to be true—they often are, especially if the website overloads you with information about many recommended good deals.
- Don't respond to spam—unsolicited email offers.
- Avoid getting hooked by offers for samples with purchases and other "freebies"—they are meant to reel in the unsuspecting.
- Know whom you're dealing with. The company's website should provide basic information (i.e. the seller's name, business address, and phone number).

OVERSTOCK iPads

Get an iPad Mini for $29.15!

Limit one per day

- Check the reputation of the business before buying—be careful because it may pocket your money and not deliver on its promises. If you've never dealt with the company before, ask friends or family if they have.

Source: Adapted from "Advice on shopping online or over the phone." Ontario Ministry of Consumer Services, www.sse.gov.on.ca/mcs/en/Pages/Online_Shopping_Intro.aspx

1. What is the purpose of the advice the writer offers?

   _____

2. What does the writer claim regarding the security of personal financial information on the Internet?

   _____

3. What is the writer's view on "freebies" and other alluring offers on shopping websites?

   _____

4. Who is the intended audience of this text?

   _____

Product Research and Purchase

Digital technology has also changed how consumers research and buy products. While online shopping has not realised the exaggerated predictions of the early dot.com days that it would put bricks-and-mortar stores out of business, it is a significant and worldwide phenomenon. According to a 2008 Nielsen research report, less than 20% of the world's population had shopped online. Looking solely at the world's online population, however, the number was an astounding 85%! Large industrial countries such as Japan, South Korea, the United Kingdom, the United States and Germany were all 94% or above.

The Internet has reshaped the way that people buy big-ticket items, like automobiles, even when the product is eventually bought in a physical store. Not that long ago, the starting point for purchasing a car was a trip to a few dealerships to collect brochures that had all the product specifications and prices. This first trip often started the negotiation process with the salesman.

Today, car buyers are gathering all the information they need on the Internet before they even think about stepping into a showroom. Manufacturers' sites, auto-information sites (such as <edmunds.com> and Kelley Blue Book <kbb.com>), auto-buying sites (such as <cars.com>), car magazine sites, car blogs and so on, allow customers to research, build, price and compare cars at home. By the time the customer gets to the dealership, he or she is ready to buy. They know what car they want, what they want in it, and what price they should be paying. Automotive brochures are now largely useless, except as a nice souvenir of the car you have already bought. This process has taken a tremendous amount of power out of the hands of auto-dealers and salespeople and put it right into the hands of the consumer.

Source: Excerpted from B. Sheehan, *Basics Marketing 02: Online Marketing* (Lausanne, Switzerland: AVA Publishing, 2010), p. 21.

1. What is the main idea of the text?

   a) Online shopping will prevail over conventional shopping.

   b) Digital technology gives too much power to online businesses.

   c) Most of the world's population has access to online shopping.

   d) Digital technology has modified our shopping habits.

2. Why does the process of researching a product take power away from auto-dealers and salespeople?

   _____

3. Who is the intended audience of this text?

   _____

These three texts have different purposes and audiences and, therefore, present the same issue—online commerce—from different perspectives. A critical reader will realize that while the first reading presents discounted items or free perks as a positive tool, the second warns against being lured by freebies that may not be free at all. Similarly, the first text promotes the recommendation of products to the customer, but the second reading cautions against suspiciously attractive recommendations. The difference in perspectives is explained by the different target audiences—online entrepreneurs and online consumers. In the third reading the author offers an academic look at online shopping habits, asserting that online tools empowers the consumer. This text is not directed to either entrepreneurs or consumers but rather to an audience of business or marketing students.

IDENTIFYING TECHNIQUES OF PERSUASION

In argumentative texts, the author may use the following *techniques of persuasion*:

- Presenting **support for an opinion**: citing research results, statistics
     Example: *According to the 2010 Dietary Guidelines, vegetarian eating patterns have been associated with improved health outcomes including lower levels of obesity, a reduced risk of heart disease and lower blood pressure.*

- Using **logical reasoning**: tracing causal relationships in an argument
     Example: *The earth's limited resources, including land and water, are being consumed more and more quickly as the population increases. How can*

vegetarianism help reduce the consumption of limited resources? Very simply: if you look at the two statements Land + Water = Crops *and* Land + Water + Crops = Livestock, *you can see that the limited resources are repeated in both statements. By eating meat, humans are using limited resources that create crops. Then additional limited resources plus those crops are used to create livestock. Wouldn't it make sense to just eat the crops?*

- Using **analogies and/or contrasts**: discussing a situation similar to or very different from the one in question and making conclusions based on the similarities or contrasts

    Example: *The Canadian government should revise its taxation system. The Canadian middle class has a heavy tax burden, while the economic elite pays relatively little. If this continues, Canada will resemble one of the developing Latin American countries with no middle class, but only the very poor and the super-rich.*

- Giving **examples** from personal experiences: using the author's or other people's experiences to prove the validity of the author's opinion

    Example: *Insurance companies make it so easy to sign up and pay for travel insurance but then so hard to get compensation. I once had a 12-hour delay and had to pay for a hotel, and my insurance company refused to reimburse me. They defended their decision with the fact that my connection was between two airlines: they found a small-print excuse in the policy not to pay me.*

- Using an **emotional tone**: using emotionally loaded vocabulary and examples to appeal to the reader's emotional sensitivity

    Example: *In commercial farming, a major part of the food industry, many farmers treat animals cruelly. For example, to satisfy consumers' desire for tender veal, calves are mercilessly confined in tight cages where they cannot move freely. This way the calves cannot develop tough muscle tissue. After a few months of living in these hellish conditions, the miserable animal is killed.*

- Presenting a **counter-argument** and then refuting it—recognizing the opposite point of view and proving that it is invalid or that any concern connected to it can be easily alleviated

    Example: *Meat eaters claim that it is difficult or even impossible to change deeply engrained habits and switch to vegetarianism. However, the change is not as difficult as it seems. First, there are plenty of delicious vegetarian choices for you in supermarkets and restaurants. Second, if your family eats meat and you choose not to, you can always stick to the side dishes—rice or noodles—and complement them with nutritious vegetables. Lastly, your wish to lead a healthy lifestyle will motivate you to achieve success in shifting to a vegetarian diet.*

In the text below, identify the techniques of persuasion used by the author and answer the questions that follow.

Why It's Time to Legalize Marijuana

01 Sometime this year, the millionth Canadian will be arrested for marijuana possession, Dana Larsen, activist for pot legalization, estimates. As Larsen notes, the war on drugs in Canada is mostly a war on marijuana, "and most of that is a war on marijuana users." Since the Tories came to power in 2006, and slammed the door on the previous Liberal government's muddled plans to reduce or decriminalize marijuana penalties, arrests for pot possession have jumped 41 percent. In those six years police reported more than 405,000 marijuana-related arrests, roughly equivalent to the populations of Regina and Saskatoon combined. According to Larsen, "We're seeing crime drop across Canada. [Police] feel they've got nothing better to do."

Statistics show increase in arrests for a crime the author believes insubstantial.

02 But is it the right thing to do? Most certainly that's the view of the federal government, which has been unshakable in its belief that pot[1] users are criminals, and that such criminals need arresting if Canada is to be a safer place. However, the Conservative hard line is increasingly out of step with its citizenry, and with the shifting mood in the United States, where two states— Colorado and Washington—have already legalized recreational use, where others have reduced penalties to a misdemeanour ticket. The case for legalizing personal use of cannabis hangs on two key questions. What is the cost and social impact of marijuana prohibition? And what are the risks to public health, to social order and personal safety of unleashing on Canada a vice[2] that has been prohibited for some 90 years?

The cost of prohibition

03 A 2002 Senate report pegged the annual cost of cannabis to law enforcement and the justice system at $300 million to $500 million and concluded that these costs "are disproportionately high given the drug's social and health consequences." Neil Boyd, a criminology professor at Simon Fraser University, concludes that the annual police- and court-related costs of enforcing marijuana possession in B.C. alone is estimated at $10.5 million per year.

---

[1] marijuana
[2] evil or immoral behaviour

The issue of public health and social order

04 At the heart of the crime bill, in the government's view, is public safety through criminal apprehension. But there are risks in prohibition, too. The most obvious are the gang hits and gun battles that impact the safety of Canadian streets, much of it fuelled by turf battles[3] over the illegal drug trade. Nor are criminal dealers prone to worry about contaminants in the product from dubious grow ops,[4] or the age of their customers.

05 Canadian children and youth, in fact, are the heaviest users of cannabis in the developed world, according to a UNICEF[5] report, which called child marijuana use a "significant concern" for its possible impacts on physical and mental health. Canadian youth, it speculated, believe occasional pot use is of little risk to their health. The report warned, however, that "legal sanctions against young people generally lead to even worse outcomes, not improvements in their lives."

06 Nor do Canada's sanctions curb underage use. Germany, Portugal, Belgium, Italy and the Netherlands are all countries where pot use has been decriminalized, legalized, or liberalized, and all have rates of child cannabis use that range from one-third to more than one-half *lower* than in Canada. Mason Tvert, a key strategist in Colorado's successful legalization vote, says criminalization has created an unregulated underground market of dealers who have no compunction about selling pot to minors. If you want to see the value of regulating a legal product, combined with proof-of-age requirements and public education campaigns, look to the falling rates of cigarette smoking among young people in both the U.S. and Canada, Tvert says. UNICEF also recommended that child pot use can be reduced more effectively with the same kind of public information campaigns and other aggressive measures used to curtail tobacco use.

The rewards of legalization

07 A B.C. coalition of public health officials, academics, and politicians is trying to take the emotion out of the legalization debate by building science-based counter-arguments to enforcement. One of its studies concludes B.C. would reap $500 million a year in taxation and licensing revenues from a liquor-control-board style of government regulation and sale of pot. An impact analysis for Colorado predicts a $12-million saving in enforcement costs in the first year, rising to $40 million "as courts and prisons adapt to fewer and fewer violators." It predicts combined savings and new revenue of $60 million, "with a potential for this number to double after 2017."

08 Would the federal government go to war with a province to protect a 90-year-old law built on myths, fears and hysteria; a law that crushed the ambitions of countless thousands of young people; a law that millions violate when it suits their purpose? Likely, but it would be one hell of a fight. After the legalization vote was decided in Washington in 2012, the Seattle Police Department posted a humourous online guide to pot use, entitled *Marijwhatnow?* Yes, it said, those over 21 can carry an ounce of pot. No, you can't smoke it in public. Will Seattle police help federal investigations of marijuana use in the state? Not a chance. There was, between the lines, a palpable relief that they no longer had to play bad cops to a bad law. Perhaps one day Canadians will be as lucky.

Source: Adapted from K. MacQueen, "Why it's time to legalize marijuana." *Macleans*, www2.macleans.ca/2013/06/10/why-its-time-to-legalize-marijuana, 10 June 2013.

---

[3] conflicts between gangs over the territories where drugs are sold
[4] illegal growing of marijuana plants
[5] United Nations Children's Fund

1. Fill in the chart with the examples of techniques of persuasion you identified in the text.

TECHNIQUE OF PERSUASION	EXAMPLE (PAR. #)
Research results	
Analogy	
Logical reasoning	
Emotional tone	
Counter-argument and its refutation	

2. Mark each statement as T (true) or F (false).

   a) ____ Ken MacQueen mentions Regina and Saskatoon to emphasize how insignificant the number of marijuana-related arrests is.

   b) ____ Larsen notes that crime rates have dropped across Canada, implying that this is the result of police anti-marijuana actions.

3. The author maintains that "the Conservative hard line [against marijuana] is increasingly out of step with its citizenry" (par. 2).

   a) Does the author support this claim?

   _____

   b) If not, what kind of support would be appropriate here?

   _____

4. The author mentions Colorado and Washington—two American states that have decriminalized marijuana—as a model for Canada. Do you think this comparison is appropriate?

   _____

5. According to the 2002 Senate report, are marijuana's health and social consequences significant?

   _____

6. How can keeping marijuana illegal be a danger to public safety, according to the text?

a) _____

b) _____

c) _____

7. The text states that Canadian children and youth are the heaviest users of marijuana in the developed world. What ways of fighting this phenomenon does the author suggest? Circle all that apply.

    a) Oganizing educational campaigns against marijuana use

    b) Promoting tobacco as a lesser evil to marijuana

    c) Taking harsh legal actions against marijuana possession

    d) Making marijuana laws more liberal to allow legal access for youth and children

    e) Requiring proof-of-age documents when purchasing legal marijuana

8. In paragraph 7, the author appeals to reason, rather than emotion. What is the author's main argument here?

    _____

9. According to the article, what are two ways the government would benefit financially if marijuana were legalized?

    a) _____

    b) _____

10. Are you convinced by the author's argument for legalizing marijuana? Explain.

    _____

ASSESSING AN ARGUMENT'S SUPPORT AND LOGIC

Being aware of an author's persuasive techniques makes it easier for the reader to assess the validity and effectiveness of an argument. In making this assessment, the reader should ask the following questions about the quality of the support for the argument:

- Is the *support* for the argument *relevant*? Is the support truly connected to the point the author is trying to make, or is it loosely related to the topic but not to the exact point of the argument?
- Is the *support* for the argument *sufficient*? Does the author provide enough support to prove his or her point of view?

- If the author uses *an emotional tone* to recruit the reader's support, does the tone mask *bias* (a lack of objectivity) on the part of the author? In other words, does the support evoke strong emotions in the reader that conceal the lack of relevant or sufficient support?
- Is the *logic* of the argument *valid* or is it *faulty*? In other words, does the author set out reasoning in a series of statements that follow a causal relationship?

Activity 4

Study the following arguments and assess their support and logic.

A. I am confounded by propaganda in favour of independent (private) schools, particularly when universally accessible, high-quality public education has long been the backbone of Canada's strength. On academic measurements I found that my public school peers and I easily performed at the same levels as our private school classmates in university and beyond.

1. Does the author support or criticize private schools? _____

2. Would you consider the author's support for the argument to be sufficient? Why or why not?

   _____

B. The United States is the last nation in the world still using chimpanzees in large-scale invasive science experiments. Laboratories in America are allowed to keep chimpanzees in metal cages the size of a kitchen table and deprive them of normal social interaction. For example, when she was living in captivity in one of the laboratories, chimp Foxie had five babies, including a set of twins. All were taken from her as infants— some when they were just days old. We should have compassion for these amazingly intelligent and creative animals. They should be set free. Science does not benefit from the experiments on chimpanzees.

1. What does the author try to persuade the reader to believe?

   _____

2. What emotional tone(s) does this passage invoke? _____

3. Would you consider all of the author's support for the argument to be relevant? Why or why not?

_____

C. Japan's nuclear program should be shut down immediately. It is clear that in an area with seismological risks as high as those in Japan nuclear energy plants should not be allowed. The 2011 Fukushima disaster, the result of a 9.3-magnitude earthquake, provides strong evidence for this. Six workers were killed in the disaster and 300 received significant radiation doses. Large amounts of radiation were released into the air, ground, and ocean water. It will take decades to decontaminate the areas surrounding Fukushima.

1. What does the author try to persuade the readers to believe?

_____

2. Would you consider the support for the argument to be sufficient and objective? Why or why not?

_____

D. You have probably noticed this sight in many Canadian streets: women wearing special clothing that covers their faces. These are Muslim women, usually recent immigrants from countries with male-dominated cultures. They might wear a *niqab* (the veil that leaves only the woman's eyes uncovered) or a *burka* (a cloak covering the whole body of a woman, including her face, so that she looks at the world through gauze). There has been an on-going debate in Canada as to whether face coverings in public should be allowed. We should follow the example of many other Western countries where there is no ban on religious clothing and no ban on religious freedom of their citizens.

1. What is the opinion of the writer about face coverings in Canada?

_____

2. Would you consider the support for the writer's opinion sufficient? Why or why not?

_____

The following arguments contain examples of faulty logic. In a small group, read the paragraphs and discuss why the arguments are not valid. Then use your own words to explain the problem with the author's reasoning in each case. The first passage is done for you.

A. Bill is arguing against free higher education. He says the Canadian government cannot afford to pay tuition for all students—to do so, the government would have to raise taxes substantially. In response to Bill's comments, Ann replies, "That's easy for you to say. Your parents are a doctor and a lawyer, and paying your tuition is not a problem for them."

What is the problem with Ann's reasoning?

Ann does not respond to the point Bill is making: raising taxes to cover tuition. Instead, she attacks Bill on a personal level. Ann accuses Bill of a biased opinion because his parents are well-off; however she does not actually know whether they, in fact, pay Bill's tuition or whether he pays it himself.

B. Marie is making an argument for working a part-time job while studying full-time. She thinks that it is absolutely necessary that she work part-time, even if she has a full-time course load. Recently, she has had trouble at school, failing two of her midterms. However, she says that the majority of the students she knows hold a job, so it is only right that she do the same.

What might be the problem with Marie's reasoning?

_____

_____

_____

C. Because the US and Canada share the same language and culture, the policies accepted in the US will work well in Canada too. For example, people in both countries believe that citizens have the right to defend themselves, and therefore the strict gun control laws in Canada should be revoked and more liberal gun laws, similar to those in the US, should be passed.

What is the problem with the reasoning above?

_____

_____

D. Hassan is a student from Saudi Arabia studying in Canada. He is having trouble enduring the cold Canadian winters, and tells his classmates how much he misses the heat and bright sun of his home country. Probably all people of Middle-Eastern origin, like Hassan, prefer hot weather to cold weather.

What is the problem with the reasoning above?

_____

_____

E. Studies show that students today spend much less time studying outside the classroom than students did 50 years ago. Whereas in the 1960s the study time for a full-time student was about 25 hours per week, in 2003 it was only about 14 hours per week. The cause of this drastic decline is that today's young people are not prepared to work hard. They would rather party or play sports than study.

a) What is the problem with the reasoning above?

_____

_____

b) What other probable causes of study time decline can you think of?

_____

_____

Now that you have discussed the logical faults in the each of the passages, read descriptions of the types of faulty logic below. Then match each type with the relevant paragraph on pages 108 and 109.

Paragraph _____ **Misleading analogy**: a comparison used as part of the argument is superficial or improbable

Paragraph _____ **Bandwagon**: an idea is considered to be true because many people agree with it

Paragraph _____ An attack directed against a person's character rather than their argument (sometimes referred to as an ***ad hominem*** argument)

Paragraph _____ **Oversimplification**: explaining the result by focusing on one cause, while in reality many causes are possible

Paragraph _____ **Overgeneralization**: a conclusion that inaccurately applies to a large group, while in fact only a small group can be described by it

PART TWO

Cross-Disciplinary Readings

Maintaining Law and Order

GETTING INTO THE TOPIC

How can a state ensure the safety of its citizens? Unit 6 presents possible answers to this question from the perspectives of history, urban planning, and criminology. The first selection takes you back in history to Elizabethan England (around the second half of the sixteenth century) and gives you an opportunity to compare today's legal system with one from the past. The second text ponders the question of modern city design, suggesting that the very layout of a city can make its residents safer. The final selection presents advantages and disadvantages of electronic monitoring systems, which keep an electronic eye on a person who has been convicted of a crime.

Discuss these questions to help you get into the topic.

1. Do you think Canada has strong laws to prevent and punish crime? Discuss such crimes as drunk driving, robbery, and murder. You can also compare Canadian laws to those in your home country.

2. How do you think criminals committing felonies (serious crimes) were punished about 400 years ago? Do you think the system of law and order at that time was more or less fair than it is today?

3. Do you feel safe in the city or town where you live? Give examples of how architects and urban planners can improve the safety of a city through design. The picture below will help you with the first example.

Crimes are less likely to occur in well-populated areas.

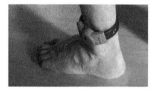

An electronic monitoring device can track a person's whereabouts.

4. Imagine that a person has been convicted of a crime and sentenced to house arrest. In your opinion, is having this person wear an electronic monitoring device an effective way to ensure that he or she does not leave home or reoffend?

READING 1

Punishment in Elizabethan England[1] History

01 The most serious crimes were treason, murder, and a range of crimes classed as felonies, including manslaughter, rape, sodomy, arson, witchcraft, burglary, robbery, and grand larceny (theft of goods worth at least 12 pence[2]). All these offences carried a mandatory death sentence, making juries sometimes reluctant to convict in felony cases: one Justice[3] complained that "most commonly the simple countryman or woman, looking no further into the loss of their own goods, are of the opinion that they would not procure a man's death for all the goods in the world," so that "upon promise to have their goods again [they] will give faint evidence, if they be not strictly looked into by the Justice."

---

[1] the second half of the sixteenth century, when the ruling monarch was Queen Elizabeth I
[2] Depending on how the calculation is done, today's equivalent of 12 pence could be as little as $20 to $50.
[3] judge

02   Someone convicted of a capital crime (any crime punishable by death) could escape death through a pardon from the crown.[4] In the case of most felonies, it was also possible for men to plead *benefit of clergy* (this option was not open to women). In the Middle Ages the clergy[5] had been exempt from secular punishment for felony, an exemption that extended to any man who could prove he was able to read. A version of the custom was still in use in the late 1500s. Benefit of clergy could only be exercised once: the convict would be branded on the thumb to mark that he had exercised this privilege (technically, he had been defrocked[6] as a clergyman). Benefit of clergy was not available to those convicted of the most serious felonies, such as burglary and robbery.

03   Most execution was by hanging, although some crimes such as poisoning and heresy (beliefs against Christianity) were punishable by burning, and treason was punishable by the triple punishment of hanging, drawing (disemboweling), and quartering (cutting the body into quarters). Nonfelonious crimes might be subject to lesser forms of corporal punishment, such as whipping, branding, or loss of a body part such as a hand or ear. Lesser punishments included fines and rituals of public humiliation, including confinement in the stocks or the pillory. The pillory confined both the head and hands: the convict was held immobile in a standing position, and vulnerable to the abuse of passers-by. The stocks confined only the legs, and most of the time only one leg was secured; the stocks were often used simply as a means of restraint rather than punishment.

04   Imprisonment was not the typical means of punishment, but its use was on the rise. Debtors might be imprisoned until they repaid their debts.

Crowds gathered to see a convict in the pillory

Serious misdemeanors might result in time at a House of Correction, a new form of institution of which the most famous was Bridewell in London: here vagrants,[7] prostitutes, and other convicts worked on treadmills to grind grain, picked apart ropes to make oakum,[8] and beat hemp plants to prepare the fibres for spinning. Imprisonment was usually for a matter of months, but sentences of life imprisonment were not unknown.

05   A snapshot view of the workings of the law can be found in the story of Jeremy Heckford, a villager from Marks Tey in Essex. In 1584 he was unemployed and in trouble with the local authorities; he fled Marks Tey, to be picked up later the same year as a vagrant in Chelmsford, where he was imprisoned on suspicion of felony.

---

[4] the power of a king or queen
[5] priests of a church
[6] stripped of the status of a clergyman
[7] people who have no home or job
[8] special fibre used in shipbuilding

No charges were pressed, and he was eventually released. By 1587 he was back in Marks Tey, where he was tried and acquitted for stealing some grain. In 1589 he was brought before the Essex Quarter Sessions court, where he was indicted for a theft valued at 2s. [shillings]— enough to qualify as a felony and send him to the gallows.[9] The jury reduced the valuation to the level of a petty larceny, and Heckford was punished by whipping. The following year he was convicted of stealing some hose and petticoats in Marks Tey. This time the valuation of 2s. was not reduced. Heckford tried to plead benefit of clergy, but failed to prove his ability to read, and so ended his life on the gallows.

06   In a society without a professional police force to enforce its laws, social control relied heavily on the use of spectacles of punishment. Hangings were public events, attended by large crowds of men, women, and children, and the sight of such punishments was considered instructive and essential in teaching the young to behave themselves. Even after execution, the remains of an executed criminal were displayed as a warning. The corpses of murderers were left in cages called gibbets to be picked clean by carrion birds, and the heads of executed traitors were impaled[10] above the gatehouse on London Bridge. Continental visitors were inevitably struck by the grisly spectacle: one Swiss visitor noted the "more than thirty skulls of noble men who had been executed and beheaded for treason and for other reasons— and their descendants are accustomed to boast of this, themselves even pointing out one of their ancestors' heads on this same bridge, believing that they will be esteemed the more because their antecedents were of such high descent that they could even covet the crown."

Source: J.L. Forgeng, *Daily life in Elizabethan England*, 2nd edition (Santa Barbara, CA: Greenwood, 2010), pp. 36–38.

---

[9] a wooden frame used for execution by hanging
[10] had a sharp pointed object pushed through

Comprehension and Skills Practice

1.   A. Match the following crimes with their definitions. You may use a dictionary for this question.

a. treason	____ the use of magic powers, especially evil ones
b. manslaughter	____ the crime of deliberately setting fire to something, especially a building
c. burglary	____ the crime of doing something that could cause danger to your country
d. arson	____ the crime of killing someone illegally but not deliberately
e. grand larceny	____ the crime of entering a building illegally and stealing things from it
f. witchcraft	____ the crime of stealing something of great value from somebody

B. Mark the statement as T (true) or F (false). Correct if the statement is false.

_____ All perpetrators of the crimes mentioned in 1A were automatically executed.

2. What is the implied main idea of paragraph 1?

 a) Jury members were not conscientious citizens and did not do their duties well.

 b) Some crimes were punished more seriously than others.

 c) Jurors cared more about their own goods than about serving justice.

 d) The legal system did not allow punishment to be varied depending on the severity of crime.

3. What were the two ways to avoid the death sentence for a convicted criminal?

 a) _____

 b) _____

4. The benefit of clergy could be used only once. How did courts ensure that a convict could not claim the benefit of clergy a second time?

 _____

5. Why do you think treason was punishable by hanging, drawing, and quartering and not just by hanging?

 _____

6. How do you think the crime of injuring someone in a fight might be punished in Elizabethan England?

 _____

7. Being confined in the pillory implied _____. Circle all that apply.

 a) possible insults, verbal or physical, from the public

 b) humiliation by passers-by

 c) being completely unable to move around

 d) having a limited freedom to move around, with one leg confined

8. Did convicts who were imprisoned contribute in any way to society? How?

 _____

9. Review the case of Jeremy Heckford.

 a) How many times did he run into trouble with the law? _____

 b) How many times was he convicted? _____

c) What punishments was he given? _____

d) What does his case illustrate about the effectiveness of Elizabethan laws? Were the laws effective? Explain your answer.

_____

_____

10. A. What is the organizational pattern of paragraph 5?

a) Process

b) Description

c) Cause-effect

d) Problem-solution

B. Why do you think the author chose to include this paragraph in the text?

_____

11. What justification does the author of this text give for the use of punishment as a public spectacle in Elizabethan England?

_____

12. Mark the inference as valid (V) or invalid (I).

_____ In other European countries the heads of executed traitors were not publicly displayed.

Vocabulary

A. Use context clues and your knowledge of word parts to determine the correct meaning of each word. Verify your answers using a dictionary if necessary.

1. felonies (par. 1): _____

2. extended (par. 2): _____

3. misdemeanors (par. 4): _____

4. spectacles (par. 6): _____

5. carrion birds (par. 6): _____

6. antecedent (par. 6): _____

B. Define the following term from the text.

benefit of clergy (par. 2): _____

READING 2

In the first part of the next reading, John Byrne, a consultant in urban design and planning, and professor of urban design in Australia, introduces a method of crime prevention through environmental design based on a set of principles known as "CPTED." The reading finishes with an extract from a Queensland government document on urban planning, which illustrates a practical application of CPTED principles as applied to street layout and design. Queensland is the second-largest state in Australia.

Designing Safer Cities

 Urban Planning

01 More than half the world's population live in cities and the proportion of urban dwellers continues to swell. Our future seems inextricably urban. In 1950, one-third of the world's population resided in urban centres but this has grown at an unprecedented rate. In 2008, for the first time, the world's population was evenly split between urban and rural areas. However in more developed nations about three-quarters of residents live in urban areas. It is unthinkable therefore that we should not try to make our cities safe and secure places in which humans can prosper, as communities, households and as individuals. This is an essential part of social sustainability and therefore of integrated sustainability.

02 Urban designers incorporate principles of "CPTED" (pronounced "sep-ted")—which stands for Crime Prevention Through Environmental Design. Its fundamental idea is that it is *possible* to use knowledge and creativity to design urban environments in ways that lessen or even prevent the incidence of crimes against people or property. The knowledge base of CPTED has been developing over decades, based on experience and research. In recent times, the idea and objectives of CPTED are found (at least in principle) in the urban planning policies of many Australian state governments and Australasian local governments.

What are the main concepts of CPTED?

03 A. *That crimes against people or property are less likely if other people are around.* They have an opportunity to intervene or assist in preventing or solving crimes, if they so care to. Their presence both discourages many would-be criminals and encourages a sense of security.

B. *That it is also important that people in adjoining buildings and spaces can see what is going on.* They too might assist and the possibility of their "passive surveillance" also can deter and give an added sense of security. They "add" to the people nearby.

C. *That this works if people care about what goes on in their community.* It is a problem if they merely watch or ignore the crimes they might see.

D. *That it's important to give people safe choices, free of high risks or unpleasant surprise, about where to be and how to anticipate and respond to problems.* Can they, for example, change routes if one seems unsafe?

04   CPTED practice encourages the legitimate use of the public parts of our cities by many people. It actively provides lots of passive surveillance of those places, avoids "hidden" spaces or traps, and also promotes community ownership of the outcomes so that those seeing what is happening care about it and do something to help. It is therefore concerned with firstly designing both the public realm and the buildings and activities at the edges of those spaces, and secondly strengthening a sense of community and its commitment to a safe city. There are naturally many interacting factors at play here to bring these together to make and sustain safer cities.

How effective is CPTED?

05   Arguably, there are no universal solutions even though we can learn from others' practical experience, and good urban environmental design

Visibility in transport nodes

responds to the particular cultural, geographical, climatic, historical and economic contexts of the inhabitants. There is always the need for balancing competing priorities, between, for example, promoting activity and surveillance and providing, with appropriate respect for privacy, places for quiet contemplation or individual enjoyment. It can be difficult to respect desire for privacy within private property, on the one hand, and to facilitate passive surveillance of the adjoining public realm, on the other.

06   As well, the way we design urban environments needs to reflect different needs of different socio-economic or cultural groups within the community and this might lead to different CPTED approaches.

07   We might attempt to make cities safe by other means including:
- By building them like armed fortresses (but that still leaves the spaces between them or, if they are big enough, within them); or
- By flooding the streets permanently with many police or other security people (but that is expensive and takes money away from other important community services); or
- By flooding the streets and parks with security cameras watched over by an army of observers somewhere, supported by instant response squads; or

Underpass: An example of a vulnerable place

- By imposing limitations on access to the public realm like curfews.

08　While at some times and in some special places a range of approaches might be desirable and worthwhile, the question remains: "Is that the way we want our community to be?" If we could lessen the need to resort to fortresses, guards, cameras and curfews by thoughtful creative practical desirable urban design, this is a preferable solution.

The urban design of neighbourhoods in Queensland: Grids and trees

09　Partly in response to changing ideas about connectivity, cars, people and mixes of land uses and partly from observation of more traditional Queensland precincts, ideas about how best to design neighbourhoods, especially with a significant residential component, have changed. In the 1970s and 1980s, the most significant design fashion (in the pursuit of safer, less trafficked and therefore more pleasant residential streets) was for "tree systems" with many separated and poorly or circuitously connected cul-de-sac ends, and with one tree usually not connected to the next, except by the main road.

10　Many now argue for a return to more traditional interconnected "grid" neighbourhoods with streets connecting many times with other streets which are often (but not always) in relatively "simple" lattice layouts. The essential feature is high street connectivity. Such neighbourhoods are to be found in many areas of Queensland and Australian cities and towns dating from the early days through into the second half of the last century, and represent some of the most desirable, high-amenity and affluent localities.

11　Such radical changes to previous industry "best practice" have significant implications for CPTED. Public transport, for example, usually can't operate doubling in and out of a series of unconnected tree systems of culs-de-sac one after another. Instead, it will stay out on the main road decreasing the likelihood of it being used, making the walk to it longer and less safe, and perhaps delivering more lonely bus stops. Having a connected lattice enables a route through a sequence of adjoining neighbourhoods to be chosen, perhaps going past local shops and facilities, overseen by housing, and so delivering a better CPTED outcome. Encouraging walking and cycling (and where motorists can see them), promoting walking to and from public transport, and having a variety of uses and therefore people in and around the neighbourhood, are all good ways of increasing safety.

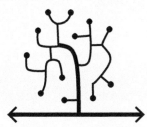

Figure 6.1 Tree system street layout

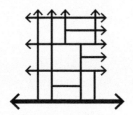

Figure 6.2 Grid street layout

Sources: Paragraphs 1–8 from J. Byrne, "Designing safer cities: CPTED." *Geodate* 23 no. 4 (August, 2010): 6–9; Paragraphs 9–11 from The State of Queensland, "Crime prevention through environmental design: Guidelines for Queensland." www.hpw.qld.gov.au/SiteCollectionDocuments/CPTEDPartA.pdf (October 2007), pp. 22–23.

1. What is the main idea of paragraph 1?

    a) We should not try to make our cities socially sustainable because only about half of the world's population lives there.

    b) Because so many people are concentrated in urban areas, we should promote their safety and security.

    c) The proportion of people living in urban areas continues to grow around the world.

    d) In developed nations, about three-quarters of the population lives in urban areas.

2. What is the main principle of CPTED?

    _____

    _____

3. Which of the following goes against the concepts of CPTED?

    a) Crowded neighbourhoods, with lots of people in the streets, facilitate crime.

    b) When residents watch the street from the windows of their houses, crime might be deterred.

    c) Public spaces should be designed such that residents feel a sense of community and therefore respond when they see a crime being committed.

    d) A city's design should offer several alternative routes to a person in case this person encounters a criminal and has to escape.

4. What is meant by *passive surveillance* (par. 3, point B)?

    _____

5. The author states that "the idea and objectives of CPTED are found (at least in principle) in the urban planning policies of many Australian state governments and Australasian local governments." He also mentions that CPTED "works if people care about what goes on in their community," and "have an opportunity to intervene or assist in preventing or solving crimes, if they so care to."

    What inference can the reader draw from these two statements?

    a) Many people in Australian cities do not care about what goes on in their community.

    b) Policy makers in Australia expect that people do care about what goes on in their community.

c) It is dangerous to intervene when a crime is occurring, and that is why Australian state governments use CPTED in their urban planning policies.

6. What are the problems that CPTED may face? Circle all that apply.

   a) In a city governed by CPTED designs, it might be difficult to create solitary places where a person spends time alone.

   b) There could be too much surveillance of public places by surrounding people.

   c) Privacy at people's homes may be lost.

   d) Cultural and socio-economic diversity within a community may lead to increased crime rates.

7. A. The author mentions several alternatives to CPTED. Does he approve of them? _____

   B. What are the disadvantages of some of these alternatives? List them below.

   _____

   _____

   _____

   C. The technique of presenting options the author considers unacceptable followed by disadvantages of these options is a form of persuasion you learned in Part I of this book. What is the name of this technique?

   _____

8. The text presents an informed opinion in paragraphs 9–11.

   A. Summarize the opinion: _____

   _____

   B. What points below support this opinion? Circle all that apply.

   a) Public transport can operate more efficiently.

   b) Walking is encouraged.

   c) Bus stops are few and difficult to access.

   d) Cycling is possible to get from one street to another.

   e) Less trafficked streets are quieter.

   f) Public places, like shops and facilities, are easily accessible by transit.

   g) More people are travelling around neighbourhoods.

9. Who would be interested in reading "Designing Safer Cities"?

   _____

A. Use context clues and your knowledge of word parts to determine the correct meaning of each word. Verify your answers using a dictionary if necessary.

1. swell (par. 1): _____

2. unprecedented (par. 1): _____

3. contemplation (par. 5): _____

4. circuitously (par. 9): _____

5. radical (par. 11): _____

B. Define the following terms from the text.

1. tree system (par. 9): _____

2. lattice layouts (par. 10): _____

READING 3

House Arrest, Electronic Monitoring, and Global Positioning Systems

 Criminology

01 *House arrest* is a program used by probation and parole agencies that requires offenders to remain in their homes at all times except for approved periods, such as travel to work or school, and occasionally for other approved destinations. As a system of social control, house arrest is typically used primarily as an initial phase of intensive probation or parole supervision, but can also be used as an alternative to pretrial detention or a jail sentence. As is the case with so many other criminal justice practices, house arrest was designed primarily to reduce financial costs to the state by reducing institutional confinement.

02 House arrest did not initially gain widespread acceptance in the criminal justice community because there was no way of ensuring offender compliance with the order, short of having officers constantly monitoring the residence. It was also viewed by the public at large as being soft on crime—"doing time in the comfort of one's home." However, house arrest gained in popularity with the advent of *electronic monitoring* (EM). EM is a system by which offenders under house arrest can be monitored for compliance using computerized technology. In modern EM systems, an electronic device worn around the offender's ankle sends a continuous signal to a receiver attached to the

offender's house phone. If the offender moves beyond 500 feet of his or her house or apartment, the transmitter records it and relays the information to a centralized computer. A probation/parole officer is then dispatched to the offender's home to investigate whether the offender has absconded or removed or tampered with the device. As of 2004, almost 13,000 offenders were under house arrest, with 90% of them being electronically monitored (Bohn & Haley, 2007).

03   An even more sophisticated method of tracking offenders is that of a *global positioning system* (GPS). GPS requires offenders to wear a removable tracking unit that constantly communicates with a non-removable ankle cuff. If communication is lost, the loss is noted by a Department of Defense satellite, which records the time and location of the loss in its database. This information is then forwarded to criminal justice authorities so that they can take action to determine why communication was lost. Unlike EM systems, the GPS can be used for surveillance as well as detention purposes. For instance, it can let authorities know if a sex offender goes within a certain distance of a schoolyard, or if a violent offender is approaching his or her victim's place of residence or work (Black & Smith, 2003). As of 2007, a total of 28 states had legislation calling for some form of electronic monitoring of sex offenders (Payne, DeMichele, & Button, 2008).

04   Payne and Gainey (2004) indicate that detractors of electronic monitoring tend to criticize it as intruding too much into the realm of privacy, and even as barbaric. Of course it is intrusive; that is the point! But it is far less intrusive than prison, and Payne and Gainey state that offenders released from jails or prisons and placed in EM programs are generally positive about the experience (not that they enjoyed it, but that it was better than the jail or prison alternative). Their findings mirror those from a larger sample of offenders on EM programs in New Zealand (Gibb & King, 2003). Many see it as jail or prison time simply served in a less restrictive and less violent environment (so much for the charge that it is barbaric), although the average experienced offender would exchange 11.35 months on EM for 12 months in prison, and although offenders overall would exchange 13.95 months on EM for 12 months in prison (Moore et al., 2008). It would seem from this and similar studies that inveterate offenders tend to prefer prison over virtually any other correctional sentence, other than straight probation.

05   Although the authors of these studies appear positive about the alleged rehabilitative promise of allowing offenders to serve time at home and thus maintaining their links to family, and although successful completion rates are high, recidivism[1] rates, which are the litmus tests[2] for any corrections program aimed at rehabilitation, were not any better than for probationers/parolees not on EM programs matched for offender risk in several Canadian provinces (Bonta, Wallace-Capretta, & Rooney, 2000). This may be viewed positively, however, as a function of the greater ability to detect noncompliance with release conditions among those under EM supervision.

06   An additional problem with EM is that because its low cost relative to incarceration is alluring to politicians, it may be (and is) used without sufficient care regarding who should be eligible for it. While offenders can be monitored and more readily arrested if they commit a crime while on EM, EM does not prevent them from committing further crimes. Several high-profile cases including rapes and murders have been committed by offenders who succeeded in removing their electronic bracelets (Reid, 2006). When cases such as these are reported, the public (which by and large would rather see

---

[1] continuing to commit crimes and seemingly being unable to stop, even after being punished
[2] a way of deciding whether something is successful

iron balls and chains attached to offenders rather than plastic bracelets) responds with charges of leniency. This is unfortunate because EM does appear to have a significant impact on prison overcrowding and on reducing correctional costs. Of course, EM can only be considered to reduce correctional costs if it is used as a substitute for incarceration, not as an addition to normal probation and parole, in which case it is an added cost.

COMPARATIVE PERSPECTIVE: ELECTRONIC MONITORING IN EUROPE

Because several European nations have found themselves burdened by overcrowded prisons over the past two decades, they have turned to electronic monitoring to ease the burden. The table produced below shows that there is widespread variation in the use of EM, ranging from a mere 0.4 per 100,000 of the population in Austria to a high of 33.2 per 100,000 in England and Wales. These rate differences reflect a number of factors, including the penal policies of the country involved, the strength of the financial and prison overcrowding burden, and the demands and fears of the public. The large differences in daily costs (the costs were converted from euros to dollars by the authors using Internet currency converters) also reflect national differences in the economy, the type of monitoring used, officer caseload sizes, and how much EM is supplemented by other surveillance and treatment methods such as probation/parole officer and social worker home visits. Some countries use the private sector to install and monitor EM equipment and others do not, while some use a combination of private and public sector workers. The sophistication of the monitoring equipment also varies from simple telephone voice recognition methods to GPS systems.

COUNTRY	POPULATION	EM RATE PER 100,000	COMPLETION RATE	DAILY COSTS
Austria	8,350,000	0.4	N/A	N/A
Belgium	10,584,000	6.3	90%	$52
Denmark	5,490,000	2.6	N/A	N/A
England & Wales	54,670,000	33.2	90%	$50
France	62,100,000	5.5	94%	N/A
Netherlands	16,440,000	5.8	93%	N/A
Norway	4,740,000	2.9	N/A	N/A
Portugal	10,640,000	4.8	N/A	$20
Scotland	5,190,000	15.4	N/A	N/A
Spain (Catalonia only)	7,200,000	1.1	85%	$10
Spain (Madrid only)	5,840,000	30.9	N/A	N/A
Sweden	9,170,000	12.1	94%	$98

Source: R. Havercamp, M. Meyer & R. Levey, "Electronic monitoring in Europe." *European Journal of Crime, Criminal Law & Criminal Justice* 12 (2004): 36–45. Copyright © Brill

The completion rates are fairly consistent across countries, and they are refreshingly high. This is possibly a function of the lower-risk offenders that are typically placed on EM in Europe. It is generally required that for an offender to be placed on EM, he or she must have a suitable residence, a functional phone line, and be working (Havercamp, Mayer, & Levy, 2004). There is also a wide range of times to be served on EM, ranging from about 3 months in England and Wales for probationers to 13 to 23 months for parolees in France (Wennerberg & Pinto, 2009).

One large-scale study of parolees released under home detention curfew (using electronic monitoring to enforce it) conducted in Britain provided very positive results (Dodgson et al., 2001). Six months after release, only 9.3% (118 out of 1,269) of the EM parolees had been reconvicted of a new crime, compared with 40.4% (558 out of 1,381) of the prisoners who were unconditionally released. Of course, all of this difference cannot be attributed to the EM program, since the groups were not matched for criminal history and those on the program were already considered to have a lower risk of reoffending. Nevertheless, the EM groups were positive about the program (it got them early release from prison), and the net financial saving to the prison service over 12 months was estimated to be £36.7 million, or about $56.25 million. The consensus in the European literature reviewed seems to be that electric monitoring "works" and that it is here to stay.

Source: M.K. Stohr, *Corrections: The Essentials* (Thousand Oaks, CA: Sage Publications, 2012), pp. 145–147.

Comprehension and Skills Practice

1. Name the four situations in which house arrest can be used.

   a) _____

   b) _____

   c) _____

   d) _____

2. What change, in the view of the general public, did EM bring to house arrest?

   _____

3. How does EM operate?

   a) The transmitter on the offender's home telephone relays information about the location of the offender to a centralized computer.

   b) The receiver sends continuous signals to a centralized computer monitored by staff.

   c) The officers wearing special electronic devices constantly monitor the offender's house.

   d) The telephone in the offender's residence generates a call to an officer if the offender stays within 500 feet of the phone.

4. Why is GPS a more sophisticated method of tracking offenders than EM?

_____

5. In paragraph 4, two criticisms aimed at EM are voiced. What is the response of EM supporters to these criticisms?

CRITICISM	RESPONSE
EM is intrusive.	
EM is barbaric.	

6. Mark each statement as T (true) or F (false).

   a) ___ Studies indicate that offenders who have experienced both a jail sentence and house arrest with EM like EM very much.

   b) ___ Experienced offenders rank straight probation as their first preference for punishment, and a prison sentence as the second.

7. Why do some researchers believe that EM programs can be rehabilitative?

   a) Under EM programs, the offender can stay at home and participate in family life.

   b) The recidivism statistics of offenders after an EM program are no higher than of those after a prison sentence.

   c) The recidivism rates of some Canadian offenders after an EM program were higher than of those after serving time in prison.

   d) Many offenders in EM programs complete their sentences without breaking the conditions set by the court.

8. Which of the following are valid inferences based on the information in paragraph 6? Circle all that apply.

   a) The author thinks that there might be more than one problem with EM.

   b) The costs of criminal justice methods are an important factor in political decisions.

   c) The fact that violent crimes have been committed by offenders sentenced to EM proves that EM is useless in tracking an offender.

d) An EM device is not completely resistant to tampering.

e) The general public can be described as conservative in its views on criminal justice.

9. Which arguments for EM does the author of this text promote? Circle all that apply.

a) Some EM methods can not only improve the chances of detention but also enable surveillance of offenders.

b) EM methods have a strong chance of preventing a crime by a monitored offender.

c) The recidivism rates of offenders after participating in an EM program are not higher than those of offenders who have served time in prison.

d) EM relieves overcrowding in prisons.

e) If applied instead of incarceration, EM saves money that otherwise would have been spent on maintaining prisons.

10. Mark each statement as T (true) or F (false), based on the information in the textbox.

a) ____ All European countries turn to EM as a widely used method of monitoring offenders.

b) ____ The more populous the country is, the more widely EM is used there.

c) ____ The large differences in daily costs of EM reflect a variety of factors, including the sophistication level of the equipment used.

d) ____ The high completion rates (the rates of completing a sentence under EM surveillance) seem to support the idea that electronic monitoring "works" in Europe.

11. Do you think the author presents an unbalanced view on the effectiveness of electronic monitoring? In other words, do you think she shows any bias (either for or against EM)? Explain your answer.

_____

_____

_____

12. Which techniques does the author of this text use to make her writing more persuasive? Give some examples.

_____

_____

_____

Use context clues and your knowledge of word parts to determine the correct meaning of each word. Verify your answers using a dictionary if necessary.

1. pretrial (par. 1): _____

2. confinement (par. 1):

    a) expenses

    b) forced stay in prison

    c) supervision

3. absconded (par. 2): _____

4. tampered (par. 2): _____

5. inveterate (par. 4):

    a) unlikely to be rehabilitated

    b) well-behaved and law-abiding

    c) having no offences in the past

6. noncompliance (par. 5): _____

UNIT REFLECTION AND SYNTHESIS

1. Match each selection with the statement that describes its approach to the problem of crime.

a. "Designing Safer Cities"	____ Crime is a serious offence against society, and therefore criminals should be publicly penalized using severe corporal methods, including capital punishment.
b. "Punishment in Elizabethan England"	____ Crime is a serious offence against our society, and therefore criminals should be punished using various methods, including some alternatives to imprisonment.
c. "House Arrest, Electronic Monitoring, and Global Positioning Systems"	____ Crime should not be tolerated in our society, and smart urban planning can help prevent it.

2. How are the means of addressing crime in Elizabethan England different from the means discussed in "Designing Safer Cities"? Summarize one main difference.

_____

_____

3. Imagine that a person living in Elizabethan England travels in a time machine to modern-day Canada. Do you think this person would see any similarities between EM and Elizabethan punishment?

_____

_____

4. A. Which of the three texts in this unit contains the most facts (rather than opinions)? _____

   B. Why do you think it is written this way?

   _____

   C. Can you identify any opinions in this text as well? If not, why do you think no opinions are presented?

   _____

   _____

5. Assess the support the authors of "Designing Safer Cities" and "House Arrest" give for their opinions.

	APPROPRIATE URBAN DESIGN CAN HELP LOWER THE CRIME RATE.	ELECTRONIC MONITORING IS AN EFFECTIVE MEANS OF REDUCING CRIME.
Is the support relevant?		
Is the support sufficient?		
Is the reasoning logical?		
Does an emotional tone hide problems with logic?		
Does the author appear biased?		

6. How are the purposes of the authors of "Designing Safer Cities" and "House Arrest" different?

"Designing Safer Cities": _____

"House Arrest": _____

7. A. Who is the audience for each text in this unit?

_____

_____

_____

B. Could the general public be the audience for all three texts? Why or why not?

_____

8. Discuss in small groups. What is your opinion about the effectiveness of

a) punishments in Elizabethan England?

b) urban planning using CPTED principles?

c) electronic monitoring?

9. How was the public involved in controlling crime in Elizabethan England? How does this public involvement differ from that described with the CPTED approach to designing cities? Fill in the Venn diagram below with similarities and differences.

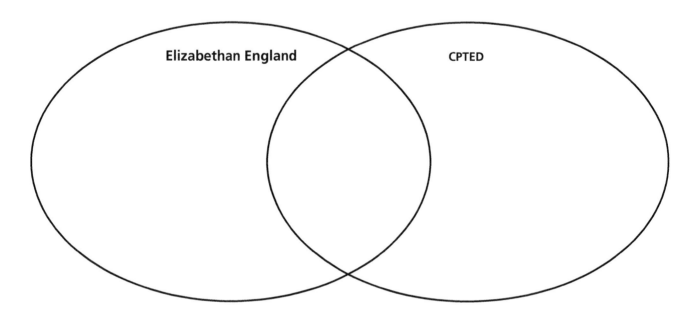

Elizabethan England CPTED

Race and Racism

GETTING INTO THE TOPIC

This unit explores the issue of race from the point of view of anthropology, sport sciences, and economics. Is it useful or appropriate to apply the concept of race when studying human diversity? Are racial terms necessary in discussing athletic achievements or economic inequalities? Is the idea of race valid at all or does it only put a racist spin on our discourse?

Discuss the following questions to help you get into the topic.

1. How would you define the term *race*? Compare your definition with the one in your dictionary. How are they similar or different?

2. Why do you think people came up with the idea of race?

3. Some people believe that genetics associated with race may be a factor in explaining why certain individuals excel at specific sports. Do you consider race to be a plausible explanation for variation in athletic achievement? Why or why not? If yes, give examples and explanations.

4. According to the US Census Bureau, net median income for white families in 2009 was about $63,000 and for African-American families, it was close to

$38,000. In Canada, the average full-time worker makes a median income of $50,699 per year, while a visible-minority worker makes $45,128. What factors do you think might contribute to this gap?

READING 1

Race

 **Anthropology**

01 The concept of race developed in the context of European exploration and conquest beginning in the fifteenth century. Europeans conquered Indigenous peoples in the Americas and established colonial political economies that soon depended on the labour of Africans imported as slaves. By the end of the nineteenth century, light-skinned Europeans had established colonial rule over large territories inhabited by darker-skinned peoples, marking the beginnings of a global racial order (see Harrison 1995; Köhler 1978; Smedley 1993; 1998; Sanjek 1994; Trouillot 1994). Both as a way of explaining the existence of the human diversity they had encountered, and as a way of justifying the domination of Indigenous peoples and the enslavement of Africans, European intellectuals argued that the human species was subdivided into "natural kinds" of human beings called races that could be sharply distinguished from one another on the basis of outward physical (or phenotypic) appearance. All individuals assigned to the same race were assumed to share many other common features, of which phenotype was only the outward index.

02 Belief in the existence of biologically distinct races (sometimes called **racialism**) was then joined to an ancient Western notion called the "Great Chain of Being," which proposed that all "natural kinds" could be ranked in a hierarchy. In the latter half of the nineteenth century, European thinkers, including many anthropologists, devised schemes for ranking the "races of mankind" from lowest to highest. Not surprisingly, the "white" northern Europeans at the apex of imperial power were placed at the top of this global hierarchy. Darker-skinned peoples, like the Indigenous inhabitants of the Americas or of Asia, were ranked somewhere in the middle. But Africans, whom Europeans had bought and sold as slaves, and whose homelands in Africa were later conquered and incorporated into European empires, ranked lowest of all.

> **racialism**: Belief in the existence of biologically distinct races.
>
> **racism**: The systematic oppression of one or more socially defined "races" by another socially defined "race" that is justified in terms of the supposedly inherent biological superiority of the rulers and the supposed inherent biological inferiority of those they rule.

In this way, the identification of races was transformed into **racism**.

03   It is important to emphasize once again that all the so-called races of human beings are imagined communities. The racial boundaries that nineteenth-century European observers thought they had discovered do not correspond to major biological discontinuities within the human species. Although our species as a whole does exhibit variation in phenotypic attributes such as skin colour, hair texture, and stature, these variations do not naturally clump into separate populations with stable boundaries that can be sharply distinguished from one another. Put another way, the traditional concept of race in Western society is biologically and genetically meaningless.

04   But even though the concept of race is biologically meaningless, racial thinking persists in the twenty-first century. Anthropologists have long argued that race is a culturally constructed social category whose members are identified on the basis of certain selected phenotypic features (such as skin colour) that all of them are said to share. The end result is a highly distorted but more or less seemingly coherent set of criteria that members of a society can use to assign people they see to one culturally defined racial category or another. Once this happens, members of society can treat racial categories as if they reflect biological reality, using them to build institutions that include or exclude particular culturally defined races. In this way, race can become "real" in its consequences, even if it has no reality in biology.

05   The social category of race is a relatively recent invention. Audrey Smedley reminds us that in the worlds of European classical antiquity, and through the Middle Ages, "no structuring of equality . . . was associated with people *because of their skin colour*" (1998: 693; emphasis in original), and Faye Harrison points out that "phenotype prejudice was not institutionalized before the sixteenth century" (1995: 51). By the nineteenth century, European thinkers were attempting to classify all humans in the world into a few, mutually exclusive racial categories. Significantly, from that time until this, as Harrison emphasizes, "blackness has come to symbolize the social bottom" (1998: 612; see also Smedley 1998: 694–5).

06   White domination of Euro-American and Euro-Canadian racial hierarchies has been a constant. However, some anthropologists who study the cultural construction of whiteness point out that, even in North America, "whiteness" is not monolithic and that the cultural attributes supposedly shared by "white people" have varied in different times and places. Some members of white ruling groups in the southern United States, for example, have traditionally distanced themselves from lower-class whites, whom they call white trash; and the meaning of whiteness in South Africa has been complicated by differences of class and culture separating British South Africans from Afrikaners (Hartigan 1997). Moreover, the sharp "caste-like" racial divide between blacks and whites in North America is currently complicated by new immigrants identified with so-called brown/Latin American/Hispanic (or Indian/Pakistani) and yellow/Asian racial categories. Harrison and others recognize that racial categorization and repression take different forms in different places. Anthropologists working in Latin America describe racial practices that do not match those characteristic of the United States and Canada.

Source: E.A. Schultz, R.H. Lavenda & R.R. Dods, *Cultural Anthropology: A Perspective on the Human Condition*, 2nd Canadian edition (Don Mills, ON: Oxford University Press, 2012), pp. 299–300.

1. Fill in the following chart, explaining the development of the concept of "race" (par. 1).

15th century:
Europeans conquer the Americas

15th to 19th centuries:

_____

_____

Europeans wanted to explain

_____

_____

Europeans needed to justify their treatment of darker-skinned people.

The concept of biologically distinct "races" became accepted.

2. Mark the statement as T (true) or F (false). Correct if the statement is false.

____ The term *race* was made up by uneducated, ignorant European citizens.

3. Highlight the definition of *race*, according to Europeans in the fifteenth through nineteenth centuries.

4. Provide a specific example from paragraph 2 explaining how racialism enabled racism.

_____

_____

5. What is the authors' opinion about "race" as a biological and genetic concept?

_____

6. Mark the statement as T (true) or F (false).

____ The author thinks that *race* is a culturally constructed social category.

7. Why do the authors use quotation marks around the word *real* in the last sentence of paragraph 4?

   a) The word refers to a specialized term.

   b) The word has a special significance within the paragraph, so the authors emphasize it.

   c) The word implies irony—although the term *race* is unreal scientifically, it is real socially.

   d) The word is taken from someone else's work; it is a part of a quotation.

8. Which technique do the authors use in paragraph 5 to persuade the reader that the social category of race is a relatively recent invention?

   _____

9. A. What is the main idea of paragraph 6? Highlight it in the text.

   B. List at least two supporting details for the main idea.

   Supporting detail 1: _____

   Supporting detail 2: _____

Vocabulary

Use context clues and your knowledge of word parts to determine the correct meaning of each word. Verify your answers using a dictionary if necessary.

1. indigenous (par. 1): _____

2. phenotype (par. 1): _____

3. apex (par. 2): _____

4. institution(s) (par. 4): _____

   a) a large important organization that has a particular purpose, for example, a university or bank

   b) a building where people with special needs are taken care of, for example because they are old or mentally ill

   c) a custom or system that has existed for a long time among a particular group of people

5. antiquity (par. 5): _____

6. monolithic (par. 6):

   a) diverse

   b) uniform

   c) traditional

READING 2

The DNA Olympics—Jamaicans Win Sprinting "Genetic Lottery"— and Why We Should All Care

Sport
Sciences

Jon Entine takes stock of the DNA London Olympics—where, as usual, African-descended athletes swept the running events while whites and Asians dominated in the water sports, field competition and strength events. What's going on here?

01 Segregation was on display in London over the past two weeks—which, surprisingly, should spark no concerns and may even help educate us all about the wonders of human biodiversity. Let me explain. Led by 100-metre world record holder Usain Bolt, Jamaican men swept the sprinting events at the London Olympics. It was a stunning feat for the small Caribbean nation. But as part of a broader trend, it's hardly surprising. Runners of West African descent are the fastest humans on earth.

02 Remarkably, the story of East African runners is the mirror image of the West African success story. While terrible at the sprints, runners from Kenya, Ethiopia, Uganda and Somalia, along with a sprinkling of North and Southern Africans, regularly dominate endurance running. And if you are an Asian or white runner? Forget about it.

03 The trends are eye opening: Athletes of African ancestry hold every major male running record, from the 100 metres to the marathon. Over the last seven Olympic men's 100-metre races, all 56 finalists have been of West African descent. Only two non-African runners,

France's Christophe Lemaire, who is white, and Australia's Irish-aboriginal Patrick Johnson, have cracked the top 500 100-metre times. There are no elite Asian sprinters—or, intriguingly, any from East or North Africa.

Cultural myths

04 What's going on here? The most frequently heard explanation is that African athletes just work harder at running. It's one of their few outlets, the story goes, to escape the trap of limited opportunities. There's a tradition of running that young athletes emulate; they've been running to

school since kindergarten; they train harder for a chance at the golden ring that athletic success offers; or athletes from other parts of the world have developed a toxic inferiority complex, a fear of "black athletes."

05 National Public Radio recently carried just such a speculative piece on Kenya, and CNN had its own version on Jamaica. Never did the word "genetics" find its way into the story. It's all nurture, they concluded—the long since scientifically discredited *tabula rasa* theory of human achievement that attributes all success to individual effort and societal "forces."

06 No one outside of the most politically correct circles really believes that. Certainly scientists don't. The director of the Copenhagen Muscle Research Institute, Bengt Saltin, the world's premier expert in human performance and race, has concluded that an athlete's "environment" accounts for no more than 20–25 percent of athletic ability. The rest comes down to the roll of the genetic dice—with each population group having distinct advantages. In other words, running success is "in the genes."

07 Here are the facts. Athletic achievements, like success of all kind, is a bio-cultural phenomenon. Yes, Usain Bolt earned his victories. He may have been born gifted but he has worked his tail off to achieve greatness. He and he alone is responsible for his gold medal haul. But humans are not blank slates. While culture, environment, individual initiative and just plain luck might influence which individuals succeed, nature—your DNA—circumscribes the possibility of even being in the game. This is Population Genetics 101. Bolt and his Jamaican teammates are members of a tiny slice of the world population—elite athletes who trace their ancestry to western and central Africa—whose body types and physiology have been uniquely shaped by thousands of years of evolution to run fast.

08 Genetically linked, highly heritable characteristics such as skeletal structure, the distribution of muscle fibre types (for example, sprinters have more natural fast twitch fibres, while distance runners are naturally endowed with more of the slow twitch variety[1]), reflex capabilities, metabolic efficiency and lung capacity are not evenly distributed among populations. Do we yet know the specific genes that contribute to on the field success? No, but that's not an argument against the powerful role of genetics in sports. We do not yet know all the factors that determine skin colour, but we know that genetics determines it. Slowly, geneticists will link human performance, including sports skills, to our DNA and more specifically to our ancestral roots—populations.

09 We cannot avoid confronting the fact of our patterned human biodiversity. Over the past decade, human genome research has moved from a study of human similarities to a focus on population-based differences. Such research offers clues to solving the mystery of disease, the Holy Grail[2] of genetics. So why do we readily accept that evolution has turned out Jews with a genetic predisposition to Tay-Sachs, Southeast Asians with a higher proclivity for beta-thalassemia and blacks who are susceptible to colorectal cancer and sickle cell disease,[3] yet find it racist to suggest that Usain Bolt can thank his West African ancestry for the most critical part of his success—his biological possibility?

10 "Differences among athletes of elite calibre are so small," said Robert Malina, a retired Michigan

---

[1] Fast twitch fibres enable short bursts of strength and speed; slow twitch fibres create fuel for continuous muscle contractions over longer periods of time.

[2] a thing that you try very hard to find or achieve, but never will

[3] Tay-Sachs, beta-thalassemia, colorectal cancer, and sickle cell disease are all diseases more likely to be found in certain populations than in others.

State University anthropologist and former editor of the *Journal of Human Genetics*, "that if you have a physique or the ability to fire muscle fibres more efficiently that might be genetically based . . . it might be very, very significant. The fraction of a second is the difference between the gold medal and fourth place."

Bio-cultural athletic hotspots

11 Although people in every population come in all shapes and sizes, body types and physiological characteristics follow a Gaussian distribution curve[4] as a result of evolutionary adaptations by our ancestors to extremely varied environmental challenges. Elite sports showcase these differences. Asians, on average, tend to be smaller with shorter extremities and long torsos—evolutionary adaptations to harsh weather encountered by Homo sapiens who migrated to Northeast Asia 40,000 years ago. China, for example, excels in many Olympic sports, for a variety of reasons. One of those reasons, according to geneticists, is that they are more flexible on average—a potential advantage in diving, gymnastics (hence the term "Chinese splits") and figure skating.

12 Whites of Eurasian ancestry are mesomorphic[5]: they have larger and relatively more muscular bodies with comparatively short limbs and thick torsos. No prototypical sprinter or marathoner here. These proportions are advantageous in sports in which strength rather than speed is at a premium. Predictably, Eurasians dominate weightlifting, wrestling and most field events, such as the shot put and hammer. At the London Olympics, with the exception of North Korea, the top lifters come from a band of Eurasian countries: China, Kazakhstan, Iran, Poland, Russia and the Ukraine. Despite the image of the sculpted African body, no African nation won an Olympic lifting medal.

13 "Evolution has shaped body types and in part athletic possibilities," Joseph Graves, Jr. told me. Graves, who is African American, is an evolutionary biologist at North Carolina Agricultural and Technical State University and UNC Greensboro. "Don't expect an Eskimo to show up on an NBA court or a Watusi[6] to win the world weight lifting championship. Differences don't necessarily correlate with skin colour, but rather with geography and climate. Endurance runners are more likely to come from East Africa and sprinters from West Africa. That's a fact. Genes play a major role in this."

Resurrecting racism?

14 Are we resurrecting racism by talking about sports in such stark black and white terms? Not at all. It's the exaggeration, not the factual core of truth that human "populations" exist that stirs fear and anger. The difficulty, of course, is sorting out how much of a trait is genetically inbred, how much may be shaped by culture and opportunity. The question is no longer *whether* these inquiries will continue but in what *manner* and to what *end*. If we hope to conquer human disease and usher in an era of personalized medicine, we need to understand the way evolution has shaped disease. And that's where sport comes into play.

15 Using sports to interrogate the complex story of human biodiversity offers some unique advantages to the fair minded amongst us. Despite considerable off-the-field disparities,

---

[4] normal-distribution bell curve, with most people falling in the middle of the scale with similar characteristics, and some at the ends of the scale with different characteristics

[5] with a body shape neither thin nor fat, with quite a lot of muscle

[6] *Eskimo* refers to an indigenous group living in the Far North across Russia, Greenland, Canada, and Alaska. (The term *Inuit*, rather than *Eskimo*, is used in Canada.) The Watusi (more commonly known as *Tutsi*) are an African ethnic group.

professional athletics remains one of the most racially and ethnically diverse professions in the world. It is the ultimate level playing field, albeit with its share of bumps and gullies. Individual athletes earn respect on the field, not by the privilege of their birth. Sports offer a unique definitiveness: there is only one high scorer, one swimmer who touches first or one runner who breaks the tape.

16   There's no need to make consideration of race in sports a taboo. In fact, sports provide the most rigid laboratory control possible—the level playing field—to guide us through the complexities of ideological correctness. Yes, celebrate the marvelous individual accomplishments we've witnessed in London . . .

bask in the real story behind The DNA Olympics. At some point, your life might depend upon on it.

Jon Entine, author of Taboo: Why Black Athletes Dominate Sports and Why We're Afraid to Talk About It *and* Abraham's Children: Race, Identity and the DNA of the Chosen People, *is founding director of the Genetic Literacy Project at the Statistical Assessment Service (STATS) at George Mason University.*

Source: Excerpted and adapted with the author's permission. Based on J. Entine, "The DNA Olympics—Jamaicans win sprinting 'genetic lottery'—and why we should all care," www.forbes.com/sites/jonentine/2012/08/12/the-dna-olympics-jamaicans-win-sprinting-genetic-lottery-and-why-we-should-all-care/

Comprehension and Skills Practice

1. A. The "segregation" referred to in paragraph 1 is between
   a) Usain Bolt and other Jamaican runners.
   b) runners of African descent and runners of European or Asian descent.
   c) male runners in London and male runners in previous Olympic games.

   B. Is the author troubled by this segregation? _____
   Which words helped you to answer?
   _____

2. A. Explain the meaning of the word *myth* in the first sub-heading.
   _____

   B. According to the author, which statements represent cultural myths about the superiority of black runners? Circle all that apply.
   a) African athletes train harder than others.
   b) African athletes have been practising running since childhood.
   c) Environment is responsible for around 20–25 percent of athletic ability.
   d) Athletes of non-African origin are intimidated by their African competitors.
   e) Athletic success is largely rooted in the athlete's genetic makeup.

C. What view does the author present to contradict these cultural myths? You may cite the text directly or rephrase in your own words.

_____

D. Which techniques of persuasion does the author use to disprove the cultural myths? Circle all that apply.

   a) Providing statistical data from sports and biology

   b) Giving examples of athletes whose experience defies these myths

   c) Referring to expert opinions

   d) Drawing an analogy between athletics and the medical field

3. Mark the statement as T (true) or F (false). Correct if the statement is false.

   ____ The author denies the role of environment and individual effort in achieving athletic success.

4. What genetically inherited characteristics does the author mention? List at least three.

   a) _____

   b) _____

   c) _____

5. Why do populations in general differ in genetic characteristics such as body type?

   _____

6. Fill in the chart describing how a body type matches the requirements of a specific sport, and the relevant origin of an athlete. Scan the text for details. The first has been done for you.

SPORT	NECESSARY BODY TYPE CHARACTERISTICS	RACIAL/GEOGRAPHIC ORIGIN OF A PROTOTYPICAL ATHLETE
100-metre race	Fast twitch muscle fibres	West Africa
Long-distance running (marathon)		
Diving, gymnastics, figure skating		
Weightlifting, wrestling, field events requiring strength		

7. The author uses the word *fact* several times in his article: "Here are the facts" (par. 7); "We cannot avoid confronting the fact of our patterned human biodiversity" (par. 9); "That's a fact" (par. 13, citing Joseph Graves, Jr.); "the factual core of truth that human 'populations' exist" (par. 14).

    A. Highlight and reread the context in which these sentences are used.

    B. Are the ideas in these contexts indeed facts? _____

    C. Why do you think the author repeats the word *fact* throughout his article?

    _____

    _____

8. According to the author, what is the accusation against those who use genetic differences to explain athletic accomplishments?

    _____

9. Why, according to the author, do sports offer unique advantages "to interrogate the complex story of human biodiversity" (par. 15)? Circle all that apply.

    a) People of different ethnicities and races compete with each other, thus making it easy to compare abilities based on genetics.

    b) Athletic achievements are easy to assess as there is a clear distinction between winners and losers.

    c) Sports carry social inequalities from off-the-field to the sports arena, thus allowing us to see that races are not equal.

    d) Individual efforts count toward winning in sports, and biological characteristics play a lesser role.

10. Scan the article for the following names and paraphrase each person's statement.

    a) Bengt Saltin

    _____

    _____

    b) Robert Malina

    _____

    _____

    c) Joseph Graves, Jr.

    _____

    _____

Use context clues and your knowledge of word parts to determine the correct meaning of each word or phrase. Verify your answers using a dictionary if necessary.

1. emulate (par. 4):
    a) admire and try to copy
    b) rebel against
    c) create

2. the roll of the genetic dice (par. 6):

    _____

3. circumscribes (par. 7):
    a) something with a circle drawn around it
    b) limited in one's powers
    c) not connected with or influenced by something

4. physique (par. 10):

    _____

5. resurrecting (par. 14):
    a) condemning
    b) bringing back into use
    c) putting an end to

6. level playing field (par. 15):

    _____

READING 3

In the final reading selection, Thomas Shapiro, Tatjana Meschede, and Sam Osoro, researchers at the Institute on Assets and Social Policy, report the results of their analysis of financial inequalities between white and African-American families in the US.

The Roots of the Widening Racial Wealth Gap: Explaining the Black-White Economic Divide

 **Economics**

01 All families need wealth to be economically secure and create opportunities for the next generation. Wealth—what we own minus what we owe—allows families to move forward by moving to better and safer neighbourhoods, investing in businesses, saving for retirement, and supporting their children's college aspirations. Having a financial cushion also provides a measure of security when a job loss or other crisis strikes. The Great Recession of 2007–2009 devastated the wealth of all families except for those with the most. The unprecedented wealth destruction during that period, accompanied by long-term high unemployment, underscores the critical importance wealth plays in weathering emergencies and helping families move along a path toward long-term financial security and opportunity.

02 Extreme wealth inequality not only hurts family well-being, it hampers economic growth in our communities and in the nation as a whole. In the US today, the richest 1 percent of households owns 37 percent of all wealth. This toxic inequality has historical underpinnings but is perpetuated[1] by policies and tax preferences that continue to favour the affluent. Most strikingly, it has resulted in an enormous wealth gap between white households and households of colour. In 2009, a representative survey of American households revealed that the median wealth of white families was $113,149 compared with $6,325 for Latino families and $5,677 for black families.

03 Looking at the *same set of families* over a 25-year period (1984–2009), our research offers key insight into how policy and the real, lived-experience of families in schools, communities, and at work affect wealth accumulation. Tracing the same households during that period, the total wealth gap between white and African-American families nearly triples, increasing from $85,000 in 1984 to $236,500 in 2009 (see Figure 7.1). To discover the major drivers behind this dramatic $152,000 increase, we tested a wide range of possible explanations, including family, labour market, and wealth characteristics. This allowed us, for the first time, to identify the primary forces behind the racial wealth gap. Our analysis found little evidence to support common perceptions about what underlies the ability to build wealth, including the notion that personal attributes and behavioural choices are key pieces of the equation. Instead, the evidence

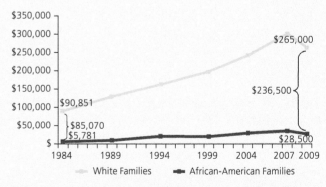

Figure 7.1 Median net worth by race, 1984–2009

---

[1] made to continue for a long time

points to policy and the configuration of both opportunities and barriers in workplaces, schools, and communities that reinforce deeply entrenched racial dynamics in how wealth is accumulated and that continue to permeate[2] the most important spheres of everyday life.

The $152,000 question: What drove the growing gap?

04 Having identified the major drivers of the racial wealth gap, we now can dig deeper to determine how similar accomplishments grow wealth *differentially by race*. Table 7.1 provides a close look at how these factors translate into differences in wealth accumulation for black and white families. We know that wealth increases through accomplishments such as job promotions, pay increases, or the purchase of a home, as well as important life and family events including receiving an inheritance and getting married. Table 7.1 highlights how similar accomplishments and life events lead to unequal wealth gains for white and African-American families. The result

is that while wealth grows for African-Americans as they achieve life advances, that growth is at a considerably lower rate than it is for whites experiencing the same accomplishments. This leads to an increase in the wealth gap.

Homeownership

05 The number of years families owned their homes was the largest predictor of the gap in wealth growth by race (Figure 7.2). Residential segregation by government design has a long legacy in this country and underpins many of the challenges African-American families face in buying homes and increasing equity.[3] There are several reasons why home equity rises so much more for whites than African-Americans:

- Because residential segregation artificially lowers demand, placing a forced ceiling on home equity for African-Americans who own homes in non-white neighborhoods;
- Because whites are far more able to give inheritances or family assistance for down payments due to historical wealth

	WHITE WEALTH GROWTH	BLACK WEALTH GROWTH
Each $1 in income increase yields	$5.19	$0.69
Each $1 in inheritance yields	.91	.20
Each $1 in family financial support yields	.35	.51
Years of homeownership	No significant impact	Significant impact
Marriage	Significant impact	No significant impact

Table 7.1 How wealth is accumulated
This table shows how key life advances and events (an increase in income, inheritance, family financial support, homeownership, and marriage) translate into the ability to increase wealth. Even with equal advances, wealth grows at far lower rates for black households, who typically need to use financial gains for everyday needs rather than long-term savings and assets.

---

[2] affect every part of something
[3] the value of a property after all charges and debts have been paid

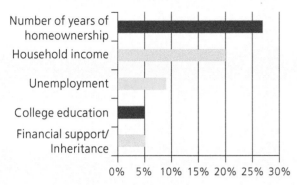

Figure 7.2 What is driving the increasing racial wealth gap?
Each factor in the graph accounts for a certain percentage of the difference in relative wealth growth between white and African-American families.

accumulation, white families buy homes and start acquiring equity an average eight years earlier than black families;

- Because whites are far more able to give family financial assistance, larger up-front payments by white homeowners lower interest rates and lending costs; and
- Due to historic differences in access to credit, typically lower incomes, and factors such as residential segregation, the homeownership rate for white families is 28.4 percent higher than the homeownership rate for black families.

06 Homes are the largest investment that most American families make and by far the biggest item in their wealth portfolio. Homeownership is an even greater part of wealth composition for black families, amounting to 53 percent of wealth for blacks and 39 percent for whites. Yet, for many years, redlining,[4] discriminatory mortgage-lending practices, lack of access to credit, and lower incomes have blocked the homeownership path for African-Americans while creating and reinforcing communities segregated by race. African-Americans, therefore, are more recent homeowners and more likely to have high-risk mortgages, hence they are more vulnerable to foreclosure[5] and volatile housing prices.

07 Figure 7.1 shows households losing wealth between 2007 and 2009 (12 percent for white families, 21 percent for African-American families), which reflects the destruction of housing wealth resulting from the foreclosure crisis and imploded housing market. Overall, half the collective wealth of African-American families was stripped away during the Great Recession due to the dominant role of home equity in their wealth portfolios and the prevalence of predatory high-risk loans in communities of colour.

Income and employment

08 Not surprisingly, increases in income are a major source of wealth accumulation for many US families. However, income gains for whites and African-Americans have a very different impact on wealth. At the respective wealth medians, every dollar increase in average income over the 25-year study period added $5.19 wealth for white households (see Table 7.1), while the same income gain only added 69 cents of wealth for African-American households.

09 The dramatic difference in wealth accumulation from similar income gains has its roots in long-standing patterns of discrimination in hiring, training, promoting, and access to benefits that have made it much harder for African-Americans to save and build assets. Due to discriminatory factors, black workers predominate in fields that are least likely to

---

[4] the discriminatory refusal of a loan, mortgage, or insurance to people in specific areas, particularly in inner-city neighbourhoods
[5] taking control of somebody's property because they have not paid back money that they borrowed to buy it

have employer-based retirement plans and other benefits, such as administration and support and food services. As a result, wealth in black families tends to be close to what is needed to cover emergency savings while wealth in white families is well beyond the emergency threshold and can be saved or invested more readily.

Inheritance

10 Most Americans inherit very little or no money, but among the families followed for 25 years whites were five times more likely to inherit than African-Americans (36 percent to 7 percent, respectively). Among those receiving an inheritance, whites received about ten times more wealth than African-Americans. Our findings show that inheritances converted to wealth more readily for white than black families: each inherited dollar contributed to 91 cents of wealth for white families compared with 20 cents for African-American families. Inheritance is more likely to add wealth to the considerably larger portfolio whites start out with since blacks, as discussed above, typically need to reserve their wealth for emergency savings.

College education

11 College readiness is greatly dependent on quality K–12 education. Neighbourhoods have grown more segregated, leaving lower-income students—especially students of colour—isolated and concentrated in lower-quality schools, and less academically prepared both to enter and complete college. Further, costs at public universities have risen 60 percent in the past two decades, with many low-income and students of colour forced to hold down jobs rather than attend college full time and graduating in deep debt. Average student debt for the class of 2011 was $26,600. Student debt is an issue that affects most graduates, but black graduates are far more vulnerable: 80 percent of black students graduate with debt compared with 64 percent of white students. More blacks than whites do not finish their undergraduate studies because financial considerations force them to leave school and earn a steady income to support themselves and their families.

Conclusion

12 It is time for a portfolio shift in public investment to grow wealth for all, not just a tiny minority. Without that shift the wealth gap between white and black households has little prospect of significantly narrowing. A healthy, fair, and equitable society cannot continue to follow such an economically unsustainable trajectory.

Source: Excerpted from T. Shapiro, T. Meschede, and S. Osoro, "The roots of the widening racial wealth gap: Explaining the black-white economic divide." Research and Policy Brief, Institute on Assets and Social Policy (IASP) (February 2013).

Comprehension and Skills Practice

1. How is wealth defined?

_____

2. What is not true about wealth?

    a) It may secure comfortable retirement.

b) It guarantees security in the case of job loss.

c) It may alleviate financial difficulty in the case of a financial crisis.

d) It allows upward movement from one neighbourhood to another.

3. Mark the statement as T (true) or F (false).

____ In the US, 37 percent of households possess 1 percent of the wealth.

4. What happened to the total wealth gap between white and African-American families between 1984 and 2009?

a) It became three times smaller.

b) It grew from $90,851 in 1984 to $265,000 in 2009.

c) It became three times larger.

d) The gap of $152,000 dramatically increased during these years.

5. Which of these explanations for the gap in wealth do the authors offer? Circle all that apply.

a) The personal qualities of some people promote their financial success while the qualities of others hamper their opportunities.

b) Historically, African-Americans were economically disadvantaged by their status as slaves.

c) Many American cities have traditionally had separate neighbourhoods based on colour.

d) Banks are more likely to give fair loans and mortgages to white people than to black people.

e) African-Americans are often employed in jobs that have strong employer-based retirement plans and benefits.

f) African-American graduates have larger student debts than white graduates.

g) The percentage of African-American college graduates with debts is higher than that of white graduates.

6. What important life advances and events affect a person's ability to accumulate wealth?

_____

7. Based on Figure 7.2, what percentage in the difference of relative wealth growth between blacks and whites does college education account for? How does this factor compare to the others shown in the graph?

_____

8. Based on Figure 7.3, which life advancement shows the largest gap in whites' and blacks' ability to increase wealth?

_____

9. A. What percentage of the wealth of African-American families is represented by homeownership?

_____

   B. Why did African-Americans suffer disproportionately as a result of the housing crisis in 2009?

_____

10. What is the organizational pattern of paragraph 8?

   a) Comparison

   b) Contrast

   c) Cause-effect

   d) Classification

11. Reread paragraph 9 paying particular attention to the cause-and-effect relationship of the information presented. Write each of the points below on the appropriate line to show cause and effect (one is done for you). Then describe in your own words each step in the cause-effect sequence explaining why African-American families have less wealth than white families.

   • few or no work benefits
   • wealth gap
   • discriminatory hiring practices
   • low emergency savings

_____   *few or no work benefits*   _____   _____

12. Complete the sentence.

   In addition to lower-quality schools that left many black students unprepared

   for entering college, _____ also
   made it difficult for these students to obtain a college education.

13. What is the purpose of the concluding paragraph in this text?

    a) It provides solutions to the problem.

    b) It restates the problem discussed before.

    c) It calls for a solution to the problem.

    d) It summarizes the text.

Vocabulary

Use context clues and your knowledge of word parts to determine the correct meaning of each word. Verify your answers using a dictionary if necessary.

1. unprecedented (par. 1): _____

2. hampers (par. 2): _____

3. underpinnings (par. 2): _____

4. imploded (par. 7): _____

5. unsustainable (par. 11): _____

UNIT REFLECTION AND SYNTHESIS

1. The authors of the three selections explore the concept of race from different perspectives. In the chart below, summarize the authors' views on race.

	"RACE"	"THE DNA OLYMPICS"	"THE WIDENING RACIAL WEALTH GAP"
Is race a biological reality?			_____
What is the significance of race as a social construct?		_____	

2. The author of "Race" comments that ". . . the traditional concept of race in Western society is biologically and genetically meaningless." What example(s) does the author of "The DNA Olympics" give to attempt to disprove this statement?

_____

_____

3. Mark each statement from the three selections as F (fact) or O (opinion).

a) ____ The concept of race developed in the context of European exploration and conquest beginning in the fifteenth century.

b) ____ It is important to emphasize once again that all the so-called races of human beings are *imagined communities.*

c) ____ Athletes of West African descent dominate sports requiring speed.

d) ____ Humans are different, the consequence of thousands of years of evolution in varying terrains.

e) ____ While wealth grows for African-Americans as they achieve life advances, that growth is at a considerably lower rate than it is for whites experiencing the same accomplishments.

f) ____ It is time for a portfolio shift in public investment to grow wealth for all, not just a tiny minority.

4. Would you describe any of the arguments made by any of the authors in this unit as biased? Why or why not?

_____

_____

5. Match each selection with its purpose.

a. "Race"	____ The author is trying to persuade the reader that it is important to revise policies leading to racially based wealth inequalities.
b. "The DNA Olympics"	____ The author is trying to persuade the reader that the idea of races should be abandoned.
c. "The Roots of the Widening Racial Wealth Gap"	____ The author is trying to persuade the reader that it is important to continue exploring differences between races as they help explain human diversity.

6. Match each selection with any of the following techniques used to make an argument. Give an example of how the technique is used in that selection.

- Presenting support for an opinion: citing research results and statistics
- Using logical reasoning: tracing causal relationships in the argument
- Using analogies and/or contrasts
- Giving examples from personal experiences
- Using an emotional tone
- Presenting a counter-argument and then refuting it

READING	TECHNIQUE	EXAMPLE
"Race"		
"The DNA Olympics"		
"The Roots of the Widening Racial Wealth Gap"		

7. In persuasive texts, authors' tones may vary from dispassionate to lively, from formal to informal, or from neutral to biased. The tone also depends on the source in which a text is published. For example, on a blog the author's tone may be enthusiastic and informal, while in an academic journal it is usually reserved and formal. Describe the tone of these three readings, paying attention to the source of each one.

READING	SOURCE	TONE
"Race"		
"The DNA Olympics"		
"The Roots of the Widening Racial Wealth Gap"		

Living with Nature

GETTING INTO THE TOPIC

This unit examines the relationship between people and nature. The first text reviews some potential implications of climate change around the world and in Canada. The second selection focuses on how economic factors can influence important decisions despite the risk of disaster due to natural causes, such as earthquakes. The final reading probes into the profound costs, both human and economic, that can result from extreme weather events.

Discuss these questions to help you get into the topic.

1. What are some possible results of global climate change? Refer to how people might be affected, as well as terrestrial or aquatic flora and fauna (plants and animals).

2. Study the map on page 155 and answer the questions that follow.

    a) What kinds of diseases may become more common with climate change?

    b) In addition to health, what other aspects of human life will be affected by climate change?

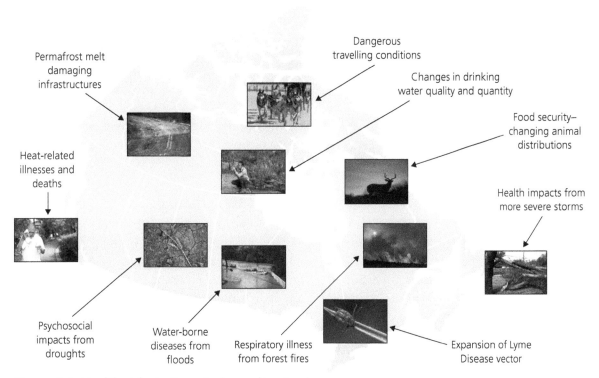

Figure 8.1 Health risks in Canada from climate change

Source: Health Canada, 2008

3. What do you know about earthquakes? Is it possible to predict an earthquake?

4. Do you think it is reasonable to construct nuclear power plants in countries located in potentially dangerous seismic zones?

5. Have you ever experienced a power outage in your home? If so, what caused it? Why do extreme weather events often result in power outages?

6. How can communities prepare for mass power outages and ease some of the potentially devastating effects?

READING 1

The first reading in this unit contains two separate excerpts united by the theme of climate change. The first, taken from an environmental studies textbook, describes some of the effects of climate change on various resource-based systems. The second part of the reading, excerpted from a human geography textbook, provides more detail on the effects of climate change, specifically rising sea levels, on human lives.

Implications of Climate Change

Environmental Studies

Terrestrial systems

01 It is conceivable that within your lifetime, many terrestrial systems, along with the associated fauna and flora, will change dramatically. For example, on the Canadian Prairies, boreal forests[1] may shift anywhere from 100 to 700 kilometres to the north, to be replaced by grasslands and more southern forest species. In the Arctic, the southern permafrost[2] border could move 500 kilometres northward, and the treeline could move from 200 to 300 kilometres to the north. Boreal forests in particular would also be affected by increases in insect infestation, disease, and fires.

02   The consequences of change to terrestrial systems could be dramatic. For example, polar bears may no longer remain to breed in Wapusk National Park in Manitoba, yet the park was created in 1996 to protect the habitat of polar bears. At the other extreme, the hoary marmot[3] in the Rockies and other areas in the Western Cordillera is likely to thrive, since changed climate leads to more avalanches, which will expand its preferred habitat of open meadow. These examples indicate that the rationale for national and provincial parks, created to protect representative ecosystems, may dramatically change as the distinctive ecosystems currently protected by such parks evolve into something totally different.

Agriculture

03 One of the major limitations on agricultural activity in most areas of Canada is our cold climate. In southern Canada, the frost-free growing season is about 200 days, and in the Far North the growing season is normally just

---

> **GLOBAL REACH OF CLIMATE CHANGE**
>
> In Canada and across the globe, we are already seeing the effects of warming temperatures and changing climate conditions. As climate change persists, we can expect, for example, further melting of glaciers and sea ice, rising sea levels, earlier springs, shifts in the distribution of animals and plants, and increasingly volatile weather. No region and no aspect of our geography will be immune; but impacts will vary in time and intensity.
>
> —NRTEE (National Round Table on the Environment and the Economy, 2010)

---

a few weeks. Furthermore, early frosts or severe winters can damage even dormant vegetation.

04   Given the above conditions, the scientific consensus is that, on balance, Canada would be one of the countries to benefit from global warming, since it would extend the growing season and reduce the damage from severe

---

[1] the northernmost and coldest forest zone of the northern hemisphere, which forms a belt across North America, Europe, and Asia
[2] a layer of soil that is permanently frozen
[3] a small mammal inhabiting the northwest mountains in North America

cold or frosts. For example, some scenarios indicate that by 2050, growing conditions in Whitehorse and Yellowknife would approximate those now found in Edmonton, and that conditions in New Brunswick would become similar to those now experienced in the Niagara Peninsula in Ontario (Hengeveld et al., 2005: 37). However, as in most situations, challenges also may arise. Many plants are vulnerable to heat stress and drought, and if temperatures increased appreciably or water became limited, crops could be adversely affected.

05   Moreover, climate change may have significant effects on food production in other regions of the world, and the first people to be hurt would be the poorest farmers. Such conditions and consequences could lead to significant increases in migration, which could cause regional instability, as well as in international migration. The latter would contribute to growing numbers of "environmental" refugees for whom Canada could be a destination of choice.

Source: P. Dearden & B. Mitchell, *Environmental Change & Challenge*, 4th edition (Don Mills, ON: Oxford University Press, 2012), pp. 206; 209–212.

CLIMATE CHANGE AND ENVIRONMENTAL REFUGEES

Future climate change is expected to have considerable impacts on natural resource systems, and it is well established that changes in the natural environment can affect human sustenance and livelihoods. This in turn can lead to instability and conflict, often followed by displacements of people and changes in occupancy and migration patterns. Therefore, as hazards and disruptions associated with climate change grow in this century, so, too, may the likelihood of related population displacements.

—McLeman and Smit (2003: 6)

Melting Ice and Rising Sea Levels

06 Human-induced global warming is expected to affect sea levels. A rise of as much as 1.5 metres (almost 5 feet) has been predicted for 2050 given current rates of melting of the Antarctic and Greenland ice sheets. If this occurs, the consequences for many currently populated areas may be catastrophic. Up to 15 percent of Egypt's arable land would be at risk, and many coastal cities such as New York and London would be below sea level. The consequences for one of the most densely populated areas in the world—coastal Bangladesh—will be disastrous unless we are able to adapt. Indeed, even before sea levels rise substantially, many coastal areas would be in danger because of storm surges.

07   The Netherlands, a more developed country, has successfully adapted to a situation where much of the current area is already almost 4 metres (13 feet) below sea level. In principle, the Netherlands model—construction of levees[1] and dikes—can be followed. Venice is already pursuing a similar strategy, constructing a flexible seawall to protect the city against Adriatic storms. But what are the costs of such projects?

---

[1] low walls built at the side of a river to prevent it from flooding

One estimate places the cost at approximately US$300 billion to protect only major areas, not including coastal margins.

08   In theory, there is an alternative to adaptation: moving away from the threatened areas. But for many people in the less developed world, this is hardly an option, and for many in the more developed world, it is culturally and economically unthinkable at the present time.

09   On the other hand, predictions of a sea-level rise are at best uncertain. In 1985, one major United States scientific committee predicted a rise of 1 metre (3 feet) by 2100, and subsequently, in 1989, amended the prediction to a rise of 0.3 metres (1 foot). Even the higher of these two is less than the prediction referred to earlier. Why such uncertainty? The principal unknown factor is the effect of warming on the Antarctic ice sheet. Instead of increasing ice melt, it is possible that, through time, warmer weather could increase snowfall, which would in turn help build up the ice sheet. However, in 2009 at a climate change conference in Copenhagen, scientists warned that the rise in sea levels would be between 1 and 2 metres by 2100, putting many of the world's coastal areas at risk.

10   The problem is serious. We need to adapt soon to an unknown situation. Dikes and population movements may or may not be needed. If they are needed, we do not know the extent of the need. In this way global uncertainty becomes local political uncertainty.

Source: W. Norton, *Human Geography*, 8th edition (Don Mills, ON: Oxford University Press, 2013), pp. 143–144.

Comprehension and Skills Practice

1. What changes are expected to occur in the flora in

    a) the Canadian Prairies?

    _____

    b) the Arctic?

    _____

2. A. Underline the main idea sentence in paragraph 2.

    B. Highlight the supporting details used in the paragraph to support the main idea.

3. Mark each inference as V (valid) or I (invalid).

    a) ____ Wapusk National Park will become too warm for polar bears to breed.

    b) ____ Hoary marmots will benefit from climate change because they will expand into higher terrain.

    c) ____ National and provincial parks will no longer be necessary as ecosystems continue to change.

4. Complete the sentences.

In southern Canada, a farmer has to take two factors into consideration.

First, an average growing season of _____ days is expected.

Second, the seeds waiting in the soil for spring growth may be damaged if

_____.

5. According to the readings, how is global warming expected to affect Canadian agriculture in general?

    a) It will limit the growing season by a few weeks.

    b) It will have a largely beneficial effect on Canadian agriculture.

    c) It will create more disadvantages than advantages for Canadian agriculture.

    d) There is no firm scientific agreement on the subject.

6. As climate change affects natural resources around the world, what global political implications may result?

    _____

7. Based on paragraph 5 and the accompanying textbox, write your own definition of the term *environmental refugees*.

    _____

8. Fill in the cause-effect chain, based on paragraph 6.

    ➡   ➡   Cities and arable lands are flooded

9. Why are Bangladesh and the Netherlands mentioned in paragraphs 6 and 7?

    _____

10. A. The text discusses the loss of land to rising sea levels. What are two possible solutions to this problem?

    a) _____

    b) _____

    B. Based on the reading, how can these solutions be evaluated?

    a) Neither solution could ever work.

    b) They are possible but too costly to implement.

c) They are both excellent solutions, as demonstrated by the examples provided.

d) One solution is too expensive, and the other is impractical.

11. Why can't scientists accurately predict the exact level of global sea rise?

_____

12. A. Based on paragraphs 9 and 10, do we know for sure that sea levels will rise in the future? Explain your answer.

_____

B. What is the latest scientific prediction on the subject of rising sea levels?

_____

13. What may the author mean by "local political uncertainty" (par. 10)? Circle all that apply.

a) Local politicians do not know how to deal with changing conditions.

b) It is not clear which decisions should be made to modify local infrastructure.

c) It is not clear who will lead in local elections.

d) It is not certain that local policies need to consider changing environmental conditions.

Vocabulary

Use context clues and your knowledge of word parts to determine the correct meaning of each word. Verify your answers using a dictionary if necessary.

1. volatile (textbox):
   a) likely to change suddenly
   b) extremely cold
   c) generally stable

2. conceivable (par. 1): _____

3. appreciably (par. 4):
   a) valuably
   b) considerably
   c) slightly

4. adversely (par. 4): _____

5. sustenance (textbox): _____

6. amended (par. 9):

   a) cancelled

   b) improved

   c) changed

READING 2

Why Japan Took the Nuclear Risk  Resource Management

When making choices about energy, there are no danger-free, cost-free solutions.

01 Three Mile Island.[1] Chernobyl.[2] Now the Fukushima nuclear power plant.[3] Within hours of the first reports of trouble at Japan's nuclear power plants, calls for abolition could be heard around the world. "Time to shut down this nation's nuclear energy program," wrote American pundit[4] Keith Olbermann. Greenpeace and other environmental groups mobilized. "The nuclear risk is not a risk that can be really controlled," said a French Green Party politician. Nuclear power must go.

02 With Japan's plants suffering explosions and officials struggling to avoid meltdowns, it's hard not to agree. Nuclear power is a demonstrable hazard. In Japan, a land constantly rattled by seismic activity, where a disaster was literally just

Smoke billows from a reactor after the explosion at Fukushima Daiichi nuclear power plant.

---

[1] an accident at a nuclear power plant in Pennsylvania, US, in 1979
[2] an accident at a nuclear power plant in the former Soviet Union (now Ukraine) in 1986; arguably the worst nuclear accident ever
[3] This article was written in March 2011, a few days after the Fukushima nuclear power plant accident.
[4] a person who knows a lot about a particular subject and who often talks about it in public

a matter of time, nuclear power is downright dangerous. Why risk it?

03   People who say that seldom mean it as a question. It's a conclusion in drag.[5] But let's treat it instead as a genuine question: Why risk it? Why should we build and operate nuclear power plants, knowing that they do pose real dangers, whatever the magnitude of those dangers may be? And why, in particular, would Japan build nuclear power plants on land that so often buckles and heaves? The answer to this second question lies in recent history. It's worth having a look because it's also a pretty good answer to the first question.

04   As recently as the 1950s, Japan was a poor country with a huge and growing population. Some far-sighted experts looked ahead and saw misery and mass starvation. But in the 1960s, Japanese manufacturing grew rapidly. Its success was based on keeping things cheap. Cheap labour. Cheap prices. Cheap quality. In the United States, the main Japanese market, "Made in Japan" meant the product cost little and was worth what it cost. Japan got wealthier. Living standards improved.

05   In the late 1960s, the American economy stumbled and in 1971 the dollar was devalued. The yen shot up. But the quality of Japanese goods had improved and so Japanese manufacturing thrived despite the rising cost of its goods. Nothing less than a miracle was underway. A nation was rising from poverty to the ranks of the wealthiest people on Earth. Some even imagined a day when Japan would lead.

06   Then, like an earthquake, the Arab oil embargo[6] struck. The Japanese miracle was built on a foundation of cheap energy—mostly oil, mostly from the Middle East. The oil embargo of late 1973 plunged the world into the frightening recession of 1974, and no one suffered worse than Japan.

07   "The recent period of Japanese glory, from 1969 to 1973, when it seemed a small, distant country would overtake the giants of the West, lasted longer than a dream, but it has ended with dramatic suddenness," wrote Donald Keene, an American professor of Japanese culture, in the New York Times. It was March 3, 1974. "The same people who only a few months ago were talking and acting as if the future held unlimited possibilities of economic expansion now gloomily announce, not without a touch of masochism, that they live in a country completely at the mercy of others for survival." Many Japanese were sure their country would sink back into poverty. The old fears of mass starvation and environmental ruin returned. "Prophecies of disaster abound," Keene noted.

08   The Japanese government responded with a sweeping, multi-pronged campaign to reduce Japan's dependency on Middle Eastern oil. Conservation and energy-efficiency was a major component. So was a rapid expansion of nuclear power. Of course, the Japanese knew their seismological reality. Indeed, Japanese earthquake science and engineering is the best in the world. But the Japanese also knew the danger of the status quo.[7] It was a trade-off.

09   The transition worked. Japan's rise resumed and within a decade it was one of the wealthiest nations in the world. It was also one of the most energy-efficient. And one of the top producers of nuclear power, with one-quarter of its electricity coming from the plants the world is watching now.

10   This story does not demonstrate that the nuclear power is right for Japan, or for anyone

---

[5] In drag refers to masking one thing as another; here the author suggests that "why risk it?" is not a sincere question, but rather an opinionated statement.

[6] the refusal of Arab countries in the Middle East to sell oil to the US and other countries from 1967–1974

[7] the situation as it is now, or as it was before a recent change

else. But it does show, I believe, that choices about energy always involve trade-offs. Which risks are acceptable? How much risk? And what are we prepared to pay to avoid or mitigate threats? There are costs and hazards associated with every choice and so these questions are unavoidable. There are no risk-free, cost-free solutions.

11 Some deny this basic reality. Certain environmental groups claim to have plans which would allow us to do away entirely with coal, oil, natural gas, and nuclear power over the next several decades. Renewable energy would replace them all. The cost could be minimal. Indeed, it would spur innovation and produce millions of new jobs.

12 It would be wonderful if it were possible. Unfortunately, it's not. One of the world's leading energy experts, Vaclav Smil of the University of Manitoba, has called these claims "not just naïve [but] profoundly irresponsible." But Smil also criticizes those at the other extreme, who see nothing undesirable about the status quo and believe any significant shift to renewable energy would be prohibitively expensive. We can do better. But it requires that we first understand basic realities, including the most basic: there are costs and risks in everything.

Source: D. Gardner, "Why Japan took the nuclear risk." *Vancouver Sun*, 18 March 2011.

Comprehension and Skills Practice

1. A. In paragraphs 2 and 3, the author cites a **rhetorical question**. Some people asked after the Fukushima disaster, "Why risk it?" What does the author suggest is the real purpose of this question, according to those who ask it?

   rhetorical question: a question asked only to make a statement or to produce an effect rather than to get an answer.

   a) To suggest that Japan has valid economic reasons to take a chance and build nuclear power stations on its territory

   b) To suggest that Japan should take a risk and continue its nuclear program

   c) To suggest that Japan should not take the risk associated with a nuclear program on seismically sensitive land

   d) To suggest that the risk was justified, even if disaster was inevitable

   B. The author, on the other hand, treats the question "Why risk it?" as a genuine question rather than a rhetorical one. How does the author answer the question "Why risk it?"

   _____

   _____

   _____

2. Provide a brief description of the stages through which the Japanese economy went.

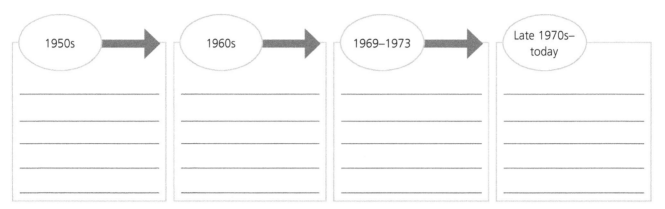

| 1950s | → | 1960s | → | 1969–1973 | → | Late 1970s– today |

3. How has the connotation of the label *Made in Japan* changed for consumers over the years?

_____

4. What weakened the Japanese economy in 1973?

   a) dollar devaluation

   b) cheap quality of Japanese goods

   c) rising costs of Japanese goods

   d) Arab oil embargo

5. What is the primary purpose of quoting Donald Keene's 1974 article in paragraph 7?

   a) to provide historical background for the general feeling of impending disaster that existed in Japan in the 1970s

   b) to prove the point that the Japanese always believed in their success and were not ready to give up

   c) to support the idea that Japanese success was built on futile dreams and could not last

   d) to introduce the tone of sadness and make the reader compassionate to the Japanese

6. Why does the author call the Japanese post-1973 energy campaign "multi-pronged" (par. 8)?

   _____

7. What was the trade-off for the Japanese (par. 8)?

   a) They gave up their economic success in return for a safe seismic situation.

   b) They traded their economic prosperity for the chances of a better future.

c) They accepted the nuclear risk for the sake of economic well-being.

d) They gave up their best seismologists for the sake of changing the present situation.

8. What is the author's view on Japan's choice to expand its nuclear program?

_____

_____

9. How would the author characterize the opinion of certain environmental groups who claim we could give up using fossil fuels and nuclear energy and switch entirely to renewable energy sources?

a) He would disagree and would characterize this opinion as biased.

b) He would disagree and would characterize this opinion as informed.

c) He would agree with this opinion and characterize it as informed.

d) He would agree with this opinion but characterize it as biased.

10. What technique(s) of persuasion does the author use to make his argument? Circle all that apply, and for each technique you circle, provide an example from the text.

TECHNIQUE	EXAMPLE
a. using analogies	
b. offering examples from personal experience	
c. using an emotional tone	
d. referring to an expert opinion	
e. providing well-researched background information	
f. assessing and refuting the opposite point of view	

11. The text states that 25 percent of Japan's energy is generated by nuclear power plants. Canada derives 15 percent of its electricity from nuclear power. Why do you think Canada uses nuclear power to a lesser degree than Japan does?

_____

Use context clues and your knowledge of word parts to determine the correct meaning of each word. Verify your answers using a dictionary if necessary.

1. abolition (par. 1): _____

2. demonstrable (par. 2): _____

3. stumbled (par. 5):
   a) accelerated
   b) became weaker
   c) was in ruins

4. abound (par. 7):
   a) are many
   b) disappear
   c) are unheard of

5. spur (par. 11): _____

READING 3

Staying Power

Electrical Engineering

Extreme storms such as Hurricane Sandy have pushed the U.S. electrical grid to its breaking point. The technology exists to keep the lights on—we just need to implement it.

01 The explosion lit up the Manhattan skyline. A sudden boom, a one-two punch of yellow light—then everything went black. After Hurricane Sandy shoved water into Con Edison's 14th Street substation in October, causing electricity to arc between capacitors, about a quarter million customers were left in the dark. Video of the high-voltage spectacle quickly went viral: it became an early, brilliant symbol of the massive storm system's most pervasive and inescapable affront—a total and lingering loss of power. Across the U.S., as far west as Indiana and from Maine to North Carolina, Sandy caused hundreds of other mass outages.

Midtown Manhattan during the post-Sandy blackout.

A tree blown down, wires ravaged by wind, a flooded power facility—each event had rippled out to affect homes far from the point of failure. The blackouts continued for weeks afterward, thwarting the region's recovery.

02 While the duration of Sandy's outages was unusual, their breadth—more than eight million homes in 21 states ultimately lost power—has become disturbingly common. In 2011, Hurricane Irene cut electricity to about 5.5 million homes. Tornadoes, ice storms, wildfires, and drought now routinely overwhelm the nation's aging electrical infrastructure, inflicting sweeping blackouts. In the early 1990s, the U.S. experienced about 20 mass outages a year; today it's well over 100. A 2012 Congressional Research Service report attributes much of the rise to an increase in extreme weather events. It also states that storm-related power failures cost the U.S. economy between $20 billion and $55 billion annually.

03 A century ago, when the foundation of today's power distribution system was laid, electric appliances were just beginning to enter homes. Over time, the nation's power use has skyrocketed, and so has the population. Demand is now rising at 1 percent a year, pushing more electricity through lines that were never intended to handle such high loads. "We sometimes joke that if Alexander Graham Bell woke up tomorrow and saw my phone, he'd be astounded," says David Manning, executive director of the New York State Smart Grid Consortium. "If Thomas Edison woke up tomorrow and saw the grid, he could not only recognize it, he could probably fix it."

04 A modern grid, capable of creating and delivering efficient, reliable power even in the midst of disaster, is long overdue. Such infrastructure would be more resilient to both storms and terrorist attacks, which the National Research Council warned in November could cripple entire regions of the country for months. Many of the necessary upgrades already exist: They've been developed in labs and demonstrated in smart-grid projects across the country. Other steps just require common sense.

Stop cascading failures

05 The existing U.S. electric grid has a linear structure. Large power plants, typically located far from the customers they serve, produce most of the electricity. Transformers at the plants increase the voltage so it can be moved more efficiently to local substations, which reduce the voltage and send it out to neighbourhoods and individual homes. When a fault current, or surge, occurs anywhere along the line, automatic circuit breakers open to halt it. That's why a single felled tree can cut power to thousands of customers. And that's how overgrown trees brushing high-voltage lines in Ohio could black out 50 million people along the East Coast in 2003.

06 One way to reduce the impact of any individual failure is to replace the linear structure

with a looped one. Imagine a power line studded with five smart switches that connects back to a substation on both ends. A tree hits the line. In the old, linear system, all the customers beyond the fault point would lose power; the utility would send out a work crew to search for the cause. In the new system, switches on both sides of the fault could isolate the problem and only customers between the two switches would go dark. Then, "those switches communicate and say, 'It's right here, come and fix me,'" says John Kelly, executive director of the nonprofit Perfect Power Institute.

07   Another way to stop failures from cascading is to install a fault-current limiter, or what University of Arkansas engineer Alan Mantooth calls a "shock absorber for the grid." He's developing the refrigerator-size device at the university's National Center for Reliable Electric Power Transmission. "As bad things happen, circuit breakers just start opening and the lights go out," Mantooth says. Rather than simply stopping the electrical surge altogether, his machine can absorb the excess current and send a regulated amount down the line.

08   When large-scale change does come, it will likely arrive in high-demand areas first. "In urban centers like New York City and Los Angeles, their fault currents are getting so high that they're having to start replacing all of their circuit breakers," Mantooth says. A fault-current limiter would be a practical solution. "We would insert this guy into the grid," he says, "leave the existing circuit breaker, and limit the current so that the breaker is not overwhelmed." The new equipment helps the old equipment remain in service for longer, a much more cost-effective approach than replacing all the breakers.

Plan better backup

09 On the evening Hurricane Sandy struck, nearly all of Lower Manhattan lost power—except for much of the NYU campus. In 2010, the university completed a project to replace its 1970s-era boilers with natural-gas-powered turbines, subterranean engines that generate 11 megawatts of electricity. Waste heat from the engines creates steam to produce an additional 2.4 megawatts and hot water, a process known as co-generation. Natural disasters were not at the top of the university's list of concerns when the administration approved the project. "Number one was cost-effective production of electricity," John Bradley of New York University says. "Number two was reduction of greenhouse-gas emissions." (The system, which powers 22 buildings and heats 37, is saving the university millions of dollars each year; it's also helped reduce the campus's carbon footprint by 20 percent.)

10   When Sandy knocked out that Con Edison substation, a third benefit of NYU's self-sufficiency became clear. "My equipment sensed that loss of voltage, and the breakers opened up, isolating the NYU grid from the larger utility grid," Bradley says. For the next week, NYU was an island of power in a darkened neighbourhood. Staff set up power strips on long tables in the library and unlocked outdoor outlets for anyone to use. "You saw people from the community plugging in their laptops, iPads, and phones all over campus," Bradley says.

Invest in efficiency

11 The more power coursing through an aging infrastructure, the more vulnerable the grid will be to disruption—even without a natural disaster. Over the last three decades, U.S. household electricity usage tripled, from 30.3 million BTU per home in 1980 to 89.6 million BTU in 2009. Transformers, meanwhile, are now more than 40 years old on average, and 70 percent of transmission lines are at least 25 years old. To be resilient, the grid—and those who rely on it—must also be more efficient.

12   Many utilities have already begun to replace one ubiquitous and outmoded device: the electricity meter, generally a spinning dial mounted near a thorn bush at the back of the house and read, in person, once a month. About 40 million U.S. homes now have smart meters, devices that digitally monitor and communicate home power use as often as several times an hour. The information allows utilities to track and bill more precisely—and recognize power outages instantly.

13   In Austin, Texas, volunteers in a smart-grid project are testing tools that will help the grid work more like the Internet, with two-way energy and information flow. So far, engineers have equipped 480 houses with advanced energy-monitoring systems. Researchers at the University of Texas at Austin analyze the data with supercomputers. "We carry out the nation's deepest-ever research on how people use electricity and natural gas on literally a second-to-second basis," says Brewster McCracken, president of Pecan Street, the consortium that runs the project.

14   Companies such as Intel, Best Buy, and LG have also partnered with Pecan Street to test and develop products in a real-world setting.

For example, Sony has installed a home energy–management system that measures the power consumption of various appliances from a single outlet and can be managed through a television set–top box. Homeowners can use the real-time data to minimize their load on the grid, shifting such activities as electric-vehicle charging to periods of surplus power.

15   The American Recovery and Reinvestment Act of 2009 devoted $16 billion to installing new transmission lines and implementing smart-grid projects such as Pecan Street. It's a modest start. Truly modernizing the U.S. grid will require an investment of $673 billion, according to a recent study by the American Society of Civil Engineers. In the meantime, the costs of inaction continue to add up: Hurricane Sandy caused $69.7 billion worth of damage to New York and New Jersey. Just weeks after the storm, Governor Andrew Cuomo requested federal funding to help New York install the technology for a smarter grid. "It will be a significant investment," New York State Smart Grid Consortium's Manning says. "But Sandy has rewritten the opportunity to make the case."

Source: K. Thompson, "Staying power." *Popular Science* 282, no. 2 (February, 2013): 38–43.

Comprehension and Skills Practice

1. Scan the text to fill in the outline with major and minor supporting details.

    I.   The effect of Hurricane Sandy and other natural disasters: long-lasting and massive power outages

         A. Causes of the rise in power outages:

             1. _____

             2. _____

         B. The need for an updated electricity grid

II. Ways to modernize the grid

    A. _____

       1. Make the structure looped.

       2. _____

    B. Plan better backup (which offers the following advantages):

       1. _____

       2. Reduction of greenhouse gas emissions

    C. _____

2. Mark each statement as T (true) or F (false). Correct if the statement is false.

    a) ____ The power outage in Manhattan was caused by water flooding the electric power substation on 14th Street.

    b) ____ The failure at the 14th Street substation led to further power outages across the US as far west as Indiana.

3. In subsection "Stop cascading failures," the author explains the difficulties with the linear power grid used in the United States. Underline the sentence in paragraph 1 that states the problem with the linear power structure.

4. What kinds of natural disasters create problems for power grids?

_____

5. What statistics does the author use to demonstrate the increase in mass power outages in recent decades?

_____

6. Complete the sentences. You may use one or more words for each blank.

The current power system in the US was established _____

and was suited to the power needs of society at that time. As _____

increased and the use of power grew, the power grid has become

_____ .

7. The point of the joke about Thomas Edison is that

    a) the phone system and electrical grid are very different inventions.

    b) Thomas Edison was very talented.

    c) the phone has changed a lot since the first model came out.

    d) the electrical grid has not changed much since its inception.

8. What is the organizational pattern of paragraph 5?

    a) cause-effect

    b) comparison

    c) process

    d) problem-solution

9. What are the advantages of the looped grid as compared to the linear one? Circle all that apply.

    a) Not as many people are affected by a power outage.

    b) The looped structure consumes less electricity.

    c) It is easier to identify the location of the fault.

    d) Large power plants are located closer to the customers they serve.

10. Why does Alan Mantooth call the fault-current limiter "a shock absorber for the grid" (par. 7)?

    _____

11. How can the fault-current limiter help with a large-scale change of power grids?

    a) It will make the replacement of old circuit breakers possible.

    b) It will enable the use of old circuit breakers while ensuring power is not disrupted.

    c) It will limit the power supply to large metropolitan areas, such as New York and Los Angeles.

    d) It will make it unnecessary to upgrade the old system.

12. In the last section of the text, "Invest in efficiency," the author mentions various devices to monitor electricity usage. Match the name of each device with its description.

a. Conventional electricity meter	____ It measures the amount of electricity used in real time and communicates the measurements to utility companies.
b. Smart meter	____ It helps homeowners to schedule their electricity-consuming activities in the most efficient way and it is connected to their TV.
c. Energy-monitoring system made by Pecan Street	____ It is installed in volunteers' homes and it measures electricity use on a second-to-second basis.
d. Sony's home energy–management	____ It has to be read manually.

13. What is the author's tone in the last paragraph, where she describes the need to modernize the US power grid?

    a) She is very uncertain the budget will be found for this.

    b) She is very optimistic that modernization will take place.

    c) She communicates with seriousness the need for modernization.

    d) She does not communicate her own emotions; she just reports the assessments of others.

Vocabulary

Use context clues and your knowledge of word parts to determine the correct meaning of each word or phrase. Verify your answers using a dictionary if necessary.

1. affront (par. 1): _____

2. ravaged (par. 1):

    a) damaged badly

    b) slightly affected

    c) temporarily repaired

3. breadth (par. 2): _____

4. resilient (par. 4):

    a) vulnerable and weak under pressure

    b) able to return to normal after being damaged

    c) exposed to dangerous impacts

5. carbon footprint (par. 9): _____

6. coursing through (par. 11): _____

7. ubiquitous (par. 12):

    a) useful

    b) very common

    c) efficient

UNIT REFLECTION AND SYNTHESIS

1. Which text raises the points listed below?

a. "Implications of Climate Change"	____ Making important choices involves giving something up for the sake of achieving a benefit.
b. "Why Japan Took the Nuclear Risk"	____ Strategic planning of national and provincial conservation parks will need to be re-evaluated as a result of climate-related terrestrial changes.
c. "Staying Power"	____ If we want to be ready in the face of natural disasters, we need to bring our infrastructure up to modern standards.
	____ Farming territories will change in various parts of the world.
	____ With the rising power needs of a growing population, on one hand, and higher frequencies of natural disasters, on the other, the grid faces overwhelming challenges.

2. "Melting Ice and Rising Sea Levels" concludes with the assertion that "We need to adapt soon to an unknown situation," and politicians will have to assess the extent of the adaptations. In "Staying Power," the author gives examples of how the American power grid could be adapted to minimize the effects of natural disasters. Provide examples from the readings of how humans have adapted, or could adapt, faced with difficult situations.

READING	HUMANS HAVE ADAPTED BY . . .	HUMANS COULD ADAPT BY . . .
"Implications of Climate Change" and "Melting Ice and Rising Sea Levels"		
"Why Japan Took the Nuclear Risk"		
"Staying Power"		

3. In "Implications of Climate Change," the authors state that we can expect increasingly volatile weather as climate change advances. Do the events described in "Staying Power" support or disprove this point? Provide evidence from the text to support your answer.

_____

_____

_____

4. "Why Japan Took the Nuclear Risk" refers to a necessary balance between the old, conventional energy sources and new, alternative ones. What balance is presented in "Staying Power" regarding the use of the old and the new grid systems?

_____

_____

_____

5. Which text is an expression of the author's opinion in response to a debatable issue? What specific words, phrases, or rhetorical devices does the author use to signal that this is an opinion piece? Underline them in the text.

_____

_____

_____

6. Each of the three readings presents natural phenomena that have significant effects on human lives. Do you think that humankind is to blame for any or all of the disastrous scenarios discussed in the three readings?

_____

_____

_____

7. What is the intended audience for each of the texts in this unit? How would you describe the tone of each? Provide specific examples from the texts that helped you identify tone and audience.

READING	AUDIENCE	TONE	EXAMPLES
"Implications of Climate Change" and "Melting Ice and Rising Sea Levels"			
"Why Japan Took the Nuclear Risk"			
"Staying Power"			

8. A. Do you live or have you ever lived in a seismic zone or a region threatened by hurricanes, tornadoes, or other natural disasters?

   B. What measures should authorities take to prepare residents for natural disasters?

   _____

   _____

   _____

   C. What can individuals do to prepare for natural disasters?

   _____

   _____

   _____

UNIT 9

Transportation

Modern modes of transportation have evolved greatly over the years, but as technology and infrastructure (such as roads, highways, bridges, parking facilities, and public transit systems) have improved, there have also been negative consequences of our twenty-first century transportation. For example, while cars are now affordable for the average family and public transportation is well-developed in many urban centres, the developed world is now facing such challenges as traffic-related air pollution, congested roads, and uncertainties about the future of our fuel resources. This unit explores the topic of transportation from the perspectives of urban studies ("Traffic Jam"), transportation and sustainability studies ("Ridesharing in North America"), and business ("How Electric Cars Got Stuck in First Gear").

GETTING INTO THE TOPIC

1. Urban mobility refers to people's ability to get from one place to another within a large city—something that is becoming increasingly difficult and time-consuming in many areas. What are some ways to relieve traffic congestion in major cities?

2. What are the advantages of using a private car to commute to work or school? Why would some commuters choose public transportation instead? Note the reasons in the T-chart.

REASONS TO USE A CAR	REASONS TO USE PUBLIC TRANSPORTATION

3. Suggest incentives to get more people out of their cars and into public or alternative transportation, such as ridesharing (carpooling).

4. Is ridesharing popular where you live? How might social media increase ridesharing among commuters?

5. Study the bar graph below. Why do you think electric and hybrid automobiles do not sell as well as gas- and diesel-powered vehicles? According to the graph, when are sales of gas and diesel vehicles expected to decrease?

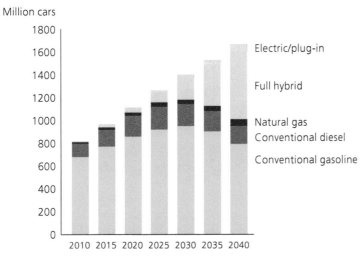

Figure 9.1 Light-duty fleet by type

READING 1

Traffic Jam

 Urban Studies

Move over megaprojects; small, creative options unlock the grid

01 Canadian cities face a litany[1] of challenges to their vibrancy and vitality. Public safety, health care, education, growing income disparity and a paucity[2] of funds are but a sampling. Amidst this long list, one issue has, nonetheless, risen to the top of the urban agenda: mobility and congestion relief.

02 Once a mundane reality, congestion is now front-page news in Canadian cities. It can make or break a politician's career. As a result, it's no wonder elected representatives are on the lookout for solutions that will make traffic and their careers flow smoothly. The problem is, many of the obvious solutions fail to have the desired effect.

03 Simply put, road congestion has risen to the top of the agenda in Canadian cities because it resonates with a diverse array of constituencies[3] who experience the effects of clogged roads on a daily basis. During the 1980s and 1990s, congestion was predominantly the concern of a handful of urban planners and environmentalists. As a result, there was underinvestment in urban transportation facilities, which has contributed to what the Canadian government now estimates is a need for $57-billion worth of new and upgraded municipal infrastructure.

04 As this underinvestment translated into congestion, a diverse set of powerful allies joined environmentalists and urban planners. Commuters were upset by the rising frequency of persistent traffic jams, which translated into a 17-percent increase in the average commute time between 1992 and 2005. Health care professionals recognized the link between increased respiratory disease and car emissions, as well as growing incidents of obesity that are linked to prolonged car usage. Business groups expressed concern about lost productivity, which Transport Canada estimates costs between $2.3-million and $3.7-billion annually. And finally, social justice activists pointed out that congestion leads to unequal access to mobility, which, in turn, can make getting to jobs and recreation opportunities difficult for those without a car.

05 The dilemma over congestion and car dependence reflects the general recognition that mobility shapes the growth, liveability and prosperity of Canadian cities. In turn, concerns

---

[1] a long boring account of a series of events, reasons, etc.
[2] a small amount; less than enough
[3] particular groups of people in society who are likely to support an idea

about traffic gridlock have made congestion relief a potent electoral issue.

The usual suspects

06 Stakeholders who promote congestion relief have their own prevailing interests. As a result, they each encourage political solutions that reflect their specific concern. This makes it difficult for politicians to find solutions that satisfy all interested parties. Furthermore, massive spending on rapid transit megaprojects has come to be seen as a politically safe approach to redressing congestion. In 2002, new rail lines were inaugurated in Toronto (Sheppard Subway) and Vancouver (Millenium Skytrain). Each cost around $1-billion. Construction is under way on subway extensions in Montreal and Vancouver. In addition, Toronto, Vancouver, and Ottawa are planning further rail expansions. Almost all of these new rail systems have been fully segregated from traffic on underground or elevated guideways. This separation translates into higher construction costs per kilometre, but is generally believed to offer a better solution to congestion. As a result, the extra cost is thought to be money well spent.

07   The popularity of urban rail as a means of addressing congestion, particularly when it is fully separated from existing roadways, stems from its appeal to a diversity of interested users. Rail is a high-quality service that can lure travelers away from their cars, while freeing up road space for remaining drivers. Retail business groups see off-road urban rail as an opportunity to support investments in public transit without reducing car accessibility or on-street parking. The shipping industry recognizes that switching car drivers to off-road public transit frees up road space for goods movement. Labour unions, as well as Canadian companies in the transportation equipment sector, promote urban rail construction as an economic development strategy. Governments view new rapid transit lines as a catalyst for high-density development around stations, which can increase the local tax base and offset construction costs. And finally, environmentalists see electric rapid transit as a way to reduce air pollution.

The reality of congestion relief

08 Despite all positive attributes of these megaprojects, they have little chance of actually alleviating road gridlock. Brian Taylor writes in the journal *Transport Policy*, "Put simply, public transport expenditures in the name of congestion reduction are growing because they are broadly popular, and not because most people believe that they are effective ways to reduce traffic congestion."

09   In reality, massive spending on recent public transit megaprojects in Canada's largest cities has failed to live up to expectations. In Toronto, despite spending over $1.3-billion on two new urban rail lines, the Toronto Transit Commission reported that the share of all trips made by transit declined to 21 percent in 2001 from 26 percent in 1986, and Statistics Canada found that commuting times in the fast-growing region increased by 16 percent between 1992 and 2005. And according to the Greater Vancouver Transportation Authority,

ridership on the Millennium Skytrain line was slower to materialize than expected, resulting in substantial operating cost deficits.

10   Shifting land-use and commuting patterns are a primary reason why rapid rail transit megaprojects have failed to either attract the expected level of passengers or meaningfully reduce congestion. As dispersed employment and residential developments have been built around the periphery of Canadian cities, complex suburb-to-suburb commuting patterns have emerged. These trips are difficult to serve by conventional public transit. This partially explains why Statistics Canada found that in 2005, the average daily commute was 41 minutes shorter by car than by public transit.

11   There are two pernicious impacts of supporting transit megaprojects that have popular appeal but are unlikely to meet expectations. First, the massive resources spent on them may have been more effectively allocated elsewhere. Second, large segments of the public, particularly in burgeoning suburban communities, may begin to believe that transit investments neither alleviate congestion nor reduce harmful emissions.

12   As a result, support has grown for initiatives known to exacerbate congestion and environmental degradation. For the first time in a generation, highway and bridge building have returned to the Canadian urban agenda as viable solutions to congestion. Taking the lead is British Columbia, where the provincial government has proposed the $3-billion Gateway program that would see Greater Vancouver blanketed with a series of new bridges and roads. These options are being suggested despite evidence by Todd Litman. In a 2001 article in the *Institute of Transportation Engineers Journal*, Litman claims that you can't build your way out of congestion.

The unusual suspects

13   Solving worsening gridlock, sprawling land-use and increasingly complex commuting patterns requires integrated programs that support a range of options. New, high-quality transit infrastructure is part of the solution, particularly when it is accompanied by transit-oriented land-use development. However, effective solutions require complementary programs—the unusual suspects—that provide both incentives and disincentives to get people out of their single occupancy vehicles and into a range of alternative modes of transportation.

14   Across Canada and around the world, there have been numerous initiatives that have encouraged the behaviour changes necessary to reduce congestion. These programs provide win-win solutions that combine benefits to corporations, commuters and transit service providers. For instance, in Vancouver, the expansion of the dedicated cycling lane network between 1995 and 2005 led to a doubling in the proportion of people who commute to work by bicycle. In Winnipeg, a pilot project to provide employees with discounted transit passes increased transit ridership by 45 percent within participating companies. And in Toronto, a year after high-occupancy vehicle lanes[4] were designated on selected highways, carpooling had more than doubled in some places, and there had been a reduction in commuting times for all drivers.

15   In California, some employers found that providing a cash subsidy to employees who don't use their parking spot can be less expensive than leasing the parking space. Moreover, a study of eight mid-sized employers that paid a "cashout" subsidy found that the share of solo-occupancy vehicle commuters decreased by 17 percent, while carpooling and transit usage increased by 64 and 50 percent respectively. And in London,

---

[4] a part of the road or highway reserved for cars with two or more people inside, designed to encourage carpooling

England, when a $12 toll charged to enter the central city was implemented in 2003, weekday inner city congestion dropped by 30 percent almost immediately. Furthermore, toll money was reinvested in public transit infrastructure and keeping fare prices stable, which made transit a more viable option.

16 To be certain, many of the programs that can reduce road congestion challenge the status quo.

They may elicit community apprehension and resistance. Overcoming these challenges requires that planning agencies listen to communities' aspirations and fears, and design programs that address them. It also requires visionary and tenacious political leadership.

Source: M. Siemiatycki, "Traffic jam." *Alternatives Journal* 33 (January, 2007): 1.

Comprehension and Skills Practice

1. Why did the issue of traffic congestion rise to the top of the urban agenda in the early 2000s?

   a) It became an important environmental problem, which environmentalists and urban planners strove to solve.

   b) Politicians became more interested in solving the problem of traffic jams.

   c) It became clear that to solve the problem, cities needed to invest significant financial resources.

   d) The problem had become worse over the previous decade and became a concern to various groups of people.

2. Match each group with a specific concern regarding congestion in Canadian cities.

a. Commuters	____ Employees arrive late to work or feel tired because of long or stressful commutes.
b. Health care professionals	
c. Business groups	____ Cities' infrastructure requires costly modifications.
d. Social justice activists	____ Car exhaust increases the risk of lung disease.
e. Environmentalists	____ People who cannot afford a car are disadvantaged with respect to employment opportunities and leisure activities.
f. Urban planners	____ Car exhaust pollutes the atmosphere.
	____ Travel to and from work is becoming more time-consuming.

3. From a politician's point of view, what is the most popular way to relieve traffic congestion?

_____

_____

4. A. What is the disadvantage of constructing underground or elevated rail systems?

_____

_____

B. According to paragraph 6, many people believe that this disadvantage is a fair price to pay for solving congestion problems. Why?

_____

_____

5. Various groups express support for expanding off-road urban rails (par. 7). Which group is associated with each of the statements below?

a) _____ Major urban transit hubs encourage high-density population growth, which increases tax revenue.

b) _____ Parking spaces near shops are not limited or eliminated by on-road rail construction.

c) _____ The construction of transit megaprojects provides job opportunities to Canadians.

d) _____ Fewer car users on the roads leave more space for shipping trucks.

6. A. What is the writer's opinion of the ability of public transit megaprojects to effectively relieve congestion?

_____

_____

B. What specific vocabulary does the writer use in the section titled "The reality of congestion relief" to reveal his opinion?

_____

_____

C. What techniques does the writer use in making his argument in order to persuade the reader of his opinion?

_____

_____

7. Fill in the missing causes and effects in the table.

CAUSE	EFFECT
During the 1980s and 1990s, few people were concerned about traffic congestion. (par. 3)	
	It is difficult for politicians to find solutions that satisfy all parties. (par. 6)
	In 2005, the average daily commute was 41 minutes shorter by car than by public transit. (par. 10)
The City of Toronto designated carpool lanes on a number of urban highways. (par. 14)	

8. Which of the following ideas would the author of the text agree with? Circle all that apply.

   a) Residential and commercial development in the suburbs is preferable to high-density development in the city.

   b) It is best to spend money on transit megaprojects.

   c) Investment in transit megaprojects does not significantly alleviate congestion.

   d) Highway and bridge building are effective solutions to traffic jams.

   e) Vancouver's $3-billion Gateway program is not a viable solution to congestion.

9. In paragraphs 13–15, the author mentions incentives and disincentives to discourage people from using their single-occupancy vehicles. Mark each measure as I (incentive) or D (disincentive) based on your understanding of these concepts.

   a) ____ A Winnipeg company provides employees with discounted transit passes.

b) ____ The City of Toronto created high-occupancy lanes on some highways.

c) ____ Some California companies pay a cash subsidy to employees who don't need a parking space.

d) ____ London City Hall charges a car toll to enter the city centre.

Vocabulary

Use context clues and your knowledge of word parts to determine the correct meaning of each word. Verify your answers using a dictionary if necessary.

1. mundane (par. 2):
   a) dramatic, exhilarating
   b) different from what is usual
   c) not interesting or exciting

2. stakeholders (par. 6): _____

3. inaugurated (par. 6):
   a) planned in advance
   b) officially opened
   c) criticized openly

4. catalyst (par. 7):
   a) a person or thing that causes a change
   b) a problem, rule, or situation that prevents somebody from doing something, or that makes something impossible
   c) a substance that makes a chemical reaction happen faster

5. periphery (par. 10): _____

6. pernicious (par. 11):
   a) beneficial
   b) insignificant
   c) harmful

READING 2

Ridesharing in North America

Transportation and Sustainability Studies

Introduction

01 Increasingly, ridesharing is being discussed as a powerful strategy to reduce congestion, emissions, and fossil fuel dependency. It is the grouping of travellers into common trips by car or van. It is also widely known in the UK as liftsharing and car sharing. Ridesharing differs from for-profit taxis and jitneys[1] in its financial motivation. When a ridesharing payment is collected, it partially covers the driver's cost. It is not intended to result in a financial gain. Moreover, the driver has a common origin and/or destination with the passengers.

02   Ridesharing's modal share has declined since the 1970s in the USA. In 1970, 20.4% of American workers commuted to work by carpool, according to the US Census. This has declined to 10.7% in 2008 (US Census Bureau, 2008). The largest drop occurred between 1980 and 1990, when carpooling declined from 19.7% to 13.4%. A drop in gasoline prices, as well as improved fuel economy and shifting social trends, contributed to this decline (Ferguson, 1997). However, ridesharing has increased slightly in recent years. From a low of 10.1% in 2004, carpooling has risen slightly and settled around 10.7% since 2005 (US Census Bureau, 2004, 2005). Similarly, ridesharing has increased somewhat since 2001 in Canada. Approximately 7% of Canadian workers commuted as a passenger in 2001; this increased to 7.7% in 2006 (Statistics Canada, 2008). Interestingly, there are seven times as many US passenger-miles for commute trips by carpool and vanpool as there are for public transit (C. Burbank, personal communication, 15 November 2009).

Background

03 Since ridesharing reduces the number of automobiles needed by travellers, it claims numerous societal benefits. Noland et al. (2006) assert that enacting policies to increase carpooling is the most effective strategy to reduce energy consumption besides prohibiting driving. Other benefits include reduced emissions, traffic congestion, and parking infrastructure demand; however, the magnitude of such benefits is unclear. The SMART 2020 report estimates that employing information and communications technology (ICT) to optimize[2] the logistics of individual road transport could abate 70 to 190 million metric tons of carbon dioxide emissions (Global e-Sustainability Initiative, 2008). Using social networking to match travellers together for carpools and vanpools is one ICT strategy.

04   On an individual level, the benefits are more tangible. Carpool and vanpool participants experience cost savings due to shared travel costs, travel-time savings by employing high-occupancy vehicle (HOV) lanes, and reduced

---

[1] buses or other vehicles carrying passengers for a low fare
[2] to make something as good as it can be

commute stress, particularly for those with longer commute distances. In addition, they often have access to preferential parking and additional incentives.

05   Despite its many benefits, there are numerous behavioural barriers to increased ridesharing use. An early study of attitudes towards carpooling found that individuals often see the attractiveness of carpooling but are disinclined to sacrifice the flexibility and convenience of the private automobile (Dueker and Levin, 1976). Moreover, psychological factors, such as the desire for personal space and time and an aversion to social situations, can impact ridesharing adoption (Bonsall et al., 1984). Personal security is also a concern when sharing a ride with strangers, although this is a perceived risk (M. Oliphant, personal communication, 15 July 2010).

North American ridesharing: The present

06   In this section, the authors focus on ridesharing activities from 2004 to the present. This period encompasses the ridesharing phase called: "technology-enabled ridematching." While this period continues to include casual carpooling,[3] HOV lanes, and park-and-ride ridesharing efforts, it is most notable for the widespread integration of the Internet, mobile phones, and social networking (i.e. an online community where individuals connect and interact) into ridesharing services. At present, the majority of North American ridematching services use online websites as their chief technology medium. Many of them are based on a ridesharing software platform purchased from a private company. As of July 2011, there were approximately 12 such companies in North America that offer this software. While the abundance of online ridesharing systems is promising, it has resulted in disparate, non-standardized databases that leave many programmes with a lack of critical mass.[4] Four key developments characterize the present and aim to address the common ridesharing concerns of critical mass, safety, or both.

Ridematching platform partnerships

07   From 2004 to the present, a new generation of ridematching platforms has been developed for regions and employers to use. Moreover, there has been significant growth and overall success with this strategy. Partnerships between ridematching software companies and its large-scale clients take advantage of existing common destinations and large numbers of potential members. These firms sell their ridematching software "platforms" to public agencies and employers, which are sometimes used as standalone websites for each group. While this partnership strategy has gained more users than previous ridesharing phases, it is most suited for commuters with regular schedules.

"Green trip"–sponsored incentives

08   Many public agencies and companies promote ridesharing by providing its members with incentives. One example is NuRide—an online ridesharing club with over 63 000 members in seven US metropolitan areas (NuRide, 2011). NuRide rewards points when members carpool, vanpool, take public transit, bike, walk, or telecommute for both work and personal trips. These points can be used for restaurant coupons, shopping discounts, and attraction tickets. NuRide partners with public agencies, employers, and businesses to sponsor the incentives. Similarly, RideSpring works with employer commute programmes and participating employees can enter monthly drawings for prizes from over 100 retailers (RideSpring, 2010).

---

[3] a practice of informal, on-the-spot ridesharing
[4] the minimum number of people required to make something work effectively

Activity in Washington DC Metro

Feb 2004	🗓	launch date
13,774	👤	members
$403,835	✂	rewards redeemed
2,370,864	🧍	greener trips
1,267,939	🚗	shared rides
855,496	🚊	transit trips
79,620	🚶	walking trips
93,185	🚲	biking trips
71,219	🏢	telecommutes
3,405	⬇	compressed work weeks
69,847,145	🌐	miles not driven
3,217,133	⛽	gallons of gas saved
$37,540,598	$	money saved
31,618	☁	tons of emissions prevented
161,241,749	♥	calories burned

Figure 9.2 Statistics from Washington DC where NuRide has been active for 10 years

Source: nuride.com

Social networking platforms

09 The rise of social networking platforms, such as Facebook, has enabled ridesharing companies to use this interface to match potential rides between friends or acquaintances more easily. These companies hope that social networking will build trust among participants, addressing safety considerations. One example is Zimride, which has partnered with 86 US and Canadian colleges, universities, and companies that each has its own "network" of members (Zimride, 2011). In addition to each network's website, Zimride also uses the Facebook platform to attract public users. Another service is PickupPal (2011), with over 156 000 members in 120 countries. It allows members to create their own groups based on common area, company, school, and shared interests. However, social networking may limit itself by relying on more isolated groups and excluding less tech-savvy users.

Real-time ridesharing services

10 In North America, two companies are beginning to offer real-time ridesharing services: AvegoTM and Carticipate. Real-time ridesharing uses Internet-enabled "smartphones" and automated ridematching software to organize rides in real time. This enables participants to be organized either minutes before the trip takes place or while the trip is occurring, with passengers picked up and dropped off along the way. These programmes attempt to address the inconvenience of traditional carpooling and vanpooling. As in most ridesharing services, a high subscriber base is required.

Ridesharing's future

11 Over the next decade, North American ridesharing is likely to include greater interoperability among services, technology integration, and policy support. Moreover, national agencies dedicated to ridesharing research and funding could substantially spur growth through a concerted effort to enact such policy measures (C. Burbank, personal communication, 27 July 2010). Additionally, research into the behavioural economics of modal choice is needed to determine which psychological and emotional factors are involved in choosing between driving alone and ridesharing (R. Steele, personal communication, 23 July 2010). A key lesson learned from past programmes is the importance of marketing and public education to raise awareness about ridesharing and its potential to reduce climate change and traffic congestion.

Source: Excerpted from N.D. Chan & S.A. Shaheen, "Ridesharing in North America: Past, present, and future." *Transportation Reviews* 32, no. 1 (January, 2012): 93–112.

1. How is ridesharing different from taking a taxi? Circle all that apply.

   a) Passengers pay less to the driver of a rideshare than they would pay to a taxi driver.

   b) Ridesharing reduces road congestion much more than taking a taxi does.

   c) Persons involved in ridesharing start and/or finish their journeys in the same location.

   d) Drivers who participate in ridesharing do not intend to make money.

2. Based on the statistics in paragraph 2, make an inference about which country—the U.S. or Canada—had a higher rate of carpooling in 2006.

   _____

3. A. Fill in the T-chart with the benefits of ridesharing.

BENEFITS FOR SOCIETY	BENEFITS FOR THE INDIVIDUAL

   B. Which kind of benefits are more easily observable?

   _____

4. Mark each statement as T (true) or F (false).

   a) _____ If people knew the societal benefits of ridesharing, there would be no barriers to participation.

   b) _____ Some people reject the idea of ridesharing because they believe it is not safe to get into a car with strangers.

5. According paragraph 6, what is the defining characteristic of present-day ridesharing?

   _____

6. What is the authors' assessment of the many online ridesharing platforms available today?

   a) The more ridesharing platforms there are, the better.

   b) There should be more companies that produce ridesharing software.

   c) Ridesharing platforms should be integrated and standardized.

   d) Many people know about ridesharing websites.

7. What is the main principle behind NuRide's program? Summarize in your own words.

   _____

8. Can someone receive reward points from NuRide if he/she decides to work from home instead of travelling to the office? Give evidence from the text for your answer.

   _____

9. Study Figure 9.2 from NuRide.com on page 187. What benefits does NuRide offer

   A. for the environment?

   _____

   B. for people's health?

   _____

10. Why is there hope that social networking will contribute to the perceived safety of ridesharing?

    _____

11. What are the limitations of using social networking platforms to increase ridesharing? Circle all that apply.

    a) They rely on separate groups of users and do not integrate all users into one database.

    b) They may compromise security by putting passengers at a greater risk of attack by a stranger.

    c) They require access to special apps and knowledge of how to use them, which some travellers may not have.

    d) Not enough people participate in ridesharing as a result of using different social platforms.

12. What is the main difference between Zimride and Carticipate services?

    _____

13. Match each of the following terms with its description.

a. HOV lane

b. park-and-ride

c. RideSpring

d. PickupPal

e. AvegoTM

_____ a website that allows users to pre-arrange a shared ride, based on their common location, company, or school

_____ a separate space on the road where single-occupancy vehicles are not allowed

_____ a company that uses ridematching software to let users organize a shared ride in real time

_____ an online company that encourages ridesharing by rewarding participants through prize lotteries

_____ a designated area outside of the city centre where drivers leave their cars and continue their commute using public transit

14. The authors refer to a number of areas in which certain developments would help increase ridesharing. In each area, note what policies or developments would be beneficial.

AREA	NECESSARY DEVELOPMENTS
Ridesharing technology	
Ridesharing research	
Public education	

Use context clues and your knowledge of word parts to determine the correct meaning of each word. Verify your answers using a dictionary if necessary.

1. claims (par. 3):
   a) says that something is true although it has not been proven
   b) demands something because it might be one's legal right
   c) gains, wins, or achieves something

2. abate (par. 3): _____

3. disinclined (par. 5):
   a) unwilling
   b) ready
   c) considering

4. aversion (par. 5):
   a) acceptance
   b) a strong feeling of not liking something
   c) the act of looking at or considering something very carefully

5. disparate (par. 6): _____

6. tech-savvy (par. 9): _____

7. concerted (par. 11): _____

READING 3

Most of your reading in college or university will come from textbooks or journals; however, you may also find valuable information in newspapers or magazines. Although the tone of magazines and newspapers may be more informal, you will use the same skills and strategies as you read the articles. The final reading in this unit comes from *Maclean's*, a reputable Canadian magazine, and contains several informal speech idioms.

How Electric Cars Got Stuck in First Gear  Business

**Electric cars are hitting showrooms, but people aren't buying.
Is there money to be made in green vehicles?**

01 On a recent autumn day, employees of Tesla wheeled their latest electrified creation, the Model S sedan, into the concourse of a bank tower in downtown Toronto. Over the lunch hour, a handful of curious passersby ogled[1] the dark-red vehicle's sleek lines, leather interior and giant touch-screen monitor.

02 The Model S is the second production vehicle built by the Silicon Valley–based carmaker founded by American entrepreneur Elon Musk. Its first effort, the US$109,000 Roadster, was launched in 2008 and immediately grabbed eyeballs—not only because it was the first production vehicle to use lithium-ion batteries like those found in laptops, but because it looked car-magazine cool and was capable of zero to 60 mph in as little as 3.7 seconds. Tesla, which has yet to turn a profit, built and sold only 1,800 Roadsters, but that was hardly the point. "We needed to build a proof of concept that put itself on the map pretty quickly," says Ricardo Reyes, a Tesla spokesperson.

03 Mission accomplished—sort of. With Tesla leading the way and governments throwing money at "green" industries, electric cars have gone from auto-show concept vehicles to production models, seemingly overnight. There's only one problem: consumers have so far shown little interest in vehicles that are perceived as expensive, time-consuming to recharge and having a limited driving range. "The buzz around electric cars in the marketplace is far

Most Americans say they want an electric car that can recharge in about two hours. The Nissan Leaf takes up to eight.

greater than what's actually being purchased," says Michelle Krebs, a senior analyst for the car website Edmunds.com. "Electric cars are not catching on."

04 Krebs, who appears in the documentary *Revenge of the Electric Car*—a sequel to *Who Killed the Electric Car?*, which explored GM's decision to recall and destroy its fleet of electric EV1 cars in 2003—points to sales data that showed just 21,394 "advanced drive" vehicles (which also includes hybrids and diesels) sold in the key U.S. market in October. That's down 12 percent from the previous year. Meanwhile, sales of conventional gas-powered cars and trucks were up 7.4 percent during the same

---

[1] stared at

period, suggesting that a bevy of smaller, more fuel-efficient models are blunting demand for alternative powertrains at current gas prices.

05   It's potentially bad news for carmakers like GM, which spent more than US$1 billion on the development of its plug-in hybrid Volt (the car runs on electricity but can switch to a gas-powered generator when the battery is depleted). Despite positive reviews, it now looks doubtful that GM will realize its 2011 sales target of 10,000 Volts, a number it has stubbornly refused to revise, even though since January it has moved just 5,544 of the cars, which each cost $41,545 before incentives. By contrast, GM's gasoline-powered Chevrolet Cruze ($15,495) has outsold the Volt by roughly 20 to one, globally.

06   GM has suggested it's a problem of supply, not demand. It recently gave U.S. dealers permission to sell their demo models, which were supposed to remain on showroom floors to attract customers. Adria MacKenzie, a spokesperson for GM's Canadian arm, says GM has sold about 200 Volts in Canada, and another 111 have been pre-sold and are now en route to dealers. "We are building as many Volts as possible to keep up with consumer demand," MacKenzie says. "These sales numbers are in line with our expectations."

07   Perhaps. But it's difficult to see how the situation will improve as GM's competitors rush into the space. In addition to Tesla, Nissan-Renault offers an all-electric car, called the Leaf—17,000 of which have been sold around the world. Ford Motor Co. has as many as five electrified vehicles in the works, while Chrysler-Fiat is planning an electric version of the Fiat 500. Mitsubishi and BMW both have electric cars coming, too.

08   It's shaping up to be a sequel to the "if we build it they will buy it" approach that nearly cratered the auto industry during the last recession—only this time it's pricey electric cars instead of cheap-to-make gas-guzzling trucks that are taking centre stage. Though having a high-tech electric car in the lineup makes for good "green" marketing and helps automakers satisfy stringent fuel economy standards, analysts note electric cars aren't cheap to develop. At some point, consumers need to do more than just marvel at them.

09   Yet recent studies show a chasm between what consumers expect from an electric car and what engineers are actually able to deliver at an affordable price. A Deloitte survey of 13,000 consumers in 17 countries found that only 63 percent of Americans would be satisfied with being able to drive 480 km before a car's battery pack was depleted, and that nearly 60 percent of U.S. respondents wanted a car that could be recharged in about two hours. By contrast, the Nissan Leaf advertises a range of just 160 km (closer to 117 km in "real world" driving conditions), and can take up to eight hours to achieve a full charge using a special charging station that can be installed in a garage and runs off a 240-volt circuit. The Leaf can also plug into standard 120-volt outlets, but the charging time is twice as long. A third option is 480-volt "fast-chargers," which would ideally be made available along highways or rest stops, and which are capable of achieving an 80 percent charge in about 30 minutes. As for the range issue, Nissan has pointed to study after study that shows most commuters drive less than 80 km per day. But that assumes people buy cars based on what they need—a fallacy[2] exposed by the enduring popularity of vehicles like the Ford Mustang or anything made by Hummer.

10   Tesla believes it can solve the consumer psychology part of the puzzle. Its Model S has

---

[2] a false idea that many people believe is true

been described as the first electric vehicle that's neither too expensive (the base model will be just over $49,000 after government incentives) nor too limiting (it has a range of 260 km, which can be boosted to 480 km with an extra battery pack that adds $20,000 to the purchase price). It has also embarked on a unique retail model by putting some 20 stores in high-end malls across North America, with the first Canadian store to open in a "premium Toronto mall" next year. The idea is to educate consumers about the technology and let them play around with it (there are cars nearby for test drives). If it sounds like the approach used by another Silicon Valley company—the one known for its iPhones and iPads—it's no coincidence. Tesla's retail strategy is being led by former Apple retail guru George Blankenship. "Apple stores are a place where people can go if they want to purchase a product, but also just sort of want to experience it and play around," says Reyes. "That's the same sort of feel we're going with for our stores."

11 Even so, the industry faces huge hurdles that may prove impossible to overcome—even if gas prices creep higher. They range from a lack of charging infrastructure to the slow pace of innovation in battery technology. And questions remain about whether electric cars can be mass-produced at a profit.

12 While the cost of building electric cars is bound to come down as the technology matures, critics point out that many of the materials needed to produce electric cars, including lithium and rare earth metals, are actually far less abundant than oil. "We're at the very pioneering stage of this," Krebs says. "We're just getting electric vehicles out on the roads and we don't know what consumer acceptance will be. But the big challenge is whether it can work as a business model."

13 In Toronto, the Tesla display continues to draw curious looks. Though Tesla says it has orders for all 6,500 of the vehicles that will be built next year, it's still a drop in the bucket for an industry that sold 11.7 million cars and light trucks in 2010 in the U.S. alone. It's too soon to say whether the electric car will be killed off this time around, but if it is, it will be because consumers—not Detroit or some shady lobby group—pulled the trigger.

Source: C. Sorensen, "How Electric Cars Got Stuck in first gear." *Maclean's* 124, 6 December 2011, 48–49.

Comprehension and Skills Practice

1. A. What was the purpose of putting the Model S sedan in the concourse of a bank tower in Toronto?

    _____

    B. What were some of the attractive features of the Model S?

    _____

2. What are the problems with electric vehicles, in the view of many car buyers?

    _____

    _____

3. A. What is Michelle Krebs's opinion of the state of electric vehicle sales? Copy one sentence from the text to answer the question.

_____

B. What technique(s) of persuasion does Krebs use to make her argument? Circle all that apply, and for each technique you circle, provide an example from the text.

TECHNIQUE	EXAMPLE
a. presenting a counter-argument and refuting it	
b. citing statistics	
c. using contrast	
d. using an emotional tone	

4. What is the best paraphrase of the following sentence from paragraph 4: ". . . a bevy of smaller, more fuel-efficient models are blunting demand for alternative powertrains at current gas prices"?

a) As gas prices today are high, small fuel-powered cars are more popular than large fuel-powered vehicles.

b) The availability of a range of compact fuel-saving cars reduces demand for green vehicles at today's gas prices.

c) At current gas prices, alternative power vehicles are preferable to even small and fuel-efficient gas models.

5. How does the GM Volt work?

_____

6. Mark each statement as F (fact) or O (opinion).

a) ____ In 2003, GM recalled and destroyed the EV1 model.

b) ___ GM sold 5,544 Volts in the period between January 2011 and the time of the article's publication.

c) ___ The sales figures of GM's Chevrolet Cruz are higher than those of the Volt.

d) ___ The sales figures of the Volt are low because GM has not built enough cars to meet the demand of customers.

e) ___ GM's sales of electric vehicles will hardly increase in the future because of strong competition from other automakers.

7. Does the author of this text approve of the "if we build it, they will buy it" (par. 8) approach? How do you know?

_____

8. A. Fill in the following table with the results of the Deloitte consumer survey.

	AMERICANS WHO AGREE WITH THE STATEMENT (%)
480 km is an acceptable driving distance between battery charges for an electric car.	
Recharging time for the battery should be about two hours.	

B. Does the Nissan Leaf electric car seem to meet the expectations of the majority of American respondents in the Deloitte survey? _____

9. A. What is the quickest recharging option for the Nissan Leaf?

_____

B. Was this option available at the time of the article's publication?

_____

10. Mark each inference as V (valid) or I (invalid) based on the information in paragraph 9.

   a) ____ Most consumers would be satisfied if 30-minute recharging units were installed along highways rest stops.

   b) ____ Because most drivers cover a distance of less than 80 kilometres per day, they are happy with the battery range of 160 kilometres offered by the Nissan Leaf.

   c) ____ The popularity of cars like the Ford Mustang and the Hummer proves that most drivers need powerful vehicles for their daily commutes.

11. Complete the sentence, based on paragraph 10.

   In addition to lowering the cost of its electric model and improving its range, Tesla can attract more buyers by _____

12. Summarize the opinion of the author regarding the future of electric cars.

   _____

   _____

Vocabulary

Use context clues and your knowledge of word parts to determine the correct meaning of each word or phrase. Verify your answers using a dictionary if necessary.

1. grabbed eyeballs (par. 2): _____

2. bevy (par. 4): _____

3. recession (par. 8):

   a) a difficult time for the economy of a country, when there is less trade and industrial activity than usual and more people are unemployed

   b) a movement of something backwards from a previous position

   c) the introduction of new things, ideas, or ways of doing something

4. stringent (par. 8):

   a) very strict and must be obeyed

   b) very strictly controlled because there is not much money

   c) surprisingly relaxed

5. chasm (par. 9): _____

6. a drop in the bucket (par. 13): _____

UNIT REFLECTION AND SYNTHESIS

1. Match each selection with its purpose.

a. "Traffic Jam"

b. "Ridesharing in North America"

c. "How Electric Cars Got Stuck in First Gear"

_____ To inform the general public, policy makers, and technology innovators about ridesharing today and in the future

_____ To persuade policy makers to solve the problem on the roads by turning to unconventional solutions instead of building more infrastructure

_____ To inform the reader of the disconnect between modern consumers' needs and wishes and the available green car technology

2. Study the sources of "Stuck in First Gear" and "Traffic Jam." How would you expect the audiences of these two texts to be different?

_____

_____

3. The author of "Traffic Jam" divides solutions to the problem of road congestion into two groups, which he calls the usual and the unusual suspects.

A. Give examples of the solutions falling under each category.

The usual suspects: _____

_____

The unusual suspects: _____

_____

B. Would ridesharing ("Ridesharing in North America") be considered a usual or an unusual suspect?

_____

4. A. The bar graph on page 177 predicts that by 2040, there will be almost as many electric and hybrid vehicles on the road as conventional gas-powered vehicles. If this prediction comes true, harmful traffic emissions and our dependency on fossil fuels would be greatly reduced. Do you think that the authors of "Traffic Jam" and "Ridesharing" would consider more electric cars an appropriate solution to the problems that they write about?

_____

_____

B. Based on your understanding of "How Electric Cars Got Stuck in First Gear," do you think the author would agree with the predictions in the graph?

_____

5. A. Often, technology plays an important role in solving modern problems. Briefly discuss the role of technology in the following.

Increasing ridesharing: _____

_____

Creating a better electric car: _____

_____

B. Can you think of any other ways in which technology will help us to overcome transportation-related environmental issues?

_____

_____

6. A. All three texts in this unit raise the issue of overcoming people's psychological barriers to change. Give three examples from the text of how people's attitudes may stand in the way of finding innovative solutions to transportation concerns. The first one is done for you.

a) Buying a car that saves fuel would be great for the environment and quite sufficient for people's daily commutes, but people prefer powerful, gas-guzzling models.

b) _____

_____

c) _____

_____

B. If you were a policy maker—an urban mayor or a government minister—what incentives or disincentives (discussed in any of the three readings) do you think would be most effective to encourage people to overcome their psychological barriers? Share your ideas with other students.

_____

_____

_____

10 Ethnocentrism

GETTING INTO THE TOPIC

This unit presents the concept of ethnocentrism from the perspectives of psychology, marketing, and political science. The first reading introduces the idea of the social and cognitive roots of prejudice, which underlies ethnocentrism. The second reading deals with ethnocentrism as a barrier to successful international marketing. The final selection discusses ethnocentrism in the context of the 9/11 terrorist attack on the United States and the war on terrorism that followed.

Discuss these questions to help you get into the topic.

1. In Canada, foreign-trained professionals are often unable to find a job because they lack "Canadian experience." When two applicants with the same qualifications apply for a position, the local person with experience working in Canada, rather than the immigrant, is often chosen. What do you think helps to explain this practice?

   a) local cultural traditions

   b) preference to hire an applicant with language proficiency

   c) racial prejudice

   d) other (explain): _____

2. Is it common for people to feel prejudiced against other races, ethnicities, or religions? If so, is it more common for people to show prejudice openly or attempt to disguise it?

3. In the early twentieth century, there was widespread prejudice on the part of Canadians, mostly of European origin, against immigrant Chinese workers. In your view, what were the roots of their prejudice?

4. What is meant by the term *ethnocentrism*? Guess the meaning of the word using your knowledge of its parts and then check your guess in a dictionary. Write down your definition.

---

5. Do you think ethnocentrism can affect a person's political beliefs? Give some examples.

READING 1

Prejudice

 **Psychology**

01 Prejudice means "prejudgement." It is an unjustifiable and usually negative attitude toward a group—often a different cultural, ethnic, or gender group. Like all attitudes, prejudice is a three-part mixture of
- *beliefs* (in this case, called stereotypes),
- *emotions* (for example, hostility or fear), and
- predisposition to *action* (to discriminate).

To *believe* that obese people are gluttonous, to *feel* dislike for an obese person, and to be hesitant to hire or date an obese person is to be prejudiced. Prejudice is a negative *attitude*. Discrimination is a negative *behaviour*.

How prejudiced are people?

02 To assess prejudice, we can observe what people say and what they do. Americans' expressed gender and racial attitudes have changed dramatically in the last half-century. Nearly everyone now agrees that women and men should receive the same pay for the same job, and that children of all races should attend the same schools.

03 Support for all forms of racial contact, including interracial dating, has also dramatically increased. Among 18- to 29-year-old Americans, 9 in 10 now say they would be fine with a family member marrying someone of a different race (Pew, 2010).

04 Yet, as *overt* prejudice wanes, *subtle* prejudice lingers. Despite increased verbal support for interracial marriage, many people admit that in socially intimate settings (dating, dancing, marrying) they would feel uncomfortable with someone of another race. And many people who *say* they feel upset with someone

making racist slurs actually, when hearing such racism, respond indifferently (Kawakami et al., 2009). In Western Europe, where many "guest workers" and refugees settled at the end of the twentieth century, "modern prejudice"—rejecting immigrant minorities as job applicants for supposedly nonracial reasons—has been replacing blatant prejudice (Jackson et el., 2001; Lester, 2004; Pettigrew, 1998, 2006). A slew of recent experiments illustrates that prejudice can be not only subtle but also automatic and unconscious.

05 Nevertheless, overt prejudice persists in many places. In the aftermath of 9/11 events and the Iraq and Afghanistan wars, 4 out of 10 Americans acknowledged "some feelings of prejudice against Muslims," and about half of non-Muslims in Western Europe and the United States perceived Muslims as "violent" (Saad, 2006; Wike & Grim, 2007). With Americans feeling threatened by Arabs, and as opposition to Islamic mosques and immigration flared in 2010, one national observer noted that "Muslims are one of the last minorities in the United States that it is still possible to demean openly" (Kristof, 2010; Lyons et al., 2010). Muslims reciprocated the negativity, with most in Jordan, Egypt, Turkey, and Britain seeing Westerners as "greedy" and "immoral."

Social roots of prejudice

06 Why does prejudice arise? Social divisions are partly responsible. We have inherited our Stone Age ancestors' need to belong, to live and love in groups. There was safety in solidarity (those who didn't band together left fewer descendants). Whether hunting, defending, or attacking, 10 hands were better than 2. Dividing the world into "us" and "them" entails racism and war, but it also provides the benefits of communal solidarity. Thus we cheer for our groups, kill for them, die for them. Indeed, we define who we are partly in terms of our groups. Through our *social identities* we associate ourselves with certain groups and contrast ourselves with others (Hogg, 1996, 2006; Turner, 1987, 2007). When Ian identifies himself as a man, an Aussie,[1] a Labourite,[2] a University of Sydney student, a Catholic, and a MacGregor, he knows who he is, and so do we.

07 Evolution prepared us, when encountering strangers, to make instant judgements: friend or foe? Those from our group, those who look like us, and also those who *sound* like us—with accents like our own—we instantly tend to like, from childhood onward (Gluszek & Dovidio, 2010; Kinzler et al., 2009). Mentally drawing a circle defines "us," the *ingroup*. But the social definition of who you are also states who you are not. People outside that circle are "them," the *outgroup*. An ingroup bias—a favouring of our own group—soon follows. Even arbitrarily creating us-them groups by tossing a coin creates this bias. In experiments, people have favoured

Canadian hockey fans use the maple leaf to identify themselves.

---

[1] a person from Australia

[2] someone who belongs to or supports the Labour party

their own group when dividing any rewards (Tajfel, 1982; Wilder, 1981).

08   The urge to distinguish enemies from friends predisposes prejudice against strangers (Whitley, 1999). To Greeks of the classical era, all non-Greeks were "barbarians." In our own era, most children believe their own school is better than all other schools in town. Many high school students form cliques—jocks, goths, skaters, gangsters, freaks, geeks—and disparage those outside their own group. Even chimpanzees have been seen to wipe clean the spot where they were touched by a chimpanzee from another group (Goodall, 1986). They also display ingroup empathy, by yawning more after seeing ingroup (rather than outgroup) members yawn (Campbell & de Waal, 2011).

09   Ingroup bias explains the cognitive power of partisanship (Cooper, 2010; Douthat, 2010). In the United States in the late 1980s, most Democrats believed inflation had risen under Republican president Ronald Reagan (it had dropped). In 2010, most Republicans believed taxes had increased under Democrat president Barack Obama (for most, they had decreased).

Cognitive roots of prejudice

10 Prejudice springs from a culture's divisions, and also from the mind's natural workings. Stereotyped beliefs are a by-product of how we cognitively simplify the world. One way we simplify our world is to categorize. A chemist categorizes molecules as organic and inorganic. Therapists categorize psychological disorders. Human beings categorize people by race, with mixed-raced people often assigned to their minority identity. Despite his mixed-race background and his rearing by a White mother and grandparents, President Obama is perceived by White Americans as Black. Researchers believe this happens because, after learning the features of a familiar racial group, the observer's selective attention is drawn to the distinctive features of the less-familiar minority. Jamin Halberstadt and his colleagues (2011) illustrated this learned-association effect by showing New Zealanders blended Chinese-Caucasian faces. Compared with Chinese participants, the Caucasian New Zealanders more readily classified ambiguous faces as Chinese (see Figure 10.1).

11   In categorizing people into groups, however, we often stereotype them. We recognize how greatly *we* differ from other individuals in *our* groups. But we overestimate the homogeneity of other groups. "They"—the members of some other group—seem to look and act alike, while "we" are more diverse (Bothwell et al., 1989). To those in one ethnic group, members of another often seem more alike than they really are in attitudes, personality, and appearance. Our

| 100% Chinese | 80% Chinese 20% Caucasian | 60% Chinese 40% Caucasian | 40% Chinese 60% Caucasian | 20% Chinese 80% Caucasian | 100% Caucasian |

Figure 10.1 Categorizing mixed-race people
When New Zealanders quickly classified 104 photos by race, those of European descent more often than those of Chinese descent classified the ambiguous middle two as Chinese (Halberstadt et al., 2011)

Speed Bump

YOU'RE BOB? SORRY, YOU RESEARCHERS ALL LOOK ALIKE TO ME.

greater recognition for own-race faces—called the other-race effect (also called the *cross-race effect* or *own-race bias*)—emerges during infancy, between 3 and 9 months of age (Gross, 2009; Kelley et al., 2007).

12   With effort and with experience, people get better at recognizing individual faces from another group (Hugenberg et al., 2010). People of European descent, for example, more accurately identify individual African faces if they have watched a great deal of basketball on television, exposing them to many African-heritage faces (Li et al., 1996). And the longer Chinese people have resided in a Western country, the less they exhibit the other-race effect (Hancock & Rhodes, 2008).

Source: Excerpted from D.G. Myers, *Psychology*, 10th edition (New York: Worth, 2013), pp. 572–579.

Comprehension and Skills Practice

1.   Read the passage and answer the questions that follow.

Michael Statson, 65, is a Caucasian patient in a Canadian hospital. During the morning rounds, a doctor with a slight Indian accent approaches his bed to examine him. Michael feels uncomfortable and anxious. In his mind, Caucasian physicians are better trained than those from Southeast Asia and more knowledgeable. Michael grudgingly lets the doctor examine him but later says to the administrator, "I'm not racist, but I'm having trouble communicating with my doctor. I don't think his English is very good. I'd really prefer if you could assign me a Canadian doctor."

A. Find three elements of prejudice in the scenario.

Belief: _____

Emotion: _____

Action: _____

B. Is it reasonable to infer that when Michael asks for a "Canadian" doctor, he is actually requesting a white doctor? Why or why not? In your opinion, does Michael display overt or subtle prejudice?

2. Mark the statement as T (true) or F (false).

____ The author of "Prejudice" is certain that prejudice against women does not exist in contemporary American society.

3. What is the topic of paragraph 4?

a) Blatant prejudice

b) Racial discrimination

c) Automatic prejudice

d) Subtle prejudice

4. Reread paragraph 4. Based on that paragraph, which of the following statements is a valid inference?

a) People who state that they would feel upset if someone made racist remarks in their company will always respond to a racist comment with criticism.

b) People who state that they would feel upset if someone made racist remarks in their company may fail to respond when it actually happens.

c) People who state that they would feel upset if someone made racist remarks in their company will act to establish justice if a racist comment is overtly hostile but will not react if the comment is made in a joking manner.

5. Which of the following statements would the author agree with?

a) Many Americans' prejudice against Muslims in the first decade of the twenty-first century was justified by the 9/11 terrorist attack.

b) Many Americans felt prejudice toward Muslims following the 9/11 events.

c) It is legal to demean members of the Muslim minority in America today.

d) The negative perception of Westerners by Muslims in the Middle East and Britain was a warranted response to American military actions in Iraq and Afghanistan.

6. What is the evolutionary reason that makes us divide people into "us" and "them"? Explain in your own words.

_____

_____

7. A. Paragraph 6 states that "we define who we are partly in terms of our groups." For example, when Ian says he is an Aussie, he is identifying himself as part of the Australian nation. What other categories does Ian use to identify himself? Would you use similar categories to identify yourself?

_____

_____

B. Paragraph 6 ends with "he [Ian] knows who he is, and so do we." Do you think that Ian's list of social identities illustrates *exactly* who Ian is as an individual?

_____

_____

8. While our sense of belonging to an ingroup provides a sense of communal solidarity, there are some disadvantages as well. What are they?

_____

_____

9. Match the researchers with their findings.

a. Campbell and de Waal

b. Wilder

c. Goodall

d. Gluszek and Dovidio

____ Similarities in appearance and accent make people like each other.

____ Even when groups are created artificially, people favour the members of their own group.

____ Chimpanzees usually clean the spot where they have been touched by a chimp from another group.

____ The frequency of yawns among chimpanzees is affected by whether or not the individual whose yawn triggers theirs belongs to their ingroup.

10. The word *barbarians* as used by ancient Greeks meant

a) people who they didn't personally know.

b) foreigners; any non-Greeks.

c) those who didn't speak Greek fluently.

11. The implied main idea of paragraph 9 is that

    a) belonging to a party makes its members unfairly prejudiced against members of an opposition party.

    b) Democrats and Republicans often exchange allegations against each other.

    c) Republican economic policies turned out to be more effective than those of the Democrats.

    d) prejudice makes citizens appreciate the effectiveness of economic policies their government is implementing.

12. Mark the statement as T (true) or F (false). Correct if the statement is false.

    ____ Categorizing is an inborn human tendency.

13. What is true of Halberstadt's experiment with blended Chinese and Caucasian faces?

    a) People prefer strangers who look like them.

    b) The visual characteristics of a less-familiar minority attract the attention of a viewer.

    c) Caucasian New Zealanders are prejudiced against Chinese.

    d) Mixed-race people are hard to define by clear categories.

14. In your own words, explain each of the following terms used in the reading.

    a) subtle prejudice (par. 4): _____

    b) ingroup bias (par. 7): _____

    c) stereotype (pars. 10-11): _____

    d) the other-race effect (par. 11): _____

15. What is the purpose of including the cartoon of the man and the penguin in the text?

_____

Vocabulary

Use context clues and your knowledge of word parts to determine the correct meaning of each word. Verify your answers using a dictionary if necessary.

1. blatant (par. 4):

    a) done in an obvious and open way without caring whether people are shocked

    b) delicate, subtle, almost unnoticeable by people

    c) modern, suitable for current times

2. aftermath (par. 5):

    a) a period before an important event

    b) the situation that exists as a result of a significant, usually negative, event

    c) complex statistics calculations happening after an event

3. foe (par. 7):

    a) stranger

    b) enemy

    c) one who looks like us

4. arbitrarily (par. 7):

    a) using power without restriction and without considering other people

    b) done in a well-planned way

    c) seemingly not based on a reason, system, or plan

5. disparage (par. 8):

    a) suggest that someone is not important or valuable

    b) physically abuse someone

    c) band together with someone

READING 2

The Self-Reference Criterion: A Major Obstacle

 Marketing

01 The key to successful international marketing is adaptation to the environmental differences from one market to another. Adaptation is a conscious effort on the part of the international marketer to anticipate the influences of both the foreign and domestic uncontrollable factors on a marketing mix and then to adjust the marketing mix to minimize the effects.

02 The primary obstacles to success in international marketing are a person's *self-reference criterion* (SRC) and an associated ethnocentrism. The SRC is an unconscious reference to one's own cultural values, experiences, and knowledge as a basis for decisions. Closely connected is ethnocentrism, that is, the notion that people in one's own company, culture, or country know

best how to do things. Ethnocentrism was particularly a problem for American managers at the beginning of the 21st century because of America's dominance in the world economy during the late 1990s. Ethnocentrism is generally a problem when managers from affluent countries work with managers and markets in less affluent countries. Both the SRC and ethnocentrism impede the ability to assess a foreign market in its true light.

03   When confronted with a set of facts, we react spontaneously on the basis of knowledge assimilated over a lifetime—knowledge that is a product of the history of our culture. We seldom stop to think about a reaction; we simply react. Thus, when faced with a problem in another culture, our tendency is to react instinctively and refer to our SRC for a solution. Our reaction, however, is based on meanings, values, symbols, and behaviour relevant to our own culture and usually different from those of the foreign culture. Such decisions are often not good ones.

04   Ethnocentrism and the SRC can influence an evaluation of the appropriateness of a domestically designed marketing mix for a foreign market. If U.S. marketers are not aware, they might evaluate a marketing mix based on U.S. experiences (i.e., their SRC) without fully appreciating the cultural differences that require adaptation. Esso, the brand name of a gasoline, was a successful name in the United States and would seem harmless enough for foreign countries; however, in Japan, the name phonetically means "stalled car," an undesirable image for gasoline. Another example is the "Pet" in Pet Milk. The name has been used for decades, yet in France, the word *pet* means, among other things, "flatulence"—again, not the desired image for canned milk. Both of these examples were real mistakes made by major companies stemming from their reliance on their SRC in making a decision.

05   When marketers take the time to look beyond their own self-reference criteria, the results are more positive. A British manufacturer of chocolate biscuits (cookies, in American English), ignoring its SRC, knew that it must package its biscuits differently to accommodate the Japanese market. Thus, in Japan, McVitie's chocolate biscuits are wrapped individually, packed in presentation cardboard boxes, and priced about three times higher than in the United Kingdom—the cookies are used as gifts in Japan and thus must look and be perceived as special. Unilever, appreciating the uniqueness of its markets, repackaged and reformulated its detergent for Brazil. One reason was that the lack of washing machines among poorer Brazilians made a simpler soap formula necessary. Also, because many people wash their clothes in rivers, the powder was packaged in plastic rather than paper so it would not get soggy. Finally, because the Brazilian poor are price conscious and buy in small quantities, the soap was packaged in small, low-priced packages. Even McDonald's modifies its traditional Big Mac in India, where it is known as the Maharaja Mac—most Indians consider cows sacred and

don't eat beef. In each of these examples, had the marketers' own self-reference criteria been the basis for decisions, none of the necessary changes would have been readily apparent based on their home-market experience.

06   Be aware, also, that not every activity within a marketing program is different from one country to another; indeed, there probably are more similarities than differences. For example, the McVitie's chocolate biscuits mentioned earlier are sold in the United States in the same package as in the United Kingdom. Such similarities, however, may lull the marketer into a false sense of apparent sameness. This apparent sameness, coupled with the self-reference criterion, is often the cause of international marketing problems. Undetected similarities do not cause problems; however, the one difference that goes undetected can create a marketing failure.

07   To avoid making errors in business decisions, the knowledgeable marketer will conduct a cross-cultural analysis that isolates the SRC influences and maintain vigilance regarding ethnocentrism. The following steps are suggested as a framework for such an analysis:

1. Define the business problem or goal in home-country cultural traits, habits, or norms.
2. Define the business problem or goal in foreign-country cultural traits, habits, or norms through consultation with natives of the target country. Make no value judgments.
3. Isolate the SRC influence in the problem and examine it carefully to see how it complicates the problem.
4. Redefine the problem without the SRC influence and solve for the optimum business goal situation.

08 An American sales manager newly posted to Japan decided that his Japanese sales representatives did not need to come into the office every day for an early morning meeting before beginning calls to clients in Tokyo. After all, that was how things were done in the United States. However, the new policy, based on both the American SRC and a modicum of ethnocentrism, produced a precipitous decline in sales performance. In his subsequent discussions with his Japanese staff, he determined that Japanese sales representatives are motivated mostly by peer pressure. Fortunately, he was able to recognize that his SRC and his American "business acumen" did not apply in this case in Tokyo. A return to the proven system of daily meetings brought sales performance back to previous levels.

09   The cross-cultural analysis approach requires an understanding of the culture of the foreign market as well as one's own culture. Surprisingly, understanding one's own culture may require additional study, because much of the cultural influence on market behaviour remains at a subconscious level and is not clearly defined.

Source: P.R. Cateora, *International Marketing*, 15th edition (Toronto: McGraw-Hill Ryerson, 2011), pp. 16–18.

1. Complete the sentences.

   a) If a manager from South Korea applies the Korean cultural standards when marketing Korean cars in India, he uses his _____.

   b) If the manager is convinced that Korean cultural standards are better than Indian ones, he exhibits _____.

2. Put the stages in the cause-effect chain in the correct order.

   a) An incorrect decision is made.

   b) Juan accumulates the knowledge, values, and symbols of his own culture over a lifetime.

   c) Juan responds without considering the cultural differences between markets, and using his SRC.

   d) Juan faces making a decision associated with marketing a product in a foreign country.

3. Mistakes in marketing such products as Esso gasoline and Pet Milk in foreign countries derived from the fact that some English words

   a) cannot be translated successfully into foreign languages.

   b) resemble foreign words that have unusual meanings.

   c) sound inappropriate for the products they name.

   d) reflect American cultural traditions.

4. Match each cause with its effect.

Causes	Effects
a. Biscuits are often used as presents in Japan.	____ The powder is packed in plastic.
b. Biscuits are wrapped in individual packages and presented in beautiful boxes.	____ Biscuits are sold at an affordable price.
c. Chocolate biscuits are a staple food item in Britain.	____ The detergent comes in small packages.
d. The Brazilian poor wash their clothes in rivers.	____ They are wrapped in beautiful individual packages and put in expensive-looking boxes.
e. The Brazilian poor cannot afford to buy expensive detergents.	____ They are sold at a price three times higher than in Britain.
f. The Brazilian poor do not own washing machines.	____ The formula for the soap is simpler.

5. Which structure does paragraph 5 follow?

   a) Main idea first, followed by supporting details

   b) Introduction, followed by main idea and supporting details

   c) Main idea first, followed by supporting details, then main idea paraphrased

6. Reread paragraph 7, paying close attention to the steps to prevent ethnocentrism in marketing. Then read the following scenario and identify how the manager approaches each of the steps. You may choose to use different colours to highlight the steps in the scenario. Discuss in small groups.

The manager of an Ethiopian coffee manufacturing company plans to market Ethiopian coffee in France. She knows that in her native country, where the beverage originated, coffee is drunk with a pinch of salt. The manager hires a research firm in France to find out about the coffee consumer habits of the French. She learns that many French people like their coffee with milk (café au lait) and sugar. The manager realizes that to market Ethiopian coffee with a picture of a steaming cup of black coffee and a recipe that includes the suggestion to add salt will not work in France. The manager decides to use an attractive picture featuring a cup of Ethiopian coffee café au lait style for her advertising campaign.

7. What is the implied main idea of paragraph 8?

_____

8. According to paragraph 8, Japanese sales representatives are motivated primarily by peer pressure, a force that is not a primary motivator for American sales people. What do you think might be the primary motivating factor for those who work in sales in North America?

_____

Use context clues and your knowledge of word parts to determine the correct meaning of each word or phrase. Verify your answers using a dictionary if necessary.

1. anticipate (par. 1): _____

2. impedes (par. 2): _____

3. stemming from (par. 4): _____

4. precipitous (par. 8): _____

5. acumen (par. 8): _____

READING 3

Terror and Ethnocentrism: Foundations of American Support for the War on Terrorism

 Political Science

01 9/11—the "day of fire" as President Bush referred to it in his second inaugural address—transformed the world. The lethal attacks on the World Trade Center in New York and the Pentagon in Washington stunned the United States and set in motion a massive redirection in U.S. policy. Within the day, President Bush declared that the United States was at war. On the evening of the 11th, in a televised address to the nation from the White House, the President

asserted, "We will make no distinction between the terrorists who committed these acts and those who harbour them. . . . None of us will ever forget this day."[1]

02   Priorities and policies shifted overnight. The President approved the creation of a new cabinet agency dedicated to homeland security. The USA PATRIOT ACT, a hugely complicated proposal to enhance the government's ability to gather intelligence within the United States and to encourage the sharing of such information between intelligence and law enforcement communities, was thrown together. By the end of October, it was the law of the land, having passed both houses of Congress by large majorities.

03   In the meantime, plans for military retaliation were going forward. On October 7, the President authorized air strikes and Special Operations attacks on vital al Qaeda and Taliban targets. Ground attacks shortly followed. By the middle of November, the Taliban had fled Kabul, and by early December, all major Afghan cities had fallen to the U.S.-led coalition forces. In "Phase Two" of the war on terrorism, the Bush Administration turned its attention to the "gathering threat" posed to the United States by Saddam Hussein.

04   In short, 9/11 set in motion a fundamental reordering of U.S. priority and policy. Our intention here is to offer an account of the foundations of American support for the "war on terrorism." We are particularly interested in determining the part played by ethnocentrism. Such an interest may seem odd. Ethnocentrism— what Daniel Levinson once called "prejudice, broadly conceived" (1949, 19)—is all but invisible in modern political analysis, and it is especially hard to find in empirical studies of

American public opinion. True enough, but a mistake, we think. Ethnocentrism is a deep human habit, an altogether commonplace inclination to divide the world into ingroups and outgroups, the former characterized by virtuosity and talent, the latter by corruption and mediocrity. Support for the war on terrorism, undertaken against a strange and shadowy enemy, should come disproportionately, we propose, from Americans possessed of an ethnocentric turn of mind.

05   To see if this is so, we analyze national survey data supplied by the 2000–2002 National Election Study. The 2000–2002 NES Panel Study is well-designed for our purposes. Respondents comprising a representative national sample of Americans of voting age were interviewed before and immediately after the 2000 election, and then again before and after the 2002 mid-term elections. By analyzing the 2000–2002 panel, we can identify whether ethnocentrism, measured before 9/11, helps account for American attitudes toward the policies, events, and authorities that have dominated national politics since that fateful day.

Ethnocentrism

06   "Ethnocentrism" is a modern word, introduced at the opening of the twentieth century by William Graham Sumner. Sumner invented the concept of ethnocentrism to name what he took to be a universal condition regarding human groups and social norms: namely, that people are convinced that their way of doing things—their folkways—are superior to the way things are done elsewhere. From *Folkways*, we learn that the Greenland Eskimo believe that Europeans wandered onto their homeland to be taught the

---

[1] www.whitehouse.gov/news/releases/2001/09/20010911-16.html

good manners that they so conspicuously lacked; that the Mbayas of South America are instructed by divine authority to take their neighbours' wives and property; that the Chinese know that persons of distinction come only from their own grand and glorious middle Kingdom; and so on.

07   Our conception of ethnocentrism is especially indebted to the writings of Daniel Levinson. In Levinson's analysis and in ours, ethnocentrism is a certain mode of thinking—a perceptual lens through which individuals understand and evaluate the world around them. Some individuals rely on this particular lens more than others do. In the extreme case,

> . . . the distinction between ingroups (those groups with which the individual identifies himself) and outgroups (with which he does not have a sense of belonging and which are regarded as antithetical to the ingroups) is of paramount importance. Outgroups are the objects of negative opinions and hostile attitudes; ingroups are the objects of positive opinions and uncritically supportive attitudes; and outgroups are regarded as properly subordinate to ingroups. (Levinson 1949, 20)

08 Ethnocentrism is a general outlook on groups and group relations, one that partitions the social world into us and them, into friend and foe. Defined this way, ethnocentrism will likely have a part to play in the story of American support for the war on terrorism. To most Americans, the adversaries in this war are unfamiliar. They come from far away and exotic places. Their language, religion, customs, and sheer physical appearance: all of it is strange. And after 9/11, not just strange, but sinister. Americans who are generally predisposed towards ethnocentrism— who as a matter of habit see the world divided into virtuous ingroups and inferior outgroups— should be especially likely to lend their support to the new war on terrorism.

Measuring ethnocentrism

09 Stereotypes are the right cognitive "container" for ethnocentrism. To measure ethnocentrism, expressed in terms of stereotypes, we draw upon a set of questions that appeared on the NES. The questions begin as follows:

> Now I have some questions about different groups in our society. I'm going to show you a seven-point scale on which the characteristics of people in a group can be rated. In the first statement a score of 1 means that you think almost all of the people in that group are "hard-working." A score of 7 means that you think almost all of the people in the group are "lazy." A score of 4 means that you think the group is not towards one end or the other, and of course you may choose any number in between that comes closest to where you think people in the group stand.
>
>   Where would you rate whites in general on this scale?

10 After being asked to judge whites on this score, respondents were then asked to make the same judgment about blacks, Asian Americans, and Hispanic Americans, in randomized order. The procedure was then repeated for two additional dimensions: "intelligent versus unintelligent" and "trustworthy versus untrustworthy."

11   In principle, the scale[2] ranges from –1 to +1, where –1 means that individuals regard outgroups to be superior in every respect to their own group; +1 means that individuals regard outgroups to be inferior in every respect to their own group. In a society free of ethnocentrism, the scale should be distributed in a tight band around 0, signifying that individuals regard outgroups and their own group to be (on average) indistinguishable. In practice, this is not what we find. The distribution of the ethnocentrism scale is not centred at zero. Rather, it is displaced to the right, in the ethnocentric direction. In

---

[2] In a section of the article not reproduced here, the authors describe how they converted the data from the NES scale (ranging from 1 to 7) to their own scale of ethnocentrism (ranging from –1 to +1).

percentage terms, a small number of Americans end up to the left of the neutral point, and many land right on or close to it, but most Americans are to be found to the right of neutrality, in the region of ethnocentrism.

Results

12 We find that American support for the war on terror is indeed derived in a significant way from ethnocentrism. Americans who believe their own group to be superior to others are also inclined to say that we should be spending more on homeland security, on keeping our borders impregnable, and on building a strong national defence. They want foreign aid cut. They think President Bush has been effective in responding to the terrorist attacks and in managing relations with other nations, and they evaluate him warmly. The effect of ethnocentrism is statistically significant and substantively sizable in each of these cases.

13 If, as we suggest, the importance of ethnocentrism to politics depends on circumstance, then support for the war on terrorism in the aftermath of 9/11 should serve as an exemplary case for several reasons. First, the war on terror lends itself to ethnocentric thinking. Second, elite discourse on the war in the United States has been saturated with language and symbols that emphasize a conflict between civilization and fanaticism. To the major networks, it was "America" that was under attack and a "Nation" that was responding with heroism and resolve (Jamieson and Waldman 2002). "Either you are with us," the President said to the nations of the world, "or you are with the terrorists." And third, there is the strong suggestion from experimental psychology that when people face serious threat their thinking simplifies (e.g., Fiske 1998; Fiske, Morling, and Stevens 1996; Wilder 1993). Category-based reasoning is one kind of simplification, and ethnocentrism is a specific kind of category-based reasoning, in which the categories are constructed in terms of ingroups and outgroups. Because many Americans experienced 9/11 as threatening (e.g., Huddy et al. 2002; Smith, Rasinski, and Toce 2001), ethnocentrism, as a way to think about what was happening and what the government should do, may have been an especially easy path to follow.

14 For a variety of reasons, then, we expect that ethnocentrism should be more important in Americans' thinking about politics in the time immediately following 9/11 than in the period running up to 9/11. As predicted, the results show that the impact of ethnocentrism is greater in the fall of 2002 than it is in the fall of 2000—greater, that it is to say, after 9/11 than before.

Conclusions

15 The effects of ethnocentrism are sizable, and they hold up across a variety of tests and specifications. But is this really surprising? If ethnocentrism is a kind of generalized suspicion of strangers, then terrorism would seem to be an easy case. Consider, though, how we have measured ethnocentrism. It would be unsurprising and quite uninformative if Americans who thought *terrorists* especially dangerous were the first to line up behind the President's policies. That is not what we have shown. We have shown, instead, that Americans who are predisposed to denigrate the character and capacity of *their fellow Americans*—white, black, Hispanic, and Asian—are the ones most likely to lend their backing to the President and his policies. Support for the war on terrorism arises in an important way from prejudice, generally conceived.

Source: Excerpted from C.D. Kam & D.R. Kinder, "Terror and ethnocentrism: Foundations of American support for the war on terrorism." *The Journal of Politics* 69, no. 2 (May, 2007): 320–338.

1. What is the main idea of paragraphs 1–3?

   _____

2. What is new about the authors' approach to researching the American war on terrorism?

   a) They research American support for the war on terrorism.

   b) They prove that 9/11 fundamentally changed American domestic and foreign policies.

   c) They maintain that ethnocentrism is a dark and unexplored subject.

   d) They claim that ethnocentrism accounts for Americans' support for the war.

3. Study the sentence "Ethnocentrism is a deep human habit, an altogether commonplace inclination to divide the world into ingroups and outgroups, the former characterized by virtuosity and talent, the latter by corruption and mediocrity."

   A. What does *the former* refer to? _____

   B. What does *the latter* refer to? _____

4. Which tool did the researchers use to conduct their study?

   a) The 2000–2002 NES Panel Study

   b) The results of the national elections in 2000

   c) Daniel Levinson's work on ethnocentrism

5. Based on paragraphs 6–8, which characteristics accurately describe ethnocentrism? Circle all that apply.

   a) Ethnocentrism is common among all peoples.

   b) Ethnocentric teachings of one human group help to make other groups more civilized.

   c) Ethnocentrism influences the way we perceive the world.

   d) Some people are more prone to ethnocentric beliefs than others.

   e) Ethnocentrism makes one view one's own group with criticism.

   f) It is easier to see the other group as inferior if that group's culture is unfamiliar.

6. A. Which qualities were the respondents surveyed on in order to measure their ethnocentrism?

   _____

B. Which groups were the respondents asked to rate?

_____

C. What were the findings of the ethnocentrism survey?

a) The scale of responses was distributed tightly around zero.

b) Most Americans were found to the left of the neutral point on the answer scale.

c) More than 50 percent of Americans considered outgroups to be superior to their own ingroups.

d) The majority of Americans were ethnocentric.

7. Mark each statement as T (true) or F (false).

a) ____ The researchers concluded that ethnocentric Americans were more supportive of the war on terrorism than non-ethnocentric Americans.

b) ____ Ethnocentrism of the respondents was more pronounced in 2000 than in 2002.

8. What claims do the authors make about the American political elite? Circle all that apply.

a) Ethnocentric patterns of thinking were exploited to mobilize support for the war on terrorism.

b) The threat of terrorism was deliberately exaggerated.

c) The elite chose category-based language in their addresses to the people.

d) The patriotic language and symbols in the media were inappropriate for the time.

9. Mark each statement as F (fact) or O (opinion).

a) ____ In 2001, many Americans supported the war on terrorism.

b) ____ Americans' ethnocentrism accounts for their support of the war on terrorism.

c) ____ In his address to the world right after 9/11, President Bush divided the world into two mutually exclusive groups: those who support America in its struggle against terrorism, and those who support terrorism.

d) ____ President Bush used ethnocentric rhetoric to fuel a conflict between the West and its enemies.

10. What conclusion do the authors make at the end of their paper?

_____

_____

_____

Use context clues and your knowledge of word parts to determine the correct meaning of each word or phrase. Verify your answers using a dictionary if necessary.

1. lethal (par. 1): _____

2. inclination (par. 4):

    a) a feeling that makes you want to do something

    b) a tendency to do something

    c) a refusal to do something

3. mediocrity (par. 4):

    a) the quality of being average or not very good

    b) the quality of being gifted

    c) not taking sides in a conflict, staying neutral

4. indebted to (par. 7): _____

5. partitions (par. 8): _____

6. sinister (par. 8): _____

7. saturated with (par. 13):

    a) filled with

    b) connected to

    c) disassociated from

UNIT REFLECTION AND SYNTHESIS

1. Match each selection with its purpose.

a. "Prejudice"	____ To persuade the reader that higher-level decisions may be made based on ethnocentrism
b. "The Self-Reference Criterion"	____ To inform the reader of the influences of ethnocentrism on economic strategies
c. "Terror and Ethnocentrism"	____ To inform the reader of the ways in which prejudice works

2. This unit presents the concept of ethnocentrism from the perspectives of psychology, marketing, and political science. Find an example of ethnocentric thinking or behaviour in each of the texts you read.

	"PREJUDICE"	"THE SELF-REFERENCE CRITERION"	"TERROR AND ETHNOCENTRISM"
Ethnocentric behaviour or thinking			

3. As cited in "Terror and Ethnocentrism," ethnocentrism is "prejudice, broadly conceived" (Levinson 1949); that is, ethnocentrism is based on prejudice. In the first selection of this unit, the author distinguishes between subtle and overt prejudice.

   Look back at all three readings. Find one example of overt prejudice and one example of subtle prejudice. Discuss your answers in small groups. Do all members of your group agree on which examples are overt and which are subtle?

   Subtle prejudice: _____

   _____

   Overt prejudice: _____

   _____

4. The author of the first selection explains that dividing people into ingroups and outgroups has evolutionary roots: "whether hunting, defending, or attacking," people seek the support of the group and rely on solidarity in numbers. How does this idea relate to Americans' support of the war on terrorism described in the last selection of the unit? Discuss in small groups.

5. According to the first reading, stereotypical thinking is a natural way in which our minds tend to work because we are hardwired to categorize things or people into groups. Which of the following is an example of such categorical thinking?

   a) Appreciating the cultural differences between India and America and creating a unique burger for the Indian market

b) Realizing that the brand name *Esso* has negative connotations in some non-English-speaking nations

c) Dividing the world into the countries that take an anti-terrorist approach and those that support terrorism

d) Planning military attacks against both the Taliban and Saddam Hussein

6. A. According to paragraph 11 in the first reading, how does the tendency to stereotype influence our perception of people in other groups?

_____

B. Now, read the following question similar to those used by researchers in the NES questionnaire discussed in the third reading: "Where would you rate whites in general on the scale of laziness?" How does this question measure stereotypical thinking of the respondents? Explain.

_____

7. While two readings in this unit are written for students, one reading addresses a more highly educated audience of experts. Which reading is this? What factors helped you decide?

_____

8. What kind of support do the authors of "The Self-Reference Criterion" present for their argument? Is the support relevant? Is it effective? Explain.

Support: _____

Relevant? _____

Sufficient? _____

9. Which texts in this unit use research results to support an opinion? Fill in the table below with examples of this technique.

TEXT	OPINION	RESEARCH RESULTS

10. Do you think the authors of any of the three selections in this unit present a biased opinion? Explain your answer.

_____

_____

_____

11. Revisit the definition you wrote for *ethnocentrism* on page 201. How does it compare to the definitions provided in the readings? Discuss in a small group.

Your definition: _____

_____

From "The Self-Reference Criterion:" Ethnocentrism is "the notion that people in one's own company, culture, or country know best how to do things."

From Sumner, cited in "Terror and Ethnocentrism:" Ethnocentrism is "a universal condition regarding human groups and social norms: namely, that people are convinced that their way of doing things—their folkways—are superior to the way things are done elsewhere."

Cancer

GETTING INTO THE TOPIC

This unit presents three perspectives on the topic of cancer, one of the leading causes of death in the developed world today. The first selection explains the biology of cancer—the processes in the body that cause it, the treatment of it, and the ways to reduce one's chances of developing it. The second selection presents cancer from an engineer's point of view—as a mechanical problem— and describes an innovative mechanics-based treatment. The final text in this unit documents a survivor's perspective on life after cancer, touching on some of the psychological, social, and economic aspects of cancer survival.

Discuss these questions to help you get into the topic.

1. What happens in the body of a person who has cancer?

2. What treatments for cancer do you know? Can cancer be cured?

3. An oncologist is a doctor who specializes in treating cancer, but there are many other professionals involved in the research or treatment of cancer. How do you think a mechanical engineer might be involved in researching treatments for cancer?

4. Do you know anyone who has survived cancer? How does he or she cope with memories of the disease?

5. How might a cancer survivor's perspective on life be different from that of a person who has never had a potentially fatal disease?

READING 1

Cancer Cells: Growing Out of Control Biology

What is cancer?

01 Cancer, which currently claims the lives of one out of every five people in the United States and other industrialized nations, is a disease of the cell cycle. Cancer cells do not respond normally to the cell cycle control system;[1] they divide excessively and can invade other tissues of the body. If unchecked, cancer cells may continue to divide until they kill the host.

02 The abnormal behaviour of cancer cells begins when a single cell undergoes transformation, a process that converts a normal cell to a cancer cell. Because a transformed cell grows abnormally, the body's immune system generally recognizes and destroys it. However, if the cell evades destruction, it may proliferate to form a *tumour*, an abnormally growing mass of body cells. If the abnormal cells remain at the original site, the lump is called a *benign tumour*. Benign tumours can cause problems if they grow large and disrupt certain organs, such as the brain, but often they can be completely removed by surgery.

03 In contrast, a *malignant tumour* is one that has begun to spread into neighbouring tissues and other parts of the body (Figure 11.1), displacing normal tissue and interrupting organ function. An individual with a malignant tumour is said to have *cancer*. Cancer cells may separate from the original tumour or secrete signal molecules that cause blood vessels to grow toward the tumour. A few tumour cells may then enter the blood or lymph[2] vessels and move to other parts of the body, where they may proliferate and form new tumours. The spread of cancer cells beyond their original site is called *metastasis*. Cancers are named according to where they originate. Liver cancer, for example, always begins in liver tissue and may spread from there.

Cancer treatment

04 Once a tumour starts growing in the body, how can it be treated? The three main types of cancer treatment are sometimes referred to as "slash, burn, and poison." Surgery to remove a

---

[1] The cell cycle control system is operated by special proteins inside the cell that send "stop" and "go-ahead" signals to control its division process.

[2] a clear liquid containing white blood cells that helps to clean the tissues of the body and helps to prevent infections from spreading

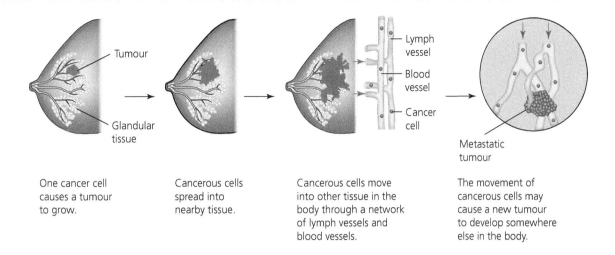

One cancer cell causes a tumour to grow.

Cancerous cells spread into nearby tissue.

Cancerous cells move into other tissue in the body through a network of lymph vessels and blood vessels.

The movement of cancerous cells may cause a new tumour to develop somewhere else in the body.

Figure 11.1 Growth and metastasis of a malignant tumour of the breast

tumour ("slash") is usually the first step. "Burn" and "poison" refer to treatments that attempt to stop cancer cells from dividing. In *radiation therapy* ("burn"), parts of the body that have cancerous tumours are exposed to concentrated beams of high-energy radiation, which can often harm cancer cells more than the normal cells of the body. However, there is sometimes enough damage to normal body cells to produce side effects such as nausea and hair loss.

05 *Chemotherapy* ("poison"), the use of drugs to disrupt cell division, is used to treat widespread or metastatic tumours. Chemotherapy drugs work in a variety of ways. Some prevent cell division by interfering with the mitotic spindle.[3] For example, paclitaxel (trade name Taxol) freezes the spindle after it forms, keeping it from functioning. Paclitaxel is made from a chemical discovered in the bark of the Pacific yew, a tree found mainly in the northwestern United States. It has fewer side effects than many other anticancer drugs and seems to be effective against some hard-to-treat cancers of the ovary and breast. Another drug, vinblastine, prevents the mitotic spindle from forming in the first place. Vinblastine was first obtained from the periwinkle plant, which is native to the tropical rain forests of Madagascar.

Cancer prevention and survival

06 Although cancer can strike anyone, there are certain lifestyle changes you can make to reduce your chances of developing cancer or increase your chances of surviving it. Not smoking, exercising adequately, avoiding overexposure to the sun, and eating a high-fibre, low-fat diet can all help to prevent cancer. Regular visits to the doctor can help identify tumours early, which is the best way to increase the chance of successful treatment.

Source: N. Campbell, J. Reece & E. Simon, *Essential Biology*, 5th edition (San Francisco: Pearson, 2013), pp. 128–129.

---

[3] a cell structure that guides the division of chromosomes (DNA-containing materials) in the cell

1. The danger of cancerous cells is that they
   a) contain special proteins that cause harm to the body.
   b) divide uncontrollably.
   c) are widespread among people in the West.
   d) are hard to detect.

2. The topic of paragraph 2 is
   a) benign tumours.
   b) surgeries as the best solution to tumours.
   c) malfunctioning of the immune system in cancer.
   d) how a tumour is formed.

3. What body part or system usually plays a crucial role in destroying an abnormal cell?
   a) The cell cycle control system
   b) The immune system
   c) Surgery
   d) Certain organs

4. Highlight the sentences in the text that define the two key terms *malignant tumour* and *benign tumour*. Then, in your own words, summarize the difference between benign and malignant tumours.

   _____

   _____

5. What plays a crucial role in allowing metastasis? Circle all that apply.
   a) Lymph and blood vessels
   b) The neighbouring tissues to those originally affected
   c) Signal molecules from the original cancerous cells
   d) Organs with disrupted function

6. How is the goal of the "slash" method of treating cancer different from those of "burn" and "poison"?

   _____

   _____

7. What is the main idea of paragraph 5?

   _____

8. What are some of the advantages of the drug paclitaxel?

   _____ and _____

9. Mark each statement as T (true) or F (false).

   a) ____ The drugs given as examples for chemotherapy in this text work on a cellular level.

   b) ____ A benign tumour is considered cancerous.

10. Which lifestyle change is not suggested in the reading as a way to prevent or reduce the chances of developing cancer?

    a) Wearing a T-shirt, loose pants, and a hat when spending a few hours on the beach

    b) Drinking alcohol in moderate amounts

    c) Biking and working out at the gym regularly

    d) Eating whole wheat bread instead of white bread

Vocabulary

A. Use context clues and your knowledge of word parts to determine the correct meaning of each word. Verify your answers using a dictionary if necessary.

1. abnormal (par. 2): _____

2. evades (par. 2): _____

3. displacing (par. 3): _____

4. secrete (par. 3): _____

5. proliferate (par. 3): _____

B. Based on the use of the word *metastasis* in the text, what do you think the word part *meta* means? Check your answer using a dictionary.

   a) cancer

   b) beyond

   c) original

   d) blood

READING 2

Infernal Mechanism

Mechanical Engineering

01 The healing arts are often held up as a field in which mechanical engineering has little purchase. Instead, we are told, medicine is a place where biology and chemistry hold the key insights. Sure, a bioengineer could fashion an artificial hip, but how could mechanical engineering hope to remedy the common cold, or cure cancer?

02 But, in truth, engineering mechanics and mechanical engineering have long been present in oncology and cancer research. The last decade has provided ample illustrations of the diversity and depth of the mechanics-to-cancer connection. Our own laboratories in Berkeley, Ohio State, and now in Houston have been active for many years in the field of mass transport inside nanopores and nanochannels,[1] and have pioneered the field of nanofluidics. Nanofluidics has a direct application to cancer therapy. For instance, these nanochannel systems can be embedded into capsules implanted in the body to release anticancer drugs with the time control that is necessary to attain maximum efficacy with greatly reduced or eliminated adverse side effects. This allows the release of drugs in accordance with a preprogrammed profile, or by external activation, or ultimately, in a self-regulated manner. Such a device can be thought of as a mechanically engineered "nanogland."[2]

03 In addition to the increased efficacy and diminished adverse side effects that accompany the release of drugs only when needed, and at the small local concentration required at the site of the implant (rather than flooding the body), these personalized nanoglands further afford the benefit of providing therapy away from the hospital setting. Such off-site treatment is particularly crucial for those in remote or under-served geographical areas, or in such extreme settings as military combat zones, humanitarian relief missions, and space travel.

04 But, in fact, an even deeper connection between mechanics and cancer has recently emerged. One of the fundamental concerns of mechanics since the discovery of simple machines is the transport of mass. If we use the word *mechanical* in this sense, rather than in a way typical in medicine or relating to mechanisms of biological action, then I can make a radical and potentially revolutionary statement: cancer is a disease of mass transport dysregulation. Simply put, cancer is a mechanical disease.

05 So, what makes a cancer a cancer? About ten years ago Dr. Douglas Hanahan and Dr. Robert

---

[1] *Nano* is a prefix meaning the size of one billionth (10^{-9}) of something; microscopic; very small.
[2] A gland is a bodily organ that produces a substance for the body to use. In this text, a *nanogland* refers to a microscopic implant designed to mimic the body's natural healing processes.

A. Weinberg identified six major hallmarks of cancer. The first hallmark is the very core of the traditional definition of cancer: "tissue invasion and metastasis." Both of these are *mechanical* aspects of the disease, as they relate to the motion and transport of organized mass units, the biological cells that make up the cancer. The second hallmark is the process of angiogenesis, or the generation of new blood vessels. The growth of cities requires expanded systems for the supply of water, food, utilities, and waste disposal; the same is true for cancers. The vasculature[3] is the key piece of the expanded system of biological facilities and services. Thus, without angiogenesis, there cannot be cancer growth. In turn, without the profound change of the dynamics of mass transport at the tissue level generated by angiogenesis, cancer would be largely a localized disease, and therefore, generally curable.

06   The remaining hallmarks of cancer all depend on the ways signals are transported in biology, within cells, and between cells. We tend to think of signals as going in a specific direction, from one point to another, since that's how most human communication works. But biological signals are most often carried by molecules that are released in the environment, inside or outside of the originating cell, or shed in the blood stream.

07   These signals "know" when they get to their intended location since they have molecular components that dock with high lock-and-key specificity to their target molecular counterparts. This docking in itself is the message transmission, and may encode a request to enhance cell proliferation or some other activity. In the biological view, the over- or under-transmission of these molecular signals has historically been linked to hyper- or hypo-production of the messenger molecules through over- or under-expression of the respective genes.

08   Given that molecular signalling is really a mass transport phenomenon, the *mechanical*, diverging view is that perhaps it is not the number of letters that counts, but rather what happened to the metaphorical postman on the

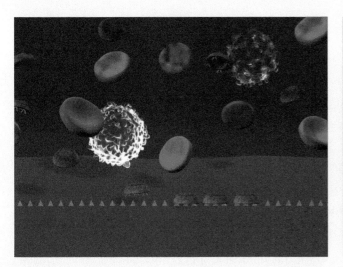

Multi-Stage Vectors (MSVs), the new drug carriers, are intended to attach to the blood vessel walls in a tumour.

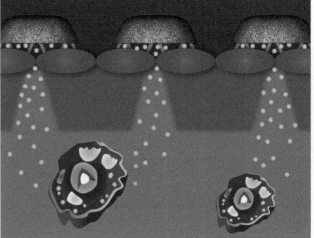

Nanoparticles released by the MSVs then seek out cancerous cells and inject them with material designed to kill that particular cancer.

---

[3] the system or arrangement of blood vessels in the body (from *vascular*, made up of, or containing blood vessels)

way to the cellular or subcellular mailbox. The actual determinants of mass transport in the body are the so-called biological barriers, including the walls of the blood vessels, the filtering organs of the body, the membranes that envelop cells and subcellular organelles. These biological barriers change essentially in the process of development of cancer. In other words, cancer is emerging as a disease of mass transport dysregulation, from the molecular to the cellular, to the tissue, organ, and organism levels.

09 A new field is now emerging, termed "transport oncophysics," that focuses on understanding the mass transport properties of all biological barriers in neoplastic pathologies.[4] Biological barriers are many, and they are sequential in nature. Any drug—nano or conventional—that is injected in the general circulation of a cancer patient must overcome all barriers to be able to discharge its therapeutic effect on the target cancer. To overcome all of the biological barriers, we have introduced a system of nanoparticles, designed to address the barriers in sequence. Called "Multi-Stage Vectors," or MSVs, they consist of particles that are released consecutively. The first stage is designed to localize on the target blood vessel walls; once there, the carriers release the second-and-later stages of a drug (see pictures on previous page).

Source: Adapted from M. Ferrari, "Infernal mechanism." *Mechanical Engineering* 132, no. 3 (March, 2010): 24–28.

---

[4] the study of diseases that involve tumours (from *neoplasm*, an abnormal growth of tissue in some part of the body, especially a tumour; and *pathology*, the scientific study of diseases)

Comprehension and Skills Practice

1. Why does the author mention an artificial hip in paragraph 1?

   a) To prove that mechanical engineers have always worked to solve medical problems

   b) As an example of mechanical engineers' contribution to cancer research

   c) To show a common opinion that mechanical engineering has a limited role in solving medical problems

   d) To make a point that mechanical engineering is as important as biology and chemistry

2. Mark the statement as T (true) or F (false).

   ____ According to the author, mechanical engineering does not have a place in the field of medicine.

3. What is NOT an advantage of anticancer drugs based on nanofluidics?

   a) The release of a drug in a time-controlled and precise manner

   b) The reduction of side effects

c) The potential availability of this treatment in remote and extreme areas

d) The ability of a patient to choose his or her own treatment

4. Knowing that mechanics relates to movement, which of the following are reasons that the author considers cancer a mechanical disease? Circle all that apply.

   a) The growth of blood vessels

   b) The transport of cells

   c) The transmission of molecular signals

   d) The development of water, food, utilities, and waste disposal systems

5. In paragraph 5, find an example of the author defining a key term. Underline the definition in the text, and then explain it in your own words.

   _____

   _____

6. What is the traditional biological view of cellular signal communication? Communication between cells occurs through

   a) the lock-and-key docking of molecules.

   b) cell replication.

   c) nanochannels used by MSVs.

   d) biological barriers, such as blood vessels or cell membranes.

7. What is special about the proposed Multi-Stage Vectors?

   a) They go against the principles of oncophysics.

   b) They will cure cancer.

   c) They are administered directly into a patient's blood.

   d) They tackle biological barriers consecutively.

8. What is the organizational pattern of paragraph 9?

   a) Cause-effect

   b) Classification

   c) Problem-solution

   d) Comparison

9. The author of "Infernal Mechanism" makes an argument for understanding and treating cancer in a non-traditional way.

   A. Which techniques does he use to make his argument? Circle all that apply.

   a) Quoting experts in the field of medicine

   b) Presenting research results

c) Recognizing a point of view different from his own

d) Sharing a personal story

e) Employing logical reasoning

f) Using clear and powerful analogies

B. Is the support for the argument relevant and sufficient? Explain.

Vocabulary

Use context clues and your knowledge of word parts to determine the correct meaning of each word or phrase. Verify your answers using a dictionary if necessary.

1. has little purchase (par. 1): _____

2. adverse (par. 2): _____

3. dysregulation (par. 4): _____

4. hallmark (par. 5): _____

5. shed (par. 6): _____

6. hyper-production (par. 7): _____

7. discharge (par. 9): _____

READING 3

What Happens When You Live?

 Health Studies

01 I am lying on a polished steel table, naked but for a thin cotton gown. Stripped of my clothes, my jewellery, my wallet, my photographs of loved ones, I watch masked people in blue gowns circle around, uncoiling tubing, pouring amber-coloured liquids into an IV, taking steel instruments out of drawers and cabinets, stuffing my hair into a paper cap. My former life already seems like a distant dream, as if I were remembering someone else's life. I have shrunk to a sentence on a medical form: "41-year-old woman with breast cancer." For the rest of my life, I will be a statistic in a tumour registry.

02 That was 15 years ago. I have survived breast cancer, a poor prognosis, chemotherapy, radiation, myriad alternative treatments, two

recurrences, and a mastectomy. My life is fairly normal . . . if you don't look closely.

03   There are more than 10 million cancer survivors in the United States today, up from a mere 3 million in 1971. With improved chemotherapy, the advent of targeted treatments, and better screening and detection methods, for many, cancer is now less a death threat than it is a chronic condition. But even after leaving the world of wigs and gamma rays and bad biopsies, we don't just live happily ever after. Oddly, many of us feel safe as long as we're getting hooked up to the IVs full of Kool-Aid-coloured chemicals, but the day our treatment ends and our hair starts to grow back, we feel as if we're being tossed to the sharks. *Now what?* we wonder. *What am I supposed to do now?*

04   Until recently, experts were still shrugging their shoulders. As the ranks of survivors swelled, the information that could improve our lives lagged behind. For decades, the medical world (understandably) focused its heavy artillery on killing cancer cells and saving lives. Only recently has a new front emerged—survivorship, the rigorous study of what happens when cancer patients live.

05   There are dozens of unknowns: Which chemotherapy treatments cause secondary cancers 20 years later? Which patients are at greatest risk of developing heart problems as a result of treatment? How many cancer survivors reach their career goals? How do people disfigured by surgery handle dating in a world obsessed with beauty and physical perfection? Until recently, the post-treatment life of a survivor was like the blank part of a medieval map labelled *Here be dragons*.[1]

06   I was hungry for information. There was a time, two or three years post-diagnosis, when all I read were books about mountain climbing—about mountain climbing disasters, to be precise. (To meet my standards, someone had to fall into a crevasse or nearly perish from hypothermia.) After accumulating an impressive armchair knowledge[2] of the use of carabiners and crampons on icy precipices, I moved on to memoirs by people who had been shipwrecked, lost en route to either pole, marooned on an island, or stranded by airplane crashes. Several years passed before it hit me that there was a connection between these survival stories and my own near brush with death: I wanted to find out what happened to people who had peered into the abyss, what they saw, and how they managed afterward.

07   Cancer is another country—especially if you're young. Doug Ulman, then a 19-year-old college student in Rhode Island, was recovering from a rare cartilage cancer that required the removal of part of his rib cage while his college dormmates were attending keg parties and dealing with midterms. "I felt about 80 years old. I had this premature maturity."

08   And if you're dating? Should you mention biopsies on the third date—or the fifth? Withhold information about your partial mastectomy when you describe yourself on Match.com? "Because I've written about having cancer, it's right there on Google," says Denise, a breast cancer survivor. "That became an issue when I started cyberdating. Once, a reporter for a major newspaper wrote me online, and for two weeks, we had a good time talking on the phone every night. When we made a date, I told him my full name. 'Good! I can look you up,' he teased. He sure did. When I got to the restaurant, there was one tall, thin, annoyed-looking guy standing outside." All flirtation was gone. Throughout dinner, her date was brusque, "acting as if he were being ripped off." He frowned while glancing repeatedly at her breasts,

---

[1] *Here be dragons* was a label denoting unknown and dangerous territory.
[2] Knowledge acquired through books or television, rather than experience, is known as armchair knowledge.

signed the cheque before they could order dessert, and fled as if from a plague-infested city. (The upside: Cancer weeds out the jerks. Like many survivors, this woman has gone on to a full, happy romantic life. As one survivor put it, "We have more to offer. Our hearts are bigger.")

09   Sigmund Freud observed that love and work are the two poles of existence, and both suffer after cancer. Younger breast cancer survivors, according to a 2002 survey by Patricia A. Ganz from UCLA, took significant hits in the "job or career" department—and no wonder. The current health care system traps many survivors or their spouses in a form of *de facto* indentured servitude, like my friend in Minneapolis who continues in a sales job she loathes, six years after a stem cell transplant: "I can't quit," she says, "I'm uninsurable."

10   "We find this all the time," says Ulman, now the director of survivorship at the Lance Armstrong Foundation, "especially with survivors between 20 and 40. The average college graduate changes jobs five or six times in his or her career—it's part of moving ahead. But cancer survivors and their partners may feel they can't take the risk." Many turn down promotions because they may need to take time off or because it is too disruptive to move away from their medical network.

11   How can an already overburdened health care system manage to sort out survivors' bank accounts, love lives, and depression, in addition to their persistent medical complaints? The experts I talked to were optimistic. "Some very smart people," David H. Johnson, MD, tells me, "are studying the issues we're talking about, and things will start to change in as little as two to five years, possibly sooner." For starters, predicts Julia H. Rowland, PhD: "you'll leave your active treatment phase with a standardized summary stating your illness, all the medications you got, the radiation you received and at which sites, and a prescription for follow-up care and surveillance." Passport for Care, being developed at the Texas Children's Cancer Center of Baylor College of Medicine, is one prototype. This secure, online, interactive resource will provide long-term pediatric cancer survivors with immediate access to abstracts of their medical histories and physician recommendations for maintaining health. The database will be up and running in two to three years; ultimately, it will be adapted for adult survivors.

12   No longer marginalized and isolated, survivors can visit websites for help, including updated information, live chats with experts, peer-to-peer support, and links to resources for depression, post-traumatic stress, and other problems. The National Coalition for Cancer Survivorship offers a website (www.canceradvocacy.org) with a "survival toolbox" and expert legal advice on insurance and employment rights.

13   We are hypersensitive to "anniversaries." Orange daylilies were blooming in lush clumps on the roadsides when I was diagnosed. Fifteen years later, it's July again, and I am barely noticing the daylilies because so many to-do lists are scrolling through my head. Until halfway through writing this article—I end up in the emergency room with blinding pelvic-abdominal pain. Lying inside the big clicking CT doughnut as eerie mechanical voices instruct me to hold my breath and let it out again, I think, *Here we go again. I had forgotten how it was.* I find out I have nothing worse than a urinary tract infection; my tests are fine, and so am I. Now the daylilies, the Queen Anne's lace,[3] the fat robins, the lush woods of summer, are fully alive for me. That is why cancer survivors are the twice-born, to borrow a word from William James.[4]

---

[3] a plant with fern-like leaves and lacy clusters of small white flowers
[4] William James (1842–1910) was an American psychologist and philosopher.

14   "I hear all the time from my patients that they look on each day as a gift," Dr. Johnson, a cancer survivor himself, tells me. "Shortly after I recovered, I was talking to an oncologist friend and I said, 'I just feel renewed.' And he said, 'You'll get over that.' But I haven't. After 15 years I still have that sense of renewal."

Source: Adapted from J. Hooper, "What happens when you live?" *Prevention* 57, no. 11 (November, 2010): 158–198.

Comprehension and Skills Practice

1. A. What event does the narrator describe in paragraph 1?

   _____

   B. What emotions do you think the narrator is experiencing while she is lying on a steel table?

   _____

2. What is the main idea of paragraph 3?

   a) More people survive cancer today than in the past.

   b) Modern medicine has made tremendous progress in detecting and treating cancer.

   c) In spite of beating the disease, many cancer survivors feel lost.

   d) Painful experiences, like wearing a wig and having biopsies, traumatize cancer survivors.

3. Which aspect of survivorship is NOT mentioned in paragraph 5?

   a) The after-effects of medical treatments

   b) Personal lives

   c) Career possibilities

   d) The role of preventive measures

4. Underline the main idea sentence of paragraph 6.

5. We can infer that "carabiners and crampons" (par. 6) are probably

   a) devices used by mountain climbers.

   b) anti-cancer drugs.

   c) kinds of memoirs.

   d) tools used by sailors.

6. Why do you think Denise's date looked annoyed (par. 8)?

_____

_____

7. How might a history of cancer get in the way of survivors' career development? Circle all that apply.

    a) Survivors may be hesitant to relocate for another job because they will have to leave their local doctors and hospital.

    b) Survivors typically feel physically weak and not energetic enough for a new career.

    c) New employers may not give medical insurance to cancer survivors.

    d) Survivors are not sure they will be able to get a medical leave, if necessary, in a new position.

8. What techniques of persuasion does the author use to convince the reader that the work aspect of a survivor's life suffers after cancer (pars. 9–10)? Circle all that apply.

    a) Quoting experts

    b) Presenting research or survey results

    c) Recognizing a point of view different from her own (counter-argument)

    d) Sharing a personal story

    e) Using an emotional tone

9. The author cites two experts, David H. Johnson, MD, and Julia H. Rowland, PhD, in paragraph 11 to provide supporting details to the main idea. What is the implied main idea in this paragraph?

_____

_____

10. What two kinds of help for survivors are discussed in paragraphs 11 and 12?

    _____ and _____

11. Mark the statement as T (true) or F (false).

    _____ Many cancer survivors have a profound appreciation for the gift of life.

12. The author of "What Happens When You Live?" expresses an opinion that life after cancer is not easy. She offers several kinds of evidence to make this opinion informed. Fill in one example for each category below.

Personal experience	*Obsessively reading about life-threatening accidents to help understand survivorship*
Experiences of other survivors	
Survey results	

13. The narrator uses several images associated with geographical spaces and geography to describe her experiences of surviving cancer. One is listed for you. Find two more images.

   a) "*... the post-treatment life of a survivor was like the blank part of a medieval map labelled 'Here be dragons.'*" (par. 5)

   b) _____

   _____

   c) _____

   _____

Vocabulary

Use context clues and your knowledge of word parts to determine the correct meaning of each word. Verify your answers using a dictionary if necessary.

1. prognosis (par. 2): _____

2. recurrence (par. 2): _____

3. disfigured (par. 5): _____

4. perish (par. 6): _____

5. prototype (par. 11): _____

6. marginalized (par. 12): _____

7. eerie (par. 13): _____

UNIT REFLECTION AND SYNTHESIS

1. The first two selections you read present different perspectives on cancer. Answer the questions in the chart below to show similarities and/ or differences between the selections. You will need to summarize the information. Some relevant paragraph numbers are indicated to help you locate the relevant information.

	"CANCER CELLS: GROWING OUT OF CONTROL"	"INFERNAL MECHANISM"
What is cancer?	(Par. 1)	(Par. 4)
How does metastasis occur?	(Par. 3)	(Par. 5)
What treatments are mentioned?		
What negative side effects, if any, do these treatments have?		
What are the advantages, if any, of the suggested treatments?		

2. Match each selection with its main thesis statement.

a. "Cancer Cells: Growing Out of Control"

b. "Infernal Mechanism"

c. "What Happens When You Live?"

____ Life after cancer is full of struggle and hope.

____ Investigating the paths of cancer cells gives hope for curing the disease.

____ There are various treatments and prevention methods for cancer—a disease of proliferating abnormal cells.

3. The author of "Cancer Cells: Growing out of Control" refers to cancer treatments as "slash, burn, and poison." Which of these treatments did the author of "What Happens When You Live?" undergo?

_____

4. Give an example of one fact and one opinion from the selections in this unit. Which is harder to find—a fact or an opinion? Why?

_____

_____

_____

_____

5. How is the purpose of "Cancer Cells: Growing out of Control" different from the purpose of "What Happens When You Live?"

_____

_____

6. A. In "Infernal Mechanism" and "What Happens When You Live" the authors use the first-person pronoun *I*. How may this affect the credibility of their texts?

_____

_____

B. Why do you think the author of "Cancer Cells: Growing out of Control" does not use *I*?

_____

_____

7. A. Who is the audience for each of the three readings?
   a) "Cancer Cells: Growing Out of Control": _____
   b) "Infernal Mechanism": _____
   c) "What Happens When You Live?": _____
   B. Explain what textual features helped you to decide.

_____

12

Gender Equality

Gender equality is generally considered to be desirable in Western society; however, although women in the Western world have many opportunities that their counterparts in other nations do not, they still face professional barriers to equality as discussed in "Gender Bias in International Business." Beyond the Western world—especially in many developing nations—gender bias tends to be more severe. In "The Global Glass Ceiling," a foreign relations specialist advises how and why multinational companies can empower women in developing countries. And in the final reading, "Born to Serve," a sociologist stresses the dire situation of elderly women and widows in India, and describes the systematic discrimination against this particular demographic.

GETTING INTO THE TOPIC

1. Are men and women treated equally in your home country? Explain.

2. Almost half of all North American workers are women; however, the number of women hired for international assignments for multinational corporations is relatively small—roughly 18 percent. Why might this be the case?

3. Are you familiar with the term *glass ceiling*? Study the cartoon. What stops the woman from reaching the sixth floor of the building? What does the cartoonist imply about the possibility of women being appointed to high-level corporate positions?

4. How can big international companies affect the lives of women in developing countries? Mark any methods companies can use to make a positive change. Do you think that any of these strategies could help to improve a corporation's bottom line, that is, the amount of money they make?

____ Employing women

____ Buying goods from local female farmers

____ Creating pro-women advertising

____ Providing career training for women

____ Teaching women to read and write

____ Giving financial grants to female entrepreneurs

5. What do you know about the status of women in developing countries, including those in Southeast Asia and the Middle East?

READING 1

Women in International Marketing 📖 Marketing

01 Gender dynamics are now taking on a new character that has long-term implications for the workplace: in a reversal of historical patterns, in most of the industrialized countries women are now in the majority on college and university campuses. Yet the gender bias against female managers that exists in some countries, coupled with myths harboured by male managers, makes many multinational companies hesitant to offer women international assignments. Although women constitute nearly half of the North American workforce, they represent relatively small percentages of the employees who are chosen for such work—barely in the neighbourhood of 18 percent. Why? The most often cited reason, that for some innate reason women have lower success rates abroad than men, is fiction. Unfortunately, such attitudes

are shared by many and probably stem from the belief that the traditional roles of women in male-dominated societies preclude them from establishing successful relationships with host-country associates. The second reason, similar to the one put forth in domestic situations, is that child-bearing and maternal responsibilities prevent women from taking, or staying in, positions that require long-term involvement and/or involve hardship situations in dangerous environments. A third issue is the often-asked question of whether it is appropriate to send women to conduct business with foreign customers in cultures where females are typically not in managerial positions. To some it appears logical that if women are not accepted in managerial roles within their own cultures, a foreign woman will not be any more acceptable.

General attitudes toward women

02 It is true that in many cultures—mostly Asian, Middle Eastern, African, and Latin American—women are not typically found in upper levels of management, and men and women are treated very differently. Indeed, a newspaper headline was scary: "Asia, Vanishing Point for as Many as 100 Million Women." The article, appearing in the *International Herald Tribune* in 1991, pointed out that the birthrate in most countries around the world is about 105 boys for every 100 girls. However, in countries like Canada or Japan, where women generally outlive men, there are about 96 men per 100 women in the population. The current numbers of men per 100 women in other Asian countries are: Korea 102, China 103, India 109, and Pakistan 106. The article describes systematic discrimination against females from birth. [. . .] Even though it is now illegal, ultra-sound units are still being used for making gender-specific abortion decisions, and all this prejudice against females is creating disruptive shortages of women.

Women in management around the world

03 If one were blind to prevailing social conditions and how strong resistance to change can be, one would expect male and female labour market participation rates and compensation levels to be nearly identical, given the successes of the feminist movement, plus the fact that female enrolment in post-secondary educational institutions has increased in every developed country over the past two decades. But this is not the case, as suggested by a number of international organizations that track the evolution of the role of women in business. One of them is the International Labour Organization (ILO), which published what is probably the most comprehensive and recent report that reviews relevant trends in various countries. The report was initially released in 2001 and updated in 2004, and is titled "Breaking Through the Glass Ceiling."

04   The report's conclusion on whether its title actually reflects current reality is relatively pessimistic. It claims women face lower employment participation rates, higher unemployment rates, and significantly lower pay levels compared to men. In general, countries in North America, South America, and Eastern Europe have a higher share of females employed in managerial positions than countries in East Asia, South Asia, and the Middle East. Women's share of legislator, senior official, and manager positions range from a low of 5 percent in South Korea to a high of almost 45 percent in the US. As shown in Figure 12.1, women are clearly underrepresented in managerial positions. Notice that the difference between the management versus total labour force shares is narrower in the more advanced countries and almost nonexistent in the US, whereas in South Korea there is an eight-fold difference between the two measures.

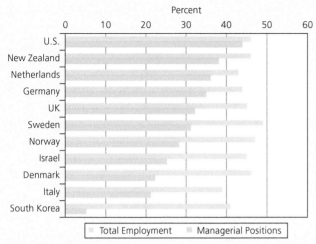

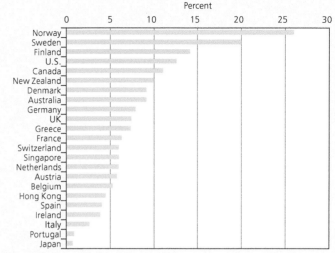

*"Managerial positions" are defined by the ILO as comprising legislator, senior official and manager positions.

Source: *Breaking Through the Glass Ceiling: Women in Management* (Update 2004, data for 2002), International Labour Organization, Geneva, Switzerland. Copyright © 2004 International Labour Organization.

Figure 12.1 Participation in the labour force and in management positions

Source: Stephanie Maier, "Research briefing: How global is good corporate governance?" Ethical Investment Research Service, August 2005 Page 12. Found at: http://www.eiris.org/files/research%20publications/howglobalisgoodcorpgov05.pdf. Data for Autumn 2004.

Figure 12.2 Women on corporate boards of directors

The ratio of female managerial positions to total employment is an important indicator of gender employment equity, but it tells us little about female participation at strategic management levels. Based on the same ILO report and other sources, it appears that gender inequity was rampant at the higher levels of the corporate world, at least until the middle of the decade. Figure 12.2 shows female participation on corporate boards in selected countries, based on data from 2004 that are comparable to the ILO time frame and were reported by the Ethical Investment Research Service (EIRS) in 2005.

05   Why does this state of affairs persist? Are men and women sufficiently different in terms of managerial capabilities that the labour market discounts female relative to male skills and efforts? According to the ILO, the answer is no, not by a long shot, and we emphatically share this view. There is no such thing as male superiority over females in performing managerial duties. On the contrary, the research suggests that each gender may have a different style of doing business, each being more effective in some situations than others. On the broader issue of the wage gap,

most labour market analysts point out that it is a product of cultural and social attitudes about the role of women. Females tend to dominate positions in health care, education, and other "feminine" occupations which generally pay less money. Also, within all occupations, whether "feminine" or "non-feminine," women tend to occupy lower job categories than men. The combination of these two factors, plus the fact that female managers have limited access to mentoring, are more commonly excluded from informal networks, and confront sexual harassment more frequently than men, results in a wage level substantially below that of men.

Women in international marketing assignments

06 Regardless of the situation that may prevail in any particular country, such external conditions should not be determining factors in whether or not a Canadian company should hire a woman for an international assignment. As world markets become more global and international competition intensifies, companies need to be represented by the most capable personnel available, from entry level to CEO. Research shows that global companies are requiring international experience for top executive positions. Executives who have had international experience are more likely to get promoted and have higher rewards, and, as with any other position, it is the organization's job to ensure that its best talent, whether male or female, partakes in such advancement; it is short-sighted business-wise, not to mention ethically unacceptable, to limit the talent pool simply because of gender. There is no reason to believe that women and men will produce different results abroad, with the possible exception of a small handful of very unique countries.

07 A key to success for either men or women often hinges on the strength of a firm's backing. When a woman manager receives training and the strong backing of her firm, she usually receives the respect commensurate with the position she holds and the firm she represents. For success, a woman needs a title that confers credibility in the culture in which she is working, and a support structure and reporting relationship that will help her get the job done. As Nancy Adler, the world-renowned organizational behaviourist of McGill University, noted more than 20 years ago, the fact that the international executive is a foreigner (*gaijin* in Japanese) matters more than gender. In short, with the power of the corporate organization behind her, resistance to her as a woman either does not materialize or is less troublesome than anticipated. Once marketing interactions begin, the willingness of a host to engage in business transactions and the respect shown to a foreign businessperson grow or diminish depending on the business skills he or she demonstrates, regardless of gender.

Source: P.R. Cateora, N. Papadopoulos, M.C. Gilly & J.L. Graham, *International Marketing*, 3rd Canadian edition (Toronto: McGraw-Hill, 2011), pp. 506–511.

Comprehension and Skills Practice

1. In paragraph 1, the authors refer to the change in historical patterns of gender dynamics. What was one of the old patterns?

   _____

2. Why did the authors include national ratios of women-to-men in paragraph 2?

   _____

   _____

3. Why would one "expect male and female labour market participation rates to be nearly identical" (par. 3)? Circle all that apply.

   a) Social conditions today promote gender equality.

   b) There has been increased recognition of women's rights within society in recent decades.

   c) Most people's ideas about gender equality have changed in favour of women.

   d) More and more women are university educated in developed countries.

4. The title of the ILO report referenced in paragraph 3 has a positive connotation for business women: "Breaking Through the Glass Ceiling." According to the text, are the report's findings compatible with this title? Give evidence from paragraph 4 to support your answer.

   _____

   _____

5. Study Figure 12.1, "Participation in the labour force and in management positions." Then look at the graph below, which shows women's participation in the labour force and in management positions in four hypothetical countries. Based on the information in the reading, in which country do you think the authors would consider the treatment of women most fair?

   a) Country A   c) Country C

   b) Country B   d) Country D

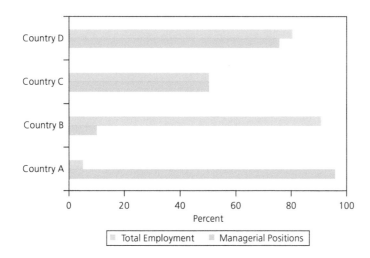

6. Study Figure 12.2. In which country is the presence of women on corporate boards of directors the highest? _____

   In which country is it the lowest? _____

7. Mark each statement as T (true) or F (false).

   a) ____ Women and men have equal managerial capabilities; therefore, there is no distinction between a female and male style of management.

   b) ____ The authors use quotation marks in the phrase *"feminine" occupations* (par. 5) when referring to certain occupations that have traditionally been performed by women. By using quotation marks, the authors are demonstrating that they do not agree with these gendered distinctions.

   c) ____ Most women occupy lower positions within a given industry than men.

8. What are two reasons why gender should not be a factor when determining a person's suitability for an international position (par. 6)?

   a) _____

   b) _____

9. Based on the information in Figure 12.2 and paragraphs 6 and 7, make an inference about the authors' opinions.

   A. Would it be a good business decision to send a capable woman to lead a Canadian business delegation to Japan? _____

   B. If no, why not? If yes, what should be done to make her assignment successful?

   _____

   _____

   _____

10. In paragraph 1, the authors list three explanations why relatively few female employees are chosen for international assignments. List each explanation, and then decide whether the authors consider it a valid reason for excluding women from international assignments. Provide clues from the text to support your assessment of the authors' opinion.

WHY FEW WOMEN ARE SENT ON INTERNATIONAL ASSIGNMENTS	DO THE AUTHORS AGREE, DISAGREE, OR OFFER NO OPINION?	TEXT CLUES
1.		
2.		
3.		

Vocabulary

Use context clues and your knowledge of word parts to determine the correct meaning of each word or phrase. Verify your answers using a dictionary if necessary.

1. preclude (par. 1): _____

2. rampant (textbox):

    a) widespread

    b) unnoticeable

    c) fictitious

3. emphatically (par. 5):

    a) partially

    b) to a lesser degree

    c) strongly

4. short-sighted (par. 6):

    a) not thinking carefully about the possible effects of something or what might happen in the future

    b) able to see things clearly only if they are very close to you

    c) meeting reasonable or necessary standards in the short term

5. pool (par. 6): _____

6. hinges on (par. 7): _____

7. commensurate with (par. 7):

    a) disproportionate to

    b) much higher than

    c) matching the importance of

READING 2

The Global Glass Ceiling: Why Empowering Women is Good for Business

 Foreign Policy

01 Over the last several decades, it has become accepted wisdom that improving the status of women is one of the most critical levers of international development. When women are educated and can earn and control income, a number of good results follow: infant mortality declines, child health and nutrition improve, agricultural productivity rises, population growth slows, economies expand, and cycles of poverty are broken.

02 But the challenges remain dauntingly large. In the Middle East, South Asia, and sub-Saharan Africa, in particular, large and persistent gender gaps in access to education, health care, technology, and income—plus a lack of basic rights and pervasive violence against women— keep women from being fully productive members of society. Entrenched gender discrimination remains a defining characteristic of life for the majority of the world's bottom two

> Governments and international organizations recognize that empowering women in the developing world is a catalyst for achieving a range of policy and development goals. It is time for multinational corporations to come to the same realization—funding education and training female business leaders is good for business.

billion people, helping sustain the gulf[1] between the most destitute and everyone else who shares this planet.

---

[1] a large difference between two groups in the way that they live

03   Narrowing that gulf demands more than the interest of the foreign aid and human rights communities, which, to date, have carried out the heavy lifting of women's empowerment in developing countries, funding projects such as schools for girls and microfinance for female entrepreneurs. It requires the involvement of the world's largest companies. Not only does the global private sector have vastly more money than governments and nongovernmental organizations, but it can wield significant leverage with its powerful brands and by extending promises of investment and employment. Some companies already promote initiatives focused on women as part of their corporate social-responsibility programs—in other words, to burnish[2] their images as good corporate citizens. But the truly transformative shift—both for global corporations and for women worldwide—will occur when companies understand that empowering women in developing economies affects their bottom lines.

The case of GE in India

04 In 2006, General Electric was facing a growing disaster. Its ultrasound technology had spread to India, and Indian human rights groups and gender activists began to accuse the company of being complicit in female feticide.[3] This was a burgeoning public relations nightmare that also threatened GE's profitable Indian ultrasound business.

05   In India, as in many other countries in South and East Asia, the heavy burden of dowry[4] payments and/or patriarchal traditions make parents prefer male children to female ones. The spread of GE's portable sonogram machines to clinics across rural India brought low-cost fetal sex screening to millions—which meant that parents could now easily abort unwanted girls. Although in 1994 the Indian government passed a law prohibiting sex-selective abortion, the problem persists. In some parts of the country, as many as 140 boys are born for every 100 girls. Comparing the cost of an abortion to a future dowry, abortion clinics lure customers with advertisements warning that it is better to "pay 500 rupees now, save 50,000 rupees later." Because abortion providers have continued to flout the 1994 law, in 2002 the Indian government amended it to make the manufacturers and distributors of sonogram equipment responsible for preventing female feticide.

06   To protect its ultrasound business and avoid legal damages, GE created a series of training programs, sales-screening procedures, and post-sale auditing processes designed to detect misuse, and it also put warning labels on its equipment. Nonetheless, GE was caught off-guard by the media campaign launched by Indian activists, who accused it of enabling female feticide. Before long, GE realized that if it hoped to continue to dominate the country's ultrasound market, it would have to confront the low status of women

Attending high school is just one way in which girls and women can be empowered.

---

[2] enhance or improve
[3] destruction or abortion of a fetus
[4] money and/or property that, in some societies, a wife or her family must pay to her husband when they get married

in Indian society. It met with activist groups and launched a poster campaign to change attitudes about women's rights. At the same time, it began to fund education for girls and to sponsor a hip, young Indian female tennis star as a progressive role model. As often happens when the private sector gets involved in the touchy subject of women's rights in the developing world, the case of GE in India was disappointingly reactive. Too often, companies act only after they face a public relations problem, whether being charged with female feticide or with hiring underage girls in sweatshops. Perhaps it is not surprising that multinational companies tend to approach the topic gingerly and belatedly, given the cultural sensitivities regarding women in many emerging markets and the fact that the senior management of local subsidiaries is often overwhelmingly male.

07 Slowly, however, attitudes are beginning to change. Partly in response to shareholder demands, some companies are becoming increasingly proactive regarding women's empowerment. In addition, investors have put more than $2 trillion into socially responsible investment funds, which weigh both financial returns and societal impact. Although supporting women's rights is not yet a primary concern of most such funds, it is becoming an increasingly high-profile component of the larger social justice agenda that dictates how and where socially responsible investment funds invest. Meanwhile, the rise of female senior managers, board members, and CEOs in Western companies is also raising the profile of women's rights in the global corporate agenda.

Expanding business, empowering women

08 A 2009 McKinsey survey of corporations with operations in emerging markets revealed that less than 20 percent of the companies had any initiatives focused on women. Their executives have simply not made the issue a strategic priority. Perhaps they should reconsider. According to the same study, three-quarters of those companies with specific initiatives to empower women in developing countries reported that their investments were already increasing their profits or that they expected them to do so soon. Such investments pay off by improving a company's talent pool and increasing employee productivity and retention. Corporations also benefit as new markets are created and existing ones expand. In the developing world especially, networks of female entrepreneurs are becoming increasingly important sales channels in places where the scarcity of roads and stores makes it difficult to distribute goods and services.

09 One example of how a corporation can simultaneously expand its business and empower women is Hindustan Unilever, India's largest consumer goods company. It launched its Shakti Entrepreneur Program in 2000 to offer microcredit grants to rural women who become door-to-door distributors of the company's household products. This sales network has now expanded to include nearly 50,000 women selling to more than three million homes across 100,000 Indian villages. Not only do these women benefit from higher self-esteem and greater status within their families, but they invest their incomes in the health, nutrition, and education of their children, thereby helping lift their communities out of poverty. Hindustan Unilever, for its part, was able to open up a previously inaccessible market.

10 Training women as local distributors of goods and services is important, of course, but so is incorporating women-owned businesses into global supply chains. As giant retailers such as Walmart and Carrefour move aggressively into emerging markets, they are trying to buy more of their products, particularly food, directly

from local producers—both to lower prices and to improve quality. With more than $400 billion in annual sales, Walmart is the world's largest retailer, so its purchasing decisions have a cascading[5] effect throughout the global supply chain. Its recent sensitivity to environmental issues, for example, is starting to transform how companies around the world produce goods. This February, it announced a plan to reduce the greenhouse gas emissions produced by its global supply chain by 20 million metric tons within five years; it plans to do this by forcing its suppliers to adjust how they source, manufacture, package, and transport their products.

11   Similarly, there are signs that Walmart is beginning to understand the importance of women's empowerment in the developing world, where it projects that most of its future growth will take place. Since almost 75 percent of its employees are women, the company has a clear interest in promoting women's economic empowerment in its new markets. Working alongside CARE, a humanitarian organization that combats global poverty, Walmart has launched several pilot programs to teach literacy and workplace skills in the developing world. In Peru, it is helping female farmers meet the company's quality-control standards. In Bangladesh, it is training local women in the garment industry to move up from fabric sorters to seamstresses and cutters. Similarly, it is developing the skills of female cashew farmers in India so that they can progress from low-level pickers to high-end processors. Walmart expects to see increased productivity, higher quality, and greater diversity in its supply chain as a result. "We aren't engaging with Walmart solely for the financial resources they bring to the table," says Helene Gayle, president and CEO of CARE. "We are working together to make change on a global level. Walmart has enormous potential to transform women's lives in the emerging markets in which it operates."

12   It is ironic, of course, that Walmart is embracing women's empowerment in emerging markets even as it fights the largest class-action sex-discrimination lawsuit in U.S. history. (Walmart is accused of discriminating against women in pay and promotions.) Undoubtedly, its women's empowerment initiatives could have multiple motivations, including diverting negative public attention. But Walmart's efforts will be sustainable only to the extent that the company considers them central to its long-term growth and profitability and not just part of a public relations strategy. The potential for its female employees and suppliers in the developing world is enormous: if Walmart sourced just one percent of its sales from women-owned businesses, it would channel billions of dollars toward women's economic empowerment— far more than what international development agencies could ever muster for such efforts.

Conclusion

13   Closing the gender gap and improving women's rights in the Middle East, South Asia, and sub-Saharan Africa may take many generations, but the benefits will be huge—not only for the individual women and their families but also for global markets. As companies seek new sources of revenue in emerging economies, they will find that gender disparities pose an obstacle to doing business. The sooner the private sector works to overcome gender inequality, the better off the world—and companies' own bottom lines— will be.

Source: Excerpted from I. Coleman, "The global glass ceiling." *Current* 524 (2010): 3–6.

---

[5] happening in rapid sequence, with one thing leading to the next

1. One of the positive results of enabling women to become educated and earn an income is declining infant mortality rates (par. 1). Explain the connection between women's education and lower infant mortality rates.

   _____

2. What examples of gender discrimination are given in paragraph 2?

   _____

3. Who are the two billion people referred to in paragraph 2?

   _____

4. According to the author, what types of organizations have the most potential to help women in developing countries?

   a) Human rights organizations

   b) Large international companies

   c) Governments who give aid to foreign countries

   d) Organizations of local citizens

5. Paragraph 3 lists three factors that make large corporations particularly influential. Match each factor with its description.

a. Powerful brands	____ Access to substantial financial resources
b. Having vast amounts of money	____ The influence of marketing and name recognition
c. Promises of investment and employment	____ Potential to hire locals and boost the local economy

6. According to the author, when will the major change occur in achieving women's empowerment?

   a) When companies realize that they have to take responsibility for improving women's position in developing countries

   b) When companies employ many local women, thus strengthening women's status

   c) When companies understand that empowering women results in higher corporate profits

   d) When companies start financing projects to educate business women

   _____

   _____

7. Explain the meaning of the advertisement line "pay 500 rupees now, save 50,000 rupees later."

_____

8. What measures did GE take in its multi-pronged approach to the problem of sex-selective abortions enabled by ultrasound screenings in India? Circle all that apply.

   a) It organized a pro-women poster campaign.

   b) It tried to make sure that its ultrasound equipment was sold to companies who would not misuse it.

   c) It worked against those companies whose management level is dominated by males.

   d) It used an Indian celebrity to promote women's rights.

   e) It sponsored learning programs for girls.

9. What is the author's opinion of GE's response?

   a) The response was appropriate and it is commended by the author.

   b) GE acted in response to the public relations problems, instead of proactively working to empower women.

   c) GE's response demonstrated that the company is sensitive to women's issues and dedicated to improving the status of women.

   d) GE acted in advance to avert a public relations scandal.

10. What is the difference between reactive and proactive approaches mentioned in paragraphs 6 and 7?

_____

_____

11. How does investing in women's programs in developing countries increase the profits of investors? List at least two ways.

_____

_____

12. Who benefits from Hindustan Unilever's employment of women as product distributors?

   a) Women

   b) Women's children

   c) Hindustan Unilever

   d) All of the above

13. Complete the sentence.

Walmart incorporates women-owned local businesses into its supply

chain by buying _____ directly from

_____ farmers and their families.

14. A. Looking at paragraphs 10–12, would you consider the author's
discussion of Walmart to be biased or unbiased? Why?

_____

_____

B. Do you think that Helene Gayle, president and CEO of CARE, presents a
biased opinion about Walmart (par. 11)? Why or why not?

_____

15. What two great motivating factors for companies to empower women in the
developing world are mentioned in the last paragraph?

a) _____

b) _____

Vocabulary

Use context clues and your knowledge of word parts to determine the correct
meaning of each word. Verify your answers using a dictionary if necessary.

1. levers (par. 1): _____

2. pervasive (par. 2): _____

3. destitute (par. 2):

a) without money, food, or other things necessary for life

b) related to or affecting women

c) having a lot of money or property

4. catalyst (textbox): _____

5. complicit (par. 4):

a) innocent

b) involved

c) ignorant

6. gingerly (par. 6):

   a) enthusiastically

   b) courageously

   c) carefully

READING 3

Born to Serve: The State of Old Women and Widows in India

 Sociology

01   The ancient Hindu scriptures[1] divide life into four stages. In the first two stages, man is a student and a householder. The third stage of life is that of retirement. When a man reaches old age and his son is ready to take over the leadership of the household, he and his wife retire. The fourth stage is one of renunciation—a removal of oneself from the bonds of familial ties and a renouncing[2] of the physical world. These stages describe primarily the role of men. According to the scriptures, a woman belongs to her father in childhood, her husband in youth and her sons in old age; a woman is never fit for independence. In the case of women, however, and especially in the case of widows, the renunciation rules are applied more strictly than they are for men. Ageism is thus formalized in the Hindu scriptures, and though these ancient texts have now lost much of their relevance and influence, the systemic[3] discrimination against aged women is ingrained in the collective psyche.

02   Nowhere is this discrimination, even cruelty, more in evidence than in the treatment of widows. With her husband dead, a widow's passion can be the cause of moral panic. She must therefore be completely neutered, desexed. The scriptures direct that she must give up ornamentation, observe fasts, emaciate the body, eat only one meal a day and sleep on the floor. She must not eat "hot" foods—such as meat or even onion and garlic—which apparently ignite sexual passion. Her hair—the source of sin and pollution—must be shaved off. The ultimate examples of forced renunciation were the thousands of widows abandoned by their families in the holy city of Benares, now known as Varanasi.

03   Labeled as worthless because their measures of worth—their husbands—were gone, widows were forced to enter "widow houses" and were often compelled to turn to prostitution in order to survive. During the British colonial rule in India, governors-general enacted legislation to

---

[1] the holy books of a particular religion (Hinduism, in this case)
[2] giving something up; stating publicly that you no longer wish to have a connection with something
[3] affecting or connected with the whole of something, as opposed to a particular part

improve the status of women. The abolition of *sati* (the practice of widows being forced to burn themselves on their husband's funeral pyre), though fiercely opposed by orthodox Hindus, was implemented in 1829 with the help of social reformists such as Raja Ram Mohan Roy, and the Widow Remarriage Act was passed in 1856.

04 Widow houses still exist in Varanasi, although they are not as numerous as they were a hundred years ago. With their heads shaven and their foreheads streaked with sandalwood, most of these widows in Varanasi, who are abandoned by their families, have to beg for a living. Chanting devotional songs the whole day is, for most, not just a route for spiritual salvation but also the only means to earn a few rupees. The proportion of widows thus afflicted, though lesser now, is still significant. And though the majority of widows in India may no longer be required to shave their hair, the mindset that a woman's identity exists only vis-à-vis the males around her has not really changed. Even today a widow is accused of being "responsible" for her husband's death. Widows are pressured to observe restrictive codes of dress and behaviour. They are excluded from religious and social life, and they are denied their property.

05 In India, social norms function to keep women financially dependent upon men. To start with, the daughter is refused an education because her father would rather educate the sons. In her adult years, the woman is denied a career because the husband requires her to serve the household and to take care of his parents. The Hindu inheritance law, whereby sons and not daughters inherit the father's wealth, propagates[4] this dependence. Throughout her life a woman remains poor because the system is structured to keep her that way.

06 The dependence of all of India's old people— both men and women—on their families is reinforced by public policy. Although the Indian Constitution provides for a welfare state, a social security system, such as is found in the United States and to an even greater extent in Europe, is completely absent. Except for the few who have held a pensionable job during their working years, the elderly have no independent means of support. For a married woman, the entitlement to a pension is linked to that of her husband and not to her age or her financial situation. Where pensions are available, they come through the men, leaving women in their state of dependency.

07 As for widows above a certain age, most Indian states do have pension plans. However, the pensions are small (less than Rs.150 [$3] per month), and the bureaucratic requirements are numerous: the applicant must have no children capable of supporting her, she must earn less than Rs.100 per month, she must be physically unfit to work, she must not beg, she must not own a house but she must have the ability to apply for a pension, make several trips to the state government offices, and so on! No wonder less than 10 percent of all widows actually receive the state's "generosity."

08 The problems of old people have traditionally been taken care of by the family network. Old-age and retirement homes are uncommon in India as old people are expected to live with their children's families. While it is true that old people can be integrated more easily into traditional families in India than in the West, in many cases these relationships become exploitative—old people, especially women, end up providing child care and doing physical labour for their children's families. The pattern of exploitation remains consistent across Indian culture: urban and rural, poor and prosperous. Education and social status do not seem to have a bearing on how old people are treated. For example, it is quite common for educated Indian immigrants in the United States to bring their

---

[4] promotes

parents to this country in order to save on hired help and child care. Is this not exploitation?

09   One clue is that despite their miserable existence, very few of the widows of Varanasi are willing to return home from the widow houses. In Varanasi, at least the widow is free to live her own life with others like herself. Back home, it is her own family that deprives her of her property, obliterates[5] her identity and ordains[6] for her a kind of social death. The key issue is that old women do not have a choice: because they do not have any other means of support, serving their children is the only way they can make ends meet. Integrating old women more closely into the lives of their children may not be the complete answer to their problems. It is time the government of India provided welfare programs and independent incomes for old people—especially for women—to ensure the rights of the elderly women are respected and the close family ties we so value are not exploited.

Source: P. Verma, "Born to serve: The state of old women and widows in India." *Off Our Backs* 35, no. 9/10 (2005): 38–39.

---

[5] destroys
[6] orders or commands

Comprehension and Skills Practice

1. What is the main difference between how the ancient Hindu scriptures describe the status of men and the status of women?

    _____

2. Which stage of life is most difficult for many women in India?
    a) Old age
    b) Youth
    c) Establishing a family
    d) Retirement from a job

3. Based on your understanding of paragraph 1, write a definition of *ageism*.

    _____

4. What is the purpose of making widows accept a poor and scarce diet, according to the scriptures?

    _____

5. What is the main idea of paragraph 4?
    a) The numbers of widow houses decreased with time.
    b) Many widows have no other choice than to make a living by begging.
    c) The dominant view on women in India is that they are identified in relation to male relatives.
    d) Widows in India suffer from an extremely low social status.

6. Where is the main idea in paragraph 5?

   a) The main idea opens the paragraph, and supporting details follow.

   b) Supporting details open the paragraph, and the main idea concludes it.

   c) The main idea is at the beginning, and it is paraphrased at the end.

   d) The main idea is in the middle of the paragraph.

7. What is the role of the state in providing for the elderly? Circle all that apply.

   a) Public policies strengthen the status of the elderly in society.

   b) All elderly people are provided with welfare allowance, based on the Indian Constitution.

   c) Only those with jobs having a pension benefit receive a government pension.

   d) Married women get pensions depending on their financial situation.

8. Circle the correct answer.

   If a widow has children who are capable of supporting her, she (**does not/ does**) receive a pension, although she might meet all the rest of the pension requirements.

9. Why does the author put the word *generosity* (par. 7) in quotation marks?

   _____

10. A. What is the author's opinion on the following points? What is your opinion? Write your answers in the chart.

	THE AUTHOR'S OPINION	MY OPINION
1. The elderly should live with their children's families, and not in old-age homes.		
2. Grandmothers should take care of their grandchildren.		

   B. How does the author support her opinion? Is her support relevant and sufficient?

   _____

   _____

11. What is the author's suggestion regarding how to improve the status of elderly women in India?

   _____

Use context clues and your knowledge of word parts to determine the correct meaning of each word or phrase. Verify your answers using a dictionary if necessary.

1. ingrained (par. 1): _____

2. emaciate (par. 2):
   a) fatten up
   b) make something thin and weak
   c) decorate

3. were . . . compelled (par. 3): _____

4. afflicted (par. 4):
   a) affected in an unpleasant way
   b) assisted by the public
   c) making substantial profits

5. propagates (par. 5): _____

6. to have a bearing (par. 8): _____

UNIT REFLECTION AND SYNTHESIS

1. Provide examples from the three readings in this unit of inequalities that women suffer. You may use information in the graphics as well as the texts.

READING	EXAMPLE
"Women in International Marketing"	
"The Global Glass Ceiling"	
"Born to Serve"	

2. "The Global Glass Ceiling" and "Born to Serve" discuss discrimination against women in India, at the very beginning of women's lives and at the end. Summarize the reasons behind this discrimination.

_____

_____

3. A. How do the first two texts—"Women in International Marketing" and "The Global Glass Ceiling"—approach the idea of empowering women? Provide examples of empowering women in the developing and developed countries by filling in the Venn diagram.

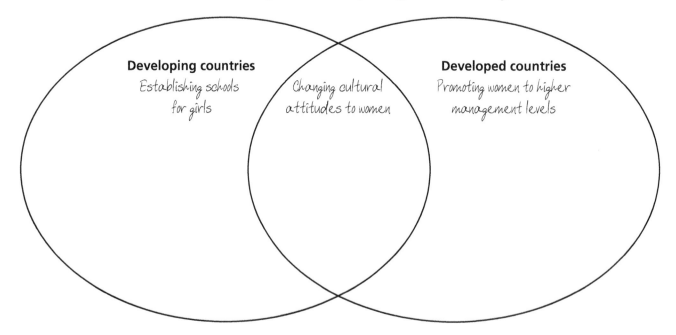

Developing countries
Establishing schools for girls

Changing cultural attitudes to women

Developed countries
Promoting women to higher management levels

B. Based on your Venn diagram, do you think the term *glass ceiling* means the same thing for women in Western society as it does for women in the developing world? Explain.

_____

_____

4. The authors of "Women in International Marketing" promote the idea of offering capable women from Western countries international assignments. How do you think female executives being hosted abroad may affect the status of local women in some Middle Eastern, South Asian, and sub-Saharan countries, where most women have lower status than in the West?

_____

_____

5. Each of the three readings advocates for elevating the status of women. For each reading, note the key player in bringing about this status change. In the next column, note the motivation for that change. One box is already filled in for you.

READING	KEY PLAYER	MOTIVATION FOR CHANGE
"Women in International Marketing"		
"The Global Glass Ceiling"		
"Born to Serve"		*concern for human rights and compassion for suffering women*

6. Although the purpose of all readings in this unit is to argue for the improvement of women's lives, each author uses different techniques of persuasion to achieve this purpose. Reflect on the differences and provide examples.

READING	TECHNIQUE(S) OF PERSUASION	EXAMPLE
"Women in International Marketing"		
"The Global Glass Ceiling"		
"Born to Serve"		

7. What is being done, or could be done, to elevate the position of women in your home country?

_____

Culture

GETTING INTO THE TOPIC

1. Imagine that one morning you find yourself alone on a small uninhabited island, forced to stay there for three months. Would you remain the same person you had always been or would your identity change as a result of losing connections with your family, colleagues, and friends?

2. A. Find the definitions of *collectivistic* and *individualistic* online or in your dictionary.

   a) collectivistic: _____

   _____

   b) individualistic: _____

   _____

   B. Which one best describes the culture you were raised in? _____

   _____

3. Read the following scenario, thinking about the contrast between individualistic and collectivistic cultures:

Michelle, a young Canadian teacher with a few years' experience teaching in a private elementary school in Toronto, has just moved to a small English-speaking village in Kenya. She is a passionate teacher and excited about the opportunity to spend a year learning about the Kenyan culture. Things began well—the schoolchildren were cheerful and enthusiastic about their work. But Michelle is starting to become frustrated. Every time she assigns work to the class, the children form small groups to discuss the assignment and complete the tasks. She is constantly reminding them that students are expected to work individually and that they will be graded individually. Eventually, her students become much less eager to learn, and she finds it difficult to motivate them to complete their tasks, even when she offers small prizes to the student with the highest grades.

How is the situation in Michelle's classroom affected by cultural differences? How might her expectations about education differ from her students' expectations?

4. Imagine the following conflict between colleagues: two doctors share the responsibility of taking care of one patient, but they disagree on the medication the patient needs. If you were a doctor in this situation, how would you resolve this disagreement?

5. Do you think the way people resolve conflicts has anything to do with the culture in which they were raised and socialized?

READING 1

Culture and the Self

Psychology

How do individualist and collectivist cultures influence people?

01 Imagine that someone were to rip away your social connections, making you a solitary refugee in a foreign land. How much of your identity would remain intact?

02   If as our solitary traveller you pride yourself on your individualism, a great deal of your identity would remain intact—the very core of your being, the sense of "me," the awareness of your personal convictions and values. Individualists (often people from North America, Western Europe, Australia, or New Zealand) give relatively greater priority to personal goals and define their identity mostly in terms of personal attributes (Schimmack et al., 2005). They strive for personal control and individual achievement. In American culture, with its relatively big *I* and small *we*, 85 percent of people have agreed that it is possible "to pretty much be who you want to be" (Sampson, 2000).

03   Individualists share the human need to belong. They join groups. But they are less focused on group harmony and doing their duty to the group (Brewer and Chen, 2007). And being more self-contained, they more easily move in and out of social groups. They feel relatively free to switch places of worship, switch jobs, or even leave their extended families and migrate to a new place. Marriage is often for as long as they both shall love.

04   If set adrift in a foreign land as a collectivist, you may experience a greater loss of identity. Cut off from family, groups, and loyal friends, you would lose the connections that have defined who you are. In a collectivist culture, group identifications provide a sense of belonging, a set of values, a network of caring individuals, an assurance of security. In return, collectivists have deeper, more stable attachments to their groups—their family, clan, or company. In South Korea, for example, people place less value on expressing a consistent, unique self-concept, and more on tradition and shared practices (Choi & Choi, 2002).

05   Valuing communal solidarity means placing a premium on preserving group spirit and ensuring that others never lose face. What people say reflects not only what they feel (their

Considerate collectivists
Japan's collectivist values, including duty to others and social harmony, were on display after the devastating 2011 earthquake and tsunami. Virtually no looting was reported, and residents remained calm and orderly, as shown here while waiting for drinking water.

inner attitudes) but what they presume others feel (Kashima et al., 1992). Avoiding direct confrontation, blunt honesty, and uncomfortable topics, collectivists often defer to others' wishes and display a polite, self-effacing humility (Markus & Kitayama, 1991). Elders and superiors receive respect, and duty to family may trump personal career and mate preference (Zhang & Kline, 2009). In new groups, people may be shy and more easily embarrassed than their individualist counterparts (Singelis et al., 1995, 1999). Compared with Westerners, people in Japanese and Chinese cultures, for example, exhibit greater shyness toward strangers and greater concern for social harmony and loyalty (Bond, 1988; Cheek & Melchior, 1990; Triandis, 1994). When the priority is "we," not "me," that individualized latte—"decaf, single shot, skinny, extra hot"—that feels so good to a North American in a coffee shop might sound more like a selfish demand in Seoul (Kim & Markus, 1999).

06   To be sure, there is diversity within cultures. Even in the most individualistic countries,

some people manifest collectivist values. Within many countries, there are also distinct cultures related to one's religion, economic status, and region (Cohen, 2009). And in collectivist Japan, a spirit of individualism marks the "northern frontier" island of Hokkaido (Kitayama et al., 2006). But in general, people (especially men) in competitive, individualist cultures have more personal freedom, are less geographically bound to their families, enjoy more privacy, and take more pride in personal achievements.

07   They even prefer unusual names, as psychologist Jean Twenge noticed while seeking a name for her first child. Over time, the most common American names listed by year on the U.S. Social Security baby names website were becoming less desirable. When she and her colleagues (2010) analyzed the first names of 325 million American babies born between 1880 and 2007, they confirmed this trend. As Figure 13.1 illustrates, the percent[age] of boys and girls given one of the 10 most common names for their birth year has plunged, especially in recent years. (No wonder my parents, who bore me in a less individualistic age, gave me such a common first name.)

08   The individualist-collectivist divide appeared in reactions to medals received during the 2000 and 2002 Olympic games. U.S. gold medal winners and the U.S. media covering them attributed the achievements mostly to the athletes themselves (Markus et al., 2006). "I think I just stayed focused," explained swimming gold medallist Misty Hyman. "It was time to show the world what I could do. I am just glad I was able to do it." Japan's gold medalist in the women's marathon, Naoko Takahashi, had a different explanation: "Here is the best coach in the world, the best manager in the world, and all of the people who support me—all of these things were getting together and became a gold medal." Even when describing friends, Westerners tend to use trait-describing adjectives ("she is helpful"),

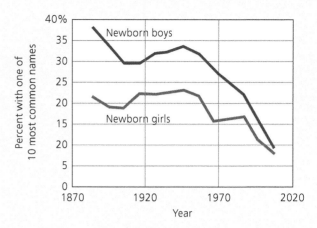

Figure 13.1 A child like no other
Americans' individualist tendencies are reflected in their choice of names for their babies. In recent years, the percentage of American babies receiving one of that year's 10 most common names has plunged. (Adapted from Twenge et al. 2010.)

whereas East Asians more often use verbs that describe behaviours in context (*"she helps her friends"*) (Heine and Buchtel, 2009; Maass et al., 2006).

09   Individualism's benefits can come at the cost of more loneliness, higher divorce and homicide rates, and more stress-related disease (Popenoe, 1993; Triandis et al., 1988). Demands for more romance and personal fulfillment in marriage can subject relationships to more pressure (Dion & Dion, 1993). In one survey, "keeping romance alive" was rated as important to good marriage by 78 percent of U.S. women but only 29 percent of Japanese women (*American Enterprise*, 1992). In China, love songs often express enduring commitment and friendship (Rothbaum & Tsang, 1998): "We will be together from now on . . . I will never change from now to forever."

10   Individualism in Western cultures has increased strikingly over the last century. What predicts such changes in one culture over time, or between differing cultures? Social history matters. Voluntary migration; a sparsely populated, challenging environment; and a

shift to a capitalist economy have fostered independence and individualism (Kitayama et al., 2009. 2010; Varnum et al., 2010). Might biology also play a role? In search of biological underpinnings to these cultural differences—remembering that everything psychological is also biological—a new subfield, *cultural neuroscience*, is studying how neurobiology and cultural traits influence each other (Ambady & Bharucha, 2009; Chiao, 2009). One researcher compared, across 29 countries, the different forms of a serotonin-regulating gene. People in collectivist cultures tended to carry a version associated with greater anxiety, though living in such cultures helps protect people from anxiety (Chiao & Blizinsky, 2010). As we will see over and again, biological, psychological, and social-cultural perspectives intersect. We are biopsychosocial creatures.

Source: D.G. Myers, *Psychology*, 10th edition (New York: Worth, 2013), pp. 150–152.

Comprehension and Skills Practice

1. Below are some descriptions of people. Decide whether each one belongs to an individualistic (I) or collectivistic (C) culture. Then highlight any lines in the text that support your answers.

    a) ＿＿ Mike is married and has a young son. His Facebook profile has many photos of himself engaged in different activities, such as skiing, hiking, and walking his dog. There are no pictures of his wife or child on Facebook. He writes that happiness in life for him is achieving professional success and enjoying vacations in different parts of the world.

    b) ＿＿ Rodrigo had lived with his elderly parents in Spain but decided to leave them and immigrate to the UK to fulfil his dream of studying philosophy at Oxford. He believes that his parents will be fine without him, and he calls them about once a month.

    c) ＿＿ Davinder lived with her only son, his wife, and their children in a spacious house in Bangalore, India. After her son's family immigrated to Canada, she became depressed. Now Davinder is waiting for her immigration visa to join her family in Canada. She will help take care of the grandchildren again.

    d) ＿＿ Matsuki has been working for the same electronics manufacturing company in Osaka, Japan, for 45 years. Now, at the age of 68, he is retiring. His boss has organized a party in Matsuki's honor, and Matsuki got a retirement gift of an expensive watch with an engraving from the company. Matsuki feels happy and sad at the same time because he is sorry to leave the place and the people he loved working for.

2. In your own words, explain the different approach to marriage in the West and in China, based on the following quotations from the text:

   "Marriage is often for as long as they both shall love."

   "We will be together from now on . . . I will never change from now to forever."

   _____

   _____

3. According to the text, one of the characteristics of a collectivistic society is avoiding blunt honesty (par. 5).

   A. Why might collectivists avoid blunt honesty?

   _____

   B. Based on your experience, provide an example of a situation involving blunt honesty in which the behaviour of individualists and collectivists would likely be different.

   _____

   _____

4. Which of the following is an expression of one's duty to family in a collectivistic culture?

   a) Both mother and father work two jobs to provide for the expensive college education of their children.

   b) The son does not marry the girl he loves because his parents disapprove. Instead, he marries the daughter of his parents' friends.

   c) An eldest son gets married and moves to a city six hours away from his parents, but visits at least three times a year because they miss him.

   d) The married couple avoid talking about their teen daughter's drug problem because it is an uncomfortable topic.

5. Why does the author refer to a "decaf, single shot, skinny, extra hot" latte order in paragraph 5? How might this coffee order sound in a coffee shop in a more collectivistic culture?

   _____

6. Mark each statement as T (true) or F (false).

   a) ____ In a collectivistic culture, all members exhibit collectivistic values to an equal degree.

   b) ____ A person's degree of collectivism or individualism may depend on his or her religion, economic status, or geographical location.

   c) ____ There is some distinction in the degree to which women and men express their individualistic values.

7. A. What is the main idea of paragraph 7?

_____

B. The author refers to his own first name. Based on his comments, what is most likely his first name?

a) Denzel   c) Dagmar

b) David   d) Delwyn

C. What does the choice of this name tell us about his parents' society?

_____

8. In paragraph 8, examples of speech representing collectivistic and individualistic styles are discussed. Explain the differences between them in your own words.

_____

_____

9. In paragraph 9, the author talks about "individualism's benefits" in relation to its problems. Fill in the table with at least three benefits and problems. You will need to refer to other paragraphs, in addition to paragraph 9, to complete this task.

INDIVIDUALISM'S BENEFITS	INDIVIDUALISM'S PROBLEMS
1.	1.
2.	2.
3.	3.

10. In the final paragraph, the author mentions factors that predict the increase of individualism in a society. Explain how the following factors may cause a culture to be more individualistic.

a) A sparsely populated, challenging environment: _____

_____

b) A shift to a capitalist economy: _____

_____

11. Myers cites research by Chiao & Blizinsky (2010) stating that "people in collectivist cultures tended to carry a [gene] associated with greater anxiety, though living in such cultures helps protect people from anxiety." Do you think this finding supports or disproves the idea that cultural differences may be explained by biological characteristics? Why or why not?

_____

Vocabulary

Use context clues and your knowledge of word parts to determine the correct meaning of each word or phrase. Verify your answers using a dictionary if necessary.

1. intact (par. 1):
    a) not damaged, complete
    b) healthy and sound
    c) disturbed

2. attributes (par. 2):
    a) goals
    b) preferences
    c) qualities

3. self-effacing (par. 5): _____

4. trump (par. 5):
    a) become more important than
    b) improve
    c) build the foundations for

5. plunged (par. 7): _____

6. subject (par. 9):
    a) topic or theme of a story or article
    b) force someone or something to undergo a particular experience
    c) cause destruction or other devastation

7. underpinnings (par. 10): _____

READING 2

Uncovering the Role of Culture in Learning, Development, and Education

 Education

Each child in kindergarten is making a book called *All About Me*. The teacher asks each child to say what is special about himself or herself, writing down these comments, with space for the child to draw a picture corresponding to each comment. One boy responds with "my brother is good at soccer and my father is good at cooking." The teacher keeps asking the boy to think about qualities of himself, prompting him: "This is all about you. Are you smart? Yes, of course you are smart, so let's say you are special because you are smart." In the end, the boy's book contained drawings with these sentences "I am special because I am smart. I am special because I am strong. I am special because I am handsome." (Zepeda, Gonzalez-Mena, Rothstein-Fisch, & Trumbull, 2006, p. 19)

01 The practice of making a book called *All About Me* is a familiar activity in many early childhood classrooms. But there may be more to this activity than what meets the eye. The teacher is likely to be thinking that identifying concepts of self will promote the child's sense of self-esteem and individuality. She may also value the child's burgeoning literacy skills. Yet, the child may be experiencing something very different. He may believe that the teacher does not like his family, and thus she does not like him. Bragging about himself may make him feel very uncomfortable. Ultimately, he may be inclined to think that his values and ideas do not matter, thwarting his concept of self—exactly the opposite of the teacher's goal (Zepeda et al., 2006).

02 The example of *All About Me* calls attention to classroom practices that, though well-intended, may be at odds with learning, eventually leading to negative feelings about school altogether. The good intentions of the teacher and the compliant but uncomfortable boy are likely to be operating with two conflicting sets of values, each invisible to the other. The teacher's goals are representative of the cultural value of individualism, the characteristic value of mainstream United States. In contrast, the boy's discomfort at being isolated from his family is characteristic of the cultural value of collectivism, the value system of many immigrant children and families. Individualism and collectivism have emerged as powerful cultural models that tie together cultural conceptions of learning and development, drawing on theory and research in developmental psychology (Greenfield & Bruner, 1966) and anthropology (Whiting & Whiting, 1973).

These two idealized developmental pathways[1] emphasize different goals for development and learning. Individualism emphasizes individual identity, independence, self-fulfillment, and standing out. Collectivism emphasizes group identity, interdependence, social responsibility, and fitting in (Greenfield, Keller, Fuligni, & Maynard, 2003).

03   Each pathway is situated in a broader sociocultural system (Keller, 1997, 2003). The individualistic pathway arises as an adaptation to a complex, urban, wealthy environment featuring a well-developed system of formal education and advanced technology. The collectivistic pathway arises as an adaptation to a small-scale, face-to-face village environment based on a subsistence economy and informal education (Greenfield, Trumbull, et al., 2006). Economic conditions and political persecution tend to incorporate people from the second kind of society into the first (Greenfield, 2009). When this happens, children and their families are exposed to two contrasting and often conflicting socializing forces that are very relevant to the care and education of many immigrant, Native American, Alaska Native, and Native Hawaiian children in the United States as well as the children of immigrant or conquered peoples in other industrialized countries, such as Australia and those of western Europe (Greenfield, Trumbull, et al., 2006).

04   On the whole, individualism emphasizes individual success, and collectivism emphasizes the success of the group as a whole (Greenfield, Trumbull, et al., 2006). In individualistic cultures, when asked to describe themselves, people tend to list trait labels referring to aspects of their personalities, such as "hard-working," "intelligent," or "athletic" (Triandis, Brislin, & Hui, 1988), as the teacher in the example above expected. In collectivistic cultures, people are more likely to embed their own personal goals with those of the group, such as their extended family or religious group (Brislin, 1993) and to think of themselves as defined by their connections to others (Markus & Kitayama, 1991). This is more or less what the boy in the opening example was doing when he tried to talk about other members of his family rather than about himself. Not surprisingly, the United States, according to some measures, is the most individualistic country in the world (Hofstede, 2001). However, this developmental pathway is hardly universal—in the 1980s, some 70% of the world's cultures could be described as collectivistic (Triandis, 1989). While increased wealth, urbanization, technology, and formal education have driven cultures and individuals around the world in an individualistic direction since the 1980s (Greenfield, 2009), major cross-cultural differences still exist.

05   Socialization practices begin at birth or even before. For example, in European American culture, expectant parents often prepare a nursery—the baby's own room—to set the stage for the development of the child's independence. This is in contrast to collectivistic cultures that utilize a family bed, where the baby sleeps with the parents.

06   Table 13.1 describes some major differences between the individualistic and collectivistic pathway of learning and development revealed by research (Greenfield, Trumbull, et al., 2006). We have selected features of each pathway that are most relevant to formal education. These pathways appear and function in ways that differentially value intelligence and knowledge. For example, in more individualistic cultures, cognitive, academic, and scientific knowledge is highly valued, particularly the accumulation of factual knowledge. Independence is demonstrated in school when children work

---

[1] a way of achieving something

DOMAIN	INDIVIDUALISTIC PATHWAY	COLLECTIVISTIC PATHWAY
Ethnotheory[2]	independence, individual success	interdependence, group/family success
Valued intelligence	cognitive, academic, scientific	social/relational
Valued knowledge	physical world, factual knowledge	social world, narrative knowledge
Models of learning	independent, active participation, praise	working in groups, observation, criticism
Communication	speaking, self-expression	comprehending, speech that is respectful to authority
Material world	personal ownership, sharing by choice	shared use, responsibility to share

Table 13.1 Contrasting cultural pathways of learning and development

alone, show what they know through speaking out and expressing themselves, and expect praise or other tangible[3] rewards for doing so. Incidentally, the importance of praise and rewards also applies to informal education at home—for example, household chores—as well as to school-based activities. In parallel fashion, the material world is also conceptualized[4] in relation to the individual. Children have individual toys and spaces; sharing takes place by permission of the owner rather than simply being assumed.

07   In contrast, collectivistic cultures value social intelligence as it relates to people, not facts or things: It is situated in a social world where knowledge about people's experiences is highly valued. Children are socialized to become interdependent with others. They work together to help and share with other members of the group, instead of being showcased for

their individual achievement (Rothstein-Fisch & Trumbull, 2008). Praise may also make them feel singled out and uncomfortable rather than make them feel good about themselves (Greenfield, Quiroz, & Raeff, 2000).

Utilizing group motivation to achieve learning in mathematics

08   During one classroom visit, an interesting classroom chart was noticed. It was a graph displaying children's names and corresponding stars next to each name indicating the level of memorized multiplication facts they had mastered. This seemed like a curiously individualistic motivational tool for children of migrant farm workers [from a collectivistic culture]. When asked about the star chart during the observation debriefing interview, the teacher explained that the students were doing poorly

---

[2] an implied idea about the ideal child in a certain culture, accompanied by beliefs about educational practices that will produce this ideal child
[3] that can be clearly seen to exist
[4] formed as an idea in your mind

in learning timed multiplication facts. She was having difficulty motivating the students, and she fell back on the star chart idea she had learned during teacher training. At the time she introduced the star chart, she conducted a class meeting that allowed her to share her concern for students' lack of math progress. She gave the students an opportunity to look at the chart and talk about it. The teacher reports,

> The students said, "Wouldn't it be neat if it would be a solid block of stars, and the whole chart was filled in," and everybody said "Yeah, yeah, that would be so neat." The students started to say they wanted to help each other. Everyone who needed help got adopted by students who had already mastered [the work]. They started helping each other pass, and they seemed to move ahead. The [more advanced] buddies put their own learning on hold in order to help their [less advanced] buddies, not for individual success, but for the success of the group. (Rothstein-Fisch et al., 2003, p. 132)

09 Thus the children were motivated to help each other study timed math facts (so that the whole group could achieve proficiency) much more than to work on increasing their own individual accumulation of stars, indicating their individual competence (Rothstein-Fisch & Trumbull, 2008).

10 Their motivation was rooted in the value of group success rather than in objects or individual awards. Incidentally, when a student was ready to be tested by the teacher at the back of the room, the teacher allowed the buddy to observe, not to provide answers but just to show support and provide encouragement. If the student was not successful, the buddy knew where to help out during the next study session. If the student was successful, the buddy would ring a special bell. This signaled to the entire class that another star had been added to "their" chart, and the children all stopped their work to applaud the individual's contribution to the group's success.

Source: C. Rothstein-Fish, P.M. Greenfield, E. Trumbull, H. Keller & B. Quiroz, "Uncovering the role of culture in learning, development, and education." In D.D. Preiss & R.J. Sternberg (Eds.), *Innovations in Educational Psychology: Perspectives on Learning, Teaching, and Human Development* (New York: Springer, 2010), pp. 269–294.

Comprehension and Skills Practice

1. A. What are the teacher's goals in assigning her students the *All About Me* activity?

    _____

    B. Is the teacher successful in achieving these goals? Why or why not?

    _____

    C. The teacher is attempting to "promote individuality." What may the student feel she is doing?

    a) Encouraging bragging

    b) Promoting independence

    c) Developing self-esteem

2. Which of the following relates to the teacher-child conflict described in the textbox? Circle all that apply.

   a) Collectivism versus individualism

   b) Positive versus negative

   c) European American versus Latin American immigrant

   d) Standing out versus fitting in

3. Paragraph 3 describes two different socio-cultural and socio-economic systems, one in which an individualistic culture is more likely and the other in which a collectivistic culture is more likely. Based on the contrasts described in this paragraph, make an inference about the definition of a "subsistence economy" (par. 3).

   a) Economy with a surplus of resources

   b) Economy in which people work hard

   c) Economy in which people make just enough to survive

   d) Economy in which there is competition for employment

4. Although American society is generally considered the most individualistic in the world, there are certain demographic groups in the country that do not conform to the individualistic culture. According to the text, which groups within America are collectivistic?

   _____

5. Mark each statement as T (true) or F (false). If the statement is false, correct it.

   a) ____ About three decades ago, most of the world was collectivistic.

   b) ____ Today, collectivistic societies represent more than 70 percent of the world cultures.

6. Review Table 13.1 on page 272. Based on your understanding of the text, label each of the examples below with the appropriate domain and pathway. The first one is done for you.

   a) A teacher awards a certificate to her best math student at the end of the school year.

   Domain: ____ethnotheory____   Pathway: ____individualistic____

   b) A five-year-old child knows the names of all the planets in the solar system.

   Domain: _____   Pathway: _____

c) A child knows the names of all families living on her street and where each of the parents is employed.

Domain: _____ Pathway: _____

d) Five siblings are doing their homework at a big table in the kitchen. The older children help the younger ones.

Domain: _____ Pathway: _____

e) After washing the family car, a child is paid $5 and runs to buy a McDonald's Happy Meal. He shares part of the meal with his younger sister when she asks him to.

Domain: _____ Pathway: _____

f) The child is quiet, polite, and talks only when his parents or grandparents ask him something.

Domain: _____ Pathway: _____

7. José, a seven-year-old boy who recently arrived to Canada from rural Mexico, is showing great progress with his English class: today he has answered all his homework story questions correctly. His teacher is very pleased with José's results. What would be the best way to reward or express praise to José, based on the ideas in the text?

_____

8. Fill in the following chart based on the section "Utilizing group motivation to achieve learning in mathematics."

What was the children's task?	
Initially, how did the teacher want to motivate the children?	
What type of motivation did the children want to complete the task?	
Did the motivational efforts work? Why or why not?	

Use context clues and your knowledge of word parts to determine the correct meaning of each word or phrase. Verify your answers using a dictionary if necessary.

1. thwarting (par. 1):

    a) boosting

    b) preventing

    c) nurturing

2. at odds (par. 2):

    a) conflicting

    b) strange

    c) embarrassing

3. compliant (par. 2): _____

4. drawing on (par. 2):

    a) creating a full picture

    b) using as a resource

    c) making comparisons between

5. embed (par. 4):

    a) contrast

    b) differentiate

    c) see as part of

6. to set the stage for (par. 5): _____

READING 3

Managing Conflict

 **Communication Studies**

01 People from most cultures prefer mutually beneficial resolutions to disagreements whenever possible (Cai and Fink, 2002). Nonetheless, the ways in which people communicate during conflicts do vary from one culture to another.

02 The kind of direct approach that characterizes many North Americans is not the norm in other parts of the world. Similarly, the assertiveness that might seem perfectly reasonable to a Canadian would be rude and insensitive in many Asian countries (Gudykunst and Ting-Toomey, 1988; Samovar et al., 2010).

03 Cultures like Japan and China value self-restraint, avoid confrontation, and place a premium on preserving and honouring the "face" of the other person. For this reason, what seems like "beating around the bush" to a Canadian would be polite to an Asian. In Japan, for example, even a simple request like "Close the door" would be too straightforward (Okabe, 1987). A more indirect statement, such as "It is somewhat cold today," would be more appropriate. To take a more important example, Japanese are reluctant to say no to a request. A more likely answer would be "Let me think about it for a while," which anyone familiar with Japanese culture would recognize as a refusal.

04 The Japanese notion of self-restraint is reflected in the important concept of *wa*, or harmony. Interpersonal harmony in Japanese culture includes a tendency for individuals to be self-critical, rather than to find fault in others.

A cross-cultural study compared Canadian and Japanese university students' willingness to accept information that they were better than other students at their university at completing a task and their reluctance to accept information that they had performed worse than their peers (Heine et al., 2000). The results of their investigation supported the idea that Canadians, on average, find it difficult to believe that they were outperformed by their average classmate but easily accept that their own performance was superior. Japanese students, in contrast, were reluctant to believe that they had outperformed the average student from their university. While North Americans, on average, are motivated to find out what is good about themselves and reluctant to find fault with themselves, Japanese tend to search for their weaknesses in order to correct them. This Japanese tendency to avoid the self-enhancement typical of more individualistic cultures and engage in significantly more self-criticism serves to enhance the collectivistic value of interpersonal harmony (*wa*) with others. There are at least two motives in collectivistic cultures related to harmony. The first is to enhance harmony and actively promote group cohesiveness, and in these instances taking a more assertive problem-solving approach to interpersonal conflict is preferred. When the motive is to avoid the disintegration of group harmony, avoidance or non-assertion are the preferred approaches to conflict resolution (Lim, 2009).

05   Similar attitudes toward conflict prevail in China, where one proverb states, "The first person to raise his voice loses the argument." Among Chinese college students (in both the People's Republic and Taiwan), the three most common methods of persuasion used are "hinting," "setting an example by one's own actions," and "strategically agreeing to whatever pleases others" (Ma and Chuang, 2001). It appears that with globalization, some of these preferences may be changing. Yan Bing Zhang and her colleagues (2005) found that while older Chinese adults still preferred an accommodating style of conflict resolution, the younger adults in their study viewed a problem-solving style just as positively as an accommodating style.

06   It isn't necessary to look at Asia to encounter cultural differences in conflict. Many First Nations people in North America approach conflict very differently than do individualistic Westerners. When disciplining their children, Aboriginal people often avoid direct criticism or reprimands. Instead, storytelling is the primary means of teaching proper behaviour (Keeshig Tobias, 1990). In addition to storytelling, parents model the behaviours expected of their children. The importance of developing and maintaining good relationships is a fundamental value of First Nations culture, and there is a belief that personal criticism is damaging and should be avoided (LaLonde, 1992).

07   The style of some other familiar cultures differs in important ways from the northern European and North American norm. These cultures see verbal disputes as a form of intimacy and even a game. For example, Canadians visiting Greece often think they are witnessing an argument when they are overhearing a friendly conversation (Tannen, 1990). Likewise, both French and Arab men (but not women) find argument stimulating (Copeland and Griggs, 1985). A comparative study of North American and Italian nursery school children showed that one of the Italian children's favourite pastimes was a kind of heated debating that Italians call *discussione* but that North Americans would regard as arguing. Likewise, research has shown that in the conversations of working-class Jewish speakers of Eastern European origin, arguments are used as a means of being sociable.

08   People from Italy, Greece, and some parts of Eastern Europe may be more willing to accept conflict because of their individualistic, low-context[1] communication style of speaking directly and avoiding uncertainty. It's not surprising that people from cultures that emphasize harmony among people with close relationships tend to handle conflicts in less direct ways. With differences like these, it is easy

Certain cultures enjoy passionate verbal disputes that North Americans might consider to be argumentative.

---

[1] In a low-context communication style, speakers are very explicit and direct, relying very little on contextual cues of a situation or culture. By contrast, in high-context communication, cultural clues play an important role, so many things are left unsaid and have to be picked up by communicators from context.

to imagine how two friends, lovers, or fellow workers from different cultural backgrounds might have trouble finding a conflict style that is comfortable for both of them.

09   Despite these differences, it is important to realize that culture is not the only factor that influences the way people think about conflict or how they act when they disagree. Some research (e.g., Beatty and McCroskey, 1997) suggests that our approach to conflict may be part of our biological makeup. Furthermore, scholarship suggests a person's self-concept is more powerful than his or her culture in determining conflict style (Oetzel et al., 2001; Ting-Toomey et al., 2001). For example, people who view themselves as mostly independent of others are likely to use a direct, solution-oriented conflict style, regardless of their cultural heritage. Those who see themselves as mostly interdependent are likely to use a style that avoids direct confrontation. And those who see themselves as both independent and interdependent are likely to have the widest variety of conflict behaviours on which to draw.

10   Beyond individual temperament and self-concept, the environment in which we are raised can shape the way we approach conflict. Parental conflict style plays a role. Parents who use spanking and other forms of corporal punishment with their children are more likely to have children who approve of using aggressive approaches to problem solving, such as hitting, with their siblings and peers (Simons and Wurtele, 2010). The influence of parental modelling and style of conflict resolution can be seen in adults as well. Research has revealed a significant relationship between the way a mother handles conflict and the style used by her adult children (Martin et al., 1997). Finally, the status of the people involved in a dispute has a powerful effect on conflict styles, at least in individualistic cultures (Kim et al., 2007). When given two conflict scenarios, one involving a classmate and the other involving a professor, students with a more individualistic orientation indicated that they would use a more argumentative approach with their classmate and feel more apprehension about the conflict with the professor. In contrast, students with a more collectivistic orientation were not more likely to be more argumentative with a peer and more avoidant with a professor, but like their more individualistic peers, they too reported feeling more apprehension about having a conflict with a professor (Kim et al., 2007).

11   Along with family influences, the "culture" of each relationship can shape how we behave (Messman and Canary, 1998). You might handle disagreements calmly in a job where rationality and civility are the norm, but shriek like a banshee[2] at home if that's the way you and a relational partner handle disputes.

Source: R.B. Adler, L.B. Rosenfeld, R.F. Proctor & C. Winder, *Interplay*, 3rd Canadian edition (Don Mills, ON: Oxford University Press, 2012), pp. 333–335.

---

[2] To shriek like a banshee is to scream or cry wildly.

1. The words in the box below relate to dealing with conflict. Place each word or phrase on the appropriate side of the T-chart, according to the way in which conflict is traditionally dealt with in North America and in China or Japan.

indirect approach	straightforwardness	hinting
assertiveness	blunt honesty	modelling
self-restraint	decisiveness	non-assertion

NORTH AMERICA	CHINA/JAPAN

2. Which example of communication would North Americans describe as "beating around the bush"?

   Your colleague lives in the same neighbourhood as you. You know that she usually drives to work, just like you. On Monday after work . . .

   a) she tells you that she has bought a new car, and she enjoys it very much.

   b) she tells you that her car broke down, and she will have to spend an extra hour travelling home from work by public transit.

   c) she asks you for a ride home because her car broke down.

   d) she says that today her husband is picking her up after work, and she is looking forward to seeing him.

3. A. Based on the information in the reading, what kind of response would you expect to the statement "It is somewhat cold today" in a Japanese classroom?

   _____

   B. What might be the response to the same statement in a Canadian classroom?

   _____

4. A. What question did Heine and colleagues (2000) try to answer in their research (par. 4)?

   _____

   B. Which cultural group scored higher on the scale of self-enhancement in this research?

   _____

   C. Complete the sentence.

   A Japanese student would probably find it _____ to accept that his or her performance was worse than that of an average peer.

5. Which personal trait helps a person from a Japanese background to live harmoniously with other people in her culture?

   _____

6. What are the two motives related to harmony in collectivistic cultures?

   _____

7. Mark each statement as T (true) or F (false).

   a) ____ Assertiveness is not used as a part of interpersonal conflict resolution in collectivistic societies.

   b) ____ Age may affect the way a person prefers to resolve conflicts.

   c) ____ As nations become more culturally integrated, through work, travel, and migration, there will likely be changes in the conflict resolution methods we traditionally associate with one culture.

8. Do you think most Westerners would agree with the Chinese saying "The first person to raise his voice loses an argument"? Why or why not?

   _____

9. Describe in your own words an "accommodating style of conflict resolution" and list methods of persuasion used in this style.

   _____

   _____

   _____

10. Underline the main idea sentence in paragraph 6. Then highlight one detail that supports this main idea.

11. A. Are conversational styles uniform among Western cultures?

_____

B. What do Italians mean by *discussione*?

_____

C. How might Canadians categorize this type of exchange?

_____

12. What can be inferred from the authors' discussion of different styles of conflict resolution?

    a) Different conflict styles create different societies: individualistic and collectivistic.

    b) Culturally different styles of conflict resolution lead to harmonious relationships between people.

    c) Colleagues from different cultural backgrounds are likely to encounter some communication problems.

    d) Partners belonging to different cultural backgrounds should not get married.

13. Paragraphs 9–11 list several factors, beyond culture, that influence our style of conflict management. Fill in the factors and provide an example for each.

FACTOR SHAPING CONFLICT STYLE	EXAMPLE
	A calm, quiet person will refrain from arguing loudly with an opponent.
Self-concept	
	Children handle conflict in a way similar to their parents.
The status of a person involved in conflict	
The norms in each individual relationship	

Vocabulary

Use context clues and your knowledge of word parts to determine the correct meaning of each word or phrase. Verify your answers using a dictionary if necessary.

1. place a premium on (par. 3): _____

2. cohesiveness (par. 4):

    a) uniqueness

    b) unity

    c) assertiveness

3. reprimands (par. 6):

    a) disapproval

    b) praises

    c) disciplinary actions

4. temperament (par. 10): _____

5. apprehension (par. 10):

    a) aggressiveness

    b) uneasiness

    c) confidence

6. civility (par. 11): _____

UNIT REFLECTION AND SYNTHESIS

1. Fill in the chart with specific examples of collectivistic and individualistic behaviours related to various relationships. Use information from all three readings.

	INDIVIDUALISTIC	COLLECTIVISTIC
Relationships with family members		
Raising children		
Relationships with peers (fellow students or colleagues)		

2. Using information from all three readings, summarize the reasons why a collectivistic culture may become more individualistic over time, especially in the twenty-first century.

_____

_____

_____

3. One of the factors influencing our conflict resolution style is our "biological makeup" ("Managing Conflict," par. 9). How is this statement about the connection between people's cultural habits and their biology either supported or contradicted in "Culture and the Self"?

_____

_____

4. Based on paragraph 8 of "Culture and the Self," people of individualistic and collectivistic backgrounds use different language to describe others: "Westerners tend to use trait-describing adjectives ("*she is helpful*"), whereas East Asians more often use verbs that describe behaviour in context ("*she helps her friends*") (Heine and Buchtel, 2009; Maass et al., 2006)."

Reread the introductory textbox in "Uncovering the Role of Culture in Learning." Which of the two sentences below would match an individualist's language? Which would match a collectivist's language?

a) My father is a good cook. _____

b) My father cooks delicious meals for us. _____

5. In "Uncovering the Role of Culture in Learning," the authors describe a conflict between a Latin American immigrant boy and a European American teacher (although the teacher does not realize that the situation involves a conflict).

Answer the following questions, based on your understanding of the second and third readings.

A. What method of conflict resolution does the boy choose?

_____

B. What are the boy's motives for choosing to resolve the conflict in this way?

_____

6. A. What recommendations would you offer to teachers and parents of students who are in a situation like the one in "Uncovering the Role of Culture in Learning"?

   _____

   B. Why is it less likely that a student from an individualistic culture would find himself or herself in a culture that is predominantly collectivistic?

   _____

   _____

7. Use information from all three readings to answer the following questions.

   What might be some negative consequences of living in an individualistic culture? Are there any negatives to living in a collectivistic society? Fill in the T-chart.

THE NEGATIVE CONSEQUENCES OF	
LIVING IN AN INDIVIDUALISTIC CULTURE	LIVING IN A COLLECTIVISTIC CULTURE

8. Do you think the authors of any of the readings in this unit are biased against the values of an individualistic culture? Explain your answer.

   _____

   _____

9. A. Who is the target audience for the readings in this unit?

   _____

   B. Do you personally find learning about the differences between collectivistic and individualistic cultures useful? Why or why not?

   _____

   _____

   _____

WORD PART	MEANING	EXAMPLE
ab-	away, from, off	*absent*; *abstemious* (not allowing yourself to have much food or alcohol or to do things that are enjoyable)
-able	having the quality of; that can or must be	*comfortable*; *calculable* (that can be calculated)
acu-	sharp, pointed	*acupuncture* (a Chinese method of treating pain and illness using special thin needles which are pushed into the skin in particular parts of the body); *acuity* (the ability to think, see, or hear clearly)
ad-	to, toward	*adapt*; *adequate*
alter	other, change	*alterable*
ante-	before, in front of	*antenatal* (before birth); *antedate* (predate)
anti-	opposed to, against; may sometimes be a variant of *ante-* (before)	*antisocial*; *antidote* (a substance that controls the effects of a poison or disease)
bene-	good	*benefit*; *benevolent* (kind, helpful, and generous)
-cess, -cede, -ceed	to go, to go back or yield	*access*; *recede* (to move gradually away from somebody or away from a previous position)
chron-	time	*chronology* (the order in which a series of events happened; a list of these events in order); *synchronize* (to happen at the same time or to move at the same speed as something)
circum-, circu-	around	*circulate*; *circumlocution* (using more words than are necessary, instead of speaking or writing in a clear, direct way)
co-, con-, com-	together, with	*cooperate*, *conflate* (to put two or more things together to make one new thing)
counter-, contra-	against, opposite	*counteract* (to do something to reduce or prevent the bad or harmful effects of something); *contradict* (to be so different from each other that one of them must be wrong)
curr-, curs-	run	*concurrent* (happening [running] at the same time); *precursor* (a person or thing that comes before somebody/something similar and that leads to or influences its development; forerunner)
de-	away from, down from	*deregulate*, *descend*
dis-	not, negate	*disappear*; *disband* (to stop something/somebody from operating as a group)
dys-	bad, abnormal	*dysfunctional*; *dystopia* (an imaginary place or state in which everything is extremely bad or unpleasant)
-ee	a noun suffix indicating a person toward whom the action is directed	*employee*; *retiree*
em-, en-	to put into, cause	*embrace* (to accept an idea, a proposal, a set of beliefs, etc); *encompass* (to include a large number or range of things; to surround or cover something completely)
equ-, equi-	equal	*equidistant*; *equipoise* (a state of balance)

WORD PART	MEANING	EXAMPLE
gen-	birth, origin	*generate* (to produce or create something); *genesis* (the beginning or origin of something)
-gnosis	know, knowledge	*diagnostic* (connected with identifying something, especially an illness)
graph-	write, record	*autograph*; *photograph*; *topography* (the physical features of an area of land)
hyper-	too much, over	*hypersensitive* (easily offended; extremely physically sensitive to particular substances, medicine, light, etc.)
il-, im-, in-, ir-	not, without	*illegal*; *impossible*; *inappropriate*; *irrelevant*
-ize	a verb suffix; to make something have a certain quality	*standardize*; *socialize*
mal-	bad, wrong	*malfunction*; *maladroit* (clumsy)
medi-	middle	*mediate* (to try to end a disagreement between two or more people or groups by talking to them and trying to find things that everyone can agree on); *median* (located in or passing through the middle)
mis-	bad, wrong	*misinterpret*; *misanthrope* (a person who hates and avoids other people)
mono-	single	*monogamy*; *monoglot* (a person who speaks only one language)
non-	not	*nonconformist*; *nonexistent*
omni-	all	*omniscient* (knowing everything)
opt-	best	*optimal*
pan-	all	*pandemic* (a disease that spreads over a whole country or the whole world)
per-	through, throughout	*perennial* (continuing for a very long time; [of plants] living for two years or more)
peri-	around, surrounding	*perimeter*; *peripatetic* (going from place to place)
phys-	related to nature or natural things	*physical*; *physician*
pre-	before	*preview*; *presuppose* (to accept something as true or existing, and act on that basis before it has been proved to be true)
proto-	original; primitive	*protocol* (the first or original version of an agreement, especially a treaty between countries, etc); *protonym* (a name used for a new species that may not yet be officially recognized)
re-	again, back	*reverse*; *relocate*
scrib-, script-	write, written	*scripture*; *prescribe*; *ascribe* (to consider or state that a book, etc., was written by a particular person; to attribute)
spect-	see, look	*inspect*; *spectator*
sub-	under	*subtitle*; *substandard*; *subterranean* (under the ground)
un-	not	*unaffected*; *unadulterated* (not mixed with other substances)
under-	below, beneath, not enough	*undercover*; *undercooked*
uni-	one	*unicorn*; *unification* (the joining of people, things, parts of a country, etc., together so that they form a single unit)
ver-	true	*verdict* (a decision that you make or an opinion that you give about something, after you have tested it or considered it carefully); *verisimilitude* (the quality of seeming to be true or real)
-vert, -vers	turn	*convert*; *subversive* (trying or likely to destroy or damage a government or political system by attacking it secretly or indirectly)
-volve	roll, turn	*evolution*

CREDITS

Literary Credits

9 In Tepperman, Lorne, and Curtis, James, *Principles of Sociology* 2/e © Oxford University Press Canada 2009. Reprinted by permission of the publisher.

13–15 Republished with permission of South-Western College Publishing, a division of Cengage Learning, *Social Psychology and Human Nature*, 3rd edition, Roy F. Baumeister and Brad Bushman, © 2014. Permission conveyed through Copyright Clearance Center, Inc.

19–21 From: PSYCHOLOGY WITH UPDATES ON DSM5, 10E by David G. Myers, Copyright 2014 by Worth Publishers. Used with permission of the publisher.

26–37 In Adler, Ronald, et al. *Interplay: The Process of Interpersonal Communication*, 3/Ce, © Oxford University Press Canada 2012. Reprinted by permission of the publisher.

38–9 *Global Connections: Canadian and World Issues,* 2E by Bruce Clark and John Wallace, © 2008 Pearson Canada pp. 1, 9-14, reprinted by permisison of Pearson Canada Inc.

40 In Schultz, Emily, Lavenda, Robert, and Dods, Roberta, *Cultural Anthropology,* 2/Ce © Oxford University Press Canada 2012. Reprinted by permission of the publisher.

44–7 Excerpted and adapted from Norton, William, Human Geography 8/e © Oxford University Press Canada 2013. Reprinted by permission of the publisher.

47–8 In Norton, William, Human Geography, 7/e © Oxford University Press Canada 2009. Reprinted by permission of the publisher.

49–51 In Norton, William, Human Geography 8/e © Oxford University Press Canada 2013. Reprinted by permission of the publisher.

52 In Norton, William, Human Geography, 7/e © Oxford University Press Canada 2009. Reprinted by permission of the publisher.

53–5 in Norton, William, Human Geography 8/e © Oxford University Press Canada 2013. Reprinted by permission of the publisher.

56 Norton, William, Human Geography, 7/e © Oxford University Press Canada 2009. Reprinted by permission of the publisher.

57–61 In Norton, William, Human Geography 8/e © Oxford University Press Canada 2013. Reprinted by permission of the publisher.

67–8 Chris Wickham and Irene Klotz (Oct. 17 2012) "New planet discovered in Earth's 'backyard'" www.reuters.com/article/2012/10/17/us-space-newplanet-idUSBRE89G0H420121017.

68 Drew Armstrong (Oct 18, 2012) "'Thunder god vine' herb kills tumours in mice: Study" *Vancouver Sun.*

68–9 Adapted from www.vancouversun.com/technology/futuretech/Face+face+with+human+barcode/6993038/story.html#ixzz29tiTFoAI.

69 From www.thestar.com/living/technology/article/1262011--curb-your-appetite-with-apps.

70–2 In Schultz, Emily, Lavenda, Robert, and Dods, Roberta, *Cultural Anthropology,* 2/Ce © Oxford University Press Canada 2012. Reprinted by permission of the publisher.

73 "Kids exposed to suicide of schoolmate more likely to attempt it, study shows'" by Alex Consiglio, May 21, 2013 www.thestar.com/life/health_wellness/news_research/2013/05/21/children_exposed_to_suicide_more_likely_to_attempt_it_study_shows.html. Reprinted with permission—Torstar Syndication Services.

73 Clark, Bruce & John Wallace (2008) *Global Connections: Canadian and World Issues,* 2E, Pearson Canada p. 25.

75 In Adler, Ronald, et al. *Interplay: The Process of Interpersonal Communication, 3/Ce* © Oxford University Press Canada 2012. Reprinted by permission of the publisher.

76–7 In Tepperman, Lorne, Albanese, Patrizia, and Curtis, James, *Sociology, 3/e* © Oxford University Press Canada 2012. Reprinted by permission of the publisher.

78–9 Presidential Commision for the Study of Bioethical Issues. www.bioethics.gov/reports/past_commissions/nbac_cloning.pdf

80 Courtesy: National Human Genome Research Institute. www.genome.gov/25020028#al-5.

81 www.iwf.org/media/2790433/Gayle_Trotter_Testimony_Gun_Violence March 2013 27, IWF, Gayle S. Trotter. United States Department of Justice.

82 www.bottledwater.org/health/water-quality

84–5 Drug addicts should be sent to isolated work camps; Brian Purdy, Postmedia News; Published: Wednesday, September 14, 2011. Reprinted by permission of the author.

86 http://supervisedinjection.vch.ca. Courtesy Vancouver Coastal Healt

86–7 Excerpted from Evan Wood's "Harper should embrace safe-injection sites: They're the law-and-order option" (Jun. 19 2013) Retrieved from:www.theglobeandmail.com/globe-debate/harper-should-embrace-safe-injection-sites-theyre-the-law-and-order-option/article12661904/. Reprinted by permission of the author.

90 "Census: One in five speaks a foreign language in Canadian homes" by Tobi Cohen for Postmedia News service, October 24, 2012. Material reprinted with the express permission of Postmedia News, a division of Postmedia Network, Inc.

91–3 'Speak English, s'il vous plait!' by Pete McMartin, *Vancouver Sun* October 25, 2012, © The Vancouver Sun. Reprinted with permission.

94–5 From *Canadian Pie* by Will Ferguson. Copyright © Will Ferguson, 2011. Reprinted by permission of Penguin Canada Books Inc.

97 Jonathan Blum, www.entrepreneur.com/article/223348. Copyright 2014. Entrepreneur Magazine. 113492:1114SH.

98 Text originally retrieved from: www.sse.gov.on.ca/mcs/en/Pages/Online_Shopping_Intro.aspx. © Queen's Printer for Ontario, 2013. Reproduced with permission.

99 © Brian Sheehan, 2010, *Basics Marketing 02: Online Marketing*, AVA UK, an imprint of Bloomsbury Publishing Plc.

101–1 "Logical Environmental Reasoning for a Vegetarian Lifestyle" (www.enviroveggie.com).

102–3 Ken MacQueen, "Why it's time to legalize marijuana" in *Maclean's Magazine* June 10, 2013. Reprinted with permission.

114–6 Republished with permission of ABC-CLIO Inc., from *Daily Life in Elizabethan England*, J.L. Forgeng, 2nd edition, © 1995. Permission conveyed through Copyright Clearance Center, Inc.

119–21 From *Geodate* 23(4), "Designing Safer Cities: CPTED" by J. Byrne. Reprinted by permission of Warringal Publications.

124–8 Republished with permission of SAGE Publications, Inc. Books, *Corrections: The Essentials*, Mary K. Stohr, © 2012. Permission conveyed through Copyright Clearance Center, Inc.

126 Table from *European Journal of Crime, Criminal Law & Criminal Justice* 12, 36-45 Havercamp, R., Meyer, R. Levey (2000) Electronic Monitoring in Europe. Reprinted by permission of the authors.

133–5 In Schultz, Emily, Lavenda, Robert, and Dods, Roberta, *Cultural Anthropology, 2/Ce* © Oxford University Press Canada 2012. Reprinted by permission of the publisher.

138–41 Excerpted and adapted from Jon Entine, "The DNA Olympics—Jamaicans winsprinting 'genetic lottery'—and why we should all care,"www.forbes.com/sites/jonentine/2012/08/12/the-dnaolympics-jamaicans-win-sprinting-genetic-lottery-andwhy-we-should-all-care/. Reprinted by permission of the author.

145–9 From Thomas Shapiro, Tatjana Meschede, and Sam Osoro. "The Roots of the Widening Racial Wealth Gap: Explaining the Black-White Economic Divide," Research and Policy Brief, Institute of Assets and Social Policy (IASP) February 2013. Reprinted with permission.

156–7 In Dearden, Philip, and Mitchell Bruce, *Environmental Change and Challenge 4/e* © Oxford University Press Canada 2012. Reprinted by permission of the publisher.

157–8 In Norton, William, *Human Geography 8/e* © Oxford University Press Canada 2013. Reprinted by permission of the publisher.

161–3 "Why Japan took the nuclear risk; When making choices about energy, there are no danger-free, cost-free solutions" by Dan Gardner, in the *Vancouver Sun*, March 18, 2011 p. A13. Material reprinted with the express permission of Postmedia News, a division of Postmedia Network, Inc.

166–9 Thompson, K. (2013). "Staying Power." *Popular Science*, 282(2), 38-43. Used with permission of *Popular Science*. Copyright © 2014. All rights reserved.

178–81 Excerpted with permission from "Traffic Jam: Move over megaprojects; small creative options unlock the grid," Matti Siemiatycki, *Alternatives*, 33:1 (2007). alternativesjournal.ca. Reprinted by permission of the author and *Alternatives*.

185–7 From *Transport Reviews*, Vol. 32, No. 1, "Ridesharing in North America: Past, Present, and Future" by N.D. Chan and S.A. Shaheen, © 2012 Taylor & Francis Ltd., http://www.informaworld.com.

192–4 Chris Sorensen, "How Electric Cars Got Stuck in First Gear" in *Maclean's Magazine*, December 6, 2011.

201–4 From: PSYCHOLOGY WITH UPDATES ON DSM5, 10E by David G. Myers, Copyright 2014 by Worth Publishers. Used with permission of the publisher.

208–10 Excerpted from *International Marketing, 15/e* by Philip Cateora et al. © 2011 McGraw Hill Education. Reprinted with permission.

213–16 Excerpted from 'Terror and Ethnocentrism: Foundation of American Support for the War on Terrorism' by Cindy D. Kam and Donald R. Kinder in *The Journal of Politics* 69 (2), May 2007 © 2007 Cambridge University Press. Reprinted with the permission of Cambridge University Press.

224–5 SIMON, ERIC j.; DICKEY, JEAN L.; REECE, JANE B.; HOGAN, KELLY A., CAMPBELL *ESSENTIAL BIOLOGY WITH PHYSIOLOGY*, 5th edition. Printed and Electronically reproduced by permission of Pearson Education, Inc. Upper Saddle River, New Jersey.

228–30 Excerpted and adapted from Ferrari, M. (March 2010), Infernal Mechanism. *Mechanical Engineering* 132 (3), 24-28. Reprinted by permission of the copyright holder. Further reproduction without permission prohibited.

232–5 Adapted from Hopper, J. (November 2005). What Happens When You Live? *Prevention* 57 (11), 158-98. Copyrighted 2014. Rodale, Inc. 114080:1114AT.

241–4 Excerpted from *International Marketing, 15/e* by Philip Cateora et al. © 2011 McGraw Hill Education. Reprinted with permission.

248–51 Coleman, I. (2010). "The Global Glass Ceiling". Current, (524), 3-6. Actually from *Foreign Affairs* May/June 2010 http://www.foreignaffairs.com/articles/66206/isobel-coleman/the-global-glass-ceiling. Reprinted by permission of FOREIGN AFFAIRS, 89(3), May/June 2010. Copyright 2010 by the Council on Foreign Relations, Inc. www.Foreign Affairs.com.

255–7 Verma, P. (2005). "Born to Serve: The State of Old Women and Widows in India." *Off Our Backs*, 35(9/10), 38-39.

263–6 From: PSYCHOLOGY WITH UPDATES ON DSM5, 10E by David G. Myers, Copyright 2014 by Worth Publishers. Used with permission of the publisher.

270–3 Republished with permission of Springer Publishing Company, Innovations in Educational *Psychology: Perspectives on Learning, Teaching, and Human Development*, D.D. Preiss & R.J. Sternberg, Eds. "Uncovering the Role of Culture in Learning, Development, and Education" by Rothstein-Fish, C., Greenfield, P.M., Trumbull, E., Keller, H., Quiroz, B., 2010. Permission conveyed through Copyright Clearance Center, Inc.

277–9 in Adler, Ronald, et al. Interplay: The Process of Interpersonal Communication, 3/Ce © Oxford University Press Canada 2012. Reprinted by permission of the publisher.

286–7 Reproduced by permission of Oxford University Press from *Oxford Advanced Learner's Dictionary 8th* Edition © Oxford University Press 2010

Photo and Figure Credits

1 © Dirk Anschütz/Corbis

3 Igor Mojzes/Thinkstock; AmmentorpDK/Thinkstock

14 Digital Vision/Thinkstock

20 Lenutaidi / Dreamstime.com

25 Goodshoot/Thinkstock

34 Wavebreakmedia Ltd/Thinkstock

40 mookandjohn/Thinkstock

43 zagart286/Thinkstock

46 Pasticcio/Thinkstock; in Norton, William, *Human Geography*, 8/e © Oxford University Press Canada 2013. Reprinted by permission of the publisher.

61 In Norton, William, *Human Geography*, 8/e © Oxford University Press Canada 2013. Reprinted by permission of the publisher.

64 © Copyright Randy Glasbergen, Galsbergen Cartoon Service.

68 ESO/L. Calçada/Nick Risinger (skysurvey.org)

70 Thinkstock

84 © ANDY CLARK/X00056/Reuters/Corbis

88 These posters were part of a public awareness campaign for hireimmigrants.ca by the Toronto Region Immigrant Employment Council (TRIEC). (Photos courtesy of TRIEC).

97 © iStock.com/Arda Guldogan

98 Thinkstock

107 © Peter Cavanagh / Alamy

111 Digital Vision/Thinkstock

114 © iStock.com / wdstock; © Steve Welsh / Alamy

115 Print Collector / Contributor / Getty Images

120 Åukasz Juszczak/Thinkstock; alice-photo/Thinkstock

121 "Crime Prevention through Environmental Design: Guidelines for Queensland," pp. 22–23. Retrieved from www.police.qldgov.au/Rsources/Internet/programs/crimeprevention. © The State of Queensland 2007

138 AP Photo/Anja Niedringhaus

145 Courtesy Institute of Assets and Social Policy (IASP). Data for this analysis are derived from the Panel Study of Income Dynamics (PSID), following nearly 1,700 working-age households from 1984-2009

147 Courtesy Institute of Assets and Social Policy (IASP). Data for this analysis are derived from the Panel Study of Income Dynamics (PSID), following nearly 1,700 working-age households from 1984-2009

155 Source map credit: © All rights reserved. *Human Health in a Changing Climate: A Canadian Assessment of Vulnerabilities and Adaptive Capacity*. Health Canada, 2008. Reproduced with permission from the Minister of Health, 2014. Photo credits : Canada Map, © Diane Labombarbe/iStockphoto; Dogsled team, © lightcatcheristockphoto; Deer, © twildlife/iStockphoto; Storm damage, © Pacificenterprise; Tick, © K-Kucharska_D-Kucharsk/iStockphotoi; Flooding, © Emmaphlema/iStockphoto; Forest fire, © ruig /iStockphoto; Drought, © audaxl/iStockphoto; Heatstroke, © nandyphotos/iStockphoto; Permafrost melt, © RyersonClark; Water quality, © BartCo/iStockphoto

161 AP Photo/Tokyo Electric Power Co.

167 © iStock.com/janniswerner

177 ExxonMobil, from ExxonMobil's 2014 Outlook for Engegy: A View to 2040. Reprinted with permission.

179 chuyu/Thinkstock

187 Courtesy NuRide

192 Thinkstock

202 Sergei Bachlakov / Shutterstock.com

203 Courtesy Dr. Jamin Halberstadt

204 Speed Bump used with the permission of Dave Coverly and the Cartoonist Group. All rights reserved.

209 AP Photos/McDonald's Corp.

229 Exerpted and adapted from Ferrari, M. (March 2010), Infernal Mechanism. Mechanical Engineering 132 (3), 24-28. Reprinted by permission of the copyright holder. Further reproduction without permission prohibited.

241 © Business Cartoons / Visual Humour

249 Paula Bronstein / Staff / Getty Images

262 © iStock.com/gnurf

264 AP Photo/Kyodo News

265 From "Fitting in or Standing Out: Trends in American Parents' Choices for Children's Names 1880-2007" by Jean M. Twenge in *Social Psychology and Personality Science*, 1 (1) Januray 2010. Reprinted by Permission of SAGE Publications.

278 John Foxx/Thinkstock

Marina Rozenberg is an instructor for Fraser International College's EAP program, affiliated with Simon Fraser University, in Vancouver, BC. At FIC, she enjoys working with students of diverse cultural and linguistic backgrounds preparing for post-secondary studies. In addition to having taught English for almost 20 years in Canada and abroad, Marina has also developed curricula in academic reading and vocabulary acquisition, two areas of special interest. Marina was born in Ukraine and moved to Israel, where she graduated from Bar Ilan University with an M.A. in English and a Teaching Diploma. She is the author of *Step Up to Academic Reading* (OUP Canada, 2012).